BUDDHIST TEXTS THROUGH THE AGES

OTHER TITLES IN THIS SERIES

Islam and the West: The Making of an Image, Norman Daniel,
    ISBN 1–85168–129–9
The Qur'an and its Exegesis, Helmut Gätje, ISBN 1–85168–118–3
The Faith and Practice of Al-Ghazali, William Montgomery Watt,
    ISBN 1–85168–062–4
What the Buddha Taught, Walpola Sri Rahula, ISBN 1–85168–142–6

RELATED TITLES PUBLISHED BY ONEWORLD:

Buddhism: A Short History, Edward Conze, ISBN 1–85168–221–X
Buddhism: A Short Introduction, Klaus K. Klostermaier,
    ISBN 1–85168–186–8
What Buddhists Believe, Elizabeth J. Harris, ISBN 1–85168–168–X

BUDDHIST TEXTS THROUGH THE AGES

Translated and edited by
Edward Conze

In collaboration with
I. B. Horner, David Snellgrove and
Arthur Waley

ONEWORLD

OXFORD

BUDDHIST TEXTS THROUGH THE AGES

Oneworld Publications
(Sales and Editorial)
185 Banbury Road
Oxford OX2 7AR
England
http://www.oneworld-publications.com

Oneworld Publications
(US Marketing Office)
160 N. Washington St.
4th floor, Boston
MA 02114
USA

ISBN 1-85168-107-8

Cover design by Design Deluxe, Bath
Printed and bound by WS Bookwell, Finland

Contents

THIRD PART

The Tantras
by David Snellgrove

FOURTH PART

Texts from China and Japan
by Arthur Waley

Introduction

A comprehensive Anthology of Buddhist Texts has never before been attempted. The documents are distributed over so many languages that no one person could aim at knowing them all. More than a dozen collections of texts from the Pali Scriptures have been published and a fairly representative collection of Mahayana passages, translated by Prof. M. Winternitz, has appeared in German.[1] But there is no corresponding publication in English for the Mahayana, and nothing in any European language for the Tantras, or for China and Japan. The overwhelming majority of the texts preserved in Sanskrit, Tibetan and the Far Eastern languages are still untranslated. Even where English translations of Mahayana texts exist, they were in most cases carried out at a time when the particular idiom of these texts was only imperfectly understood. Only in recent years has it become possible to translate accurately, and work done in the middle of the 20th century is likely to be greatly superior to anything done fifty or more years ago.

All the texts in this book have been newly translated from the originals. The book is designed as a sequel to Dr. Conze's book *Buddhism*,[2] which seemed to give a sufficiently authentic account of the development of Buddhist thought to serve as a basis for a collection of texts. In this Anthology only texts are given. They have not been encumbered with notes, on the assumption that the reader can find all the explanation that may be required in Dr. Conze's book. Considerable attention has been given to the problem of ensuring uniformity in the rendering of technical terms. A Glossary provides a list of the main terms, with their Sanskrit equivalents. In a number of cases we decided not to translate the term at all, as words such as Buddha, Dharma, Nirvana and others are likely in due course to be absorbed into the English language. In other

---

[1] *Religionsgeschichtliches Lesebuch*, ed. A. Bertholet, no. 15: Der Mahayana-Buddhismus, Tübingen, 1930.

[2] 2nd Ed., Oxford, 1953.

cases the English equivalent adopted here can be considered as a makeshift only. It is, for instance, impossible to find one English term which contains and can convey the whole wealth of meaning of a term like *moha*. Such difficulties are inherent in any translation, and we hope that the Glossary will help to reduce the dangers of misunderstanding.

The first section deals with the tradition of the *Hinayana*. The majority of the extracts chosen by Miss Horner are taken from the Pali Canon. A few passages from post-canonical works and from the old commentaries have been included. This limits the representation of the Hinayana to one school only, to the Theravadins. No extracts have been given to illustrate the traditions, or the specific doctrines, of any of the other seventeen Hinayana schools. This decision has been made merely for practical reasons, that is to say mainly because the Theravadin literature is both compact and, thanks to the editions and translations of the Pali Text Society, easily accessible. In any case, any differences found between various Hinayana sources concern only minor details of the doctrine, which fall outside the scope of this Anthology.

The question of how to present the material in this section gave rise to various difficulties. We finally agreed that, however fundamental the triad of Morality, Concentration and Wisdom may be, it would be easier, for purposes of historical information, to group the material under another Buddhist triad, that of Buddha, Dharma and Samgha. The usual order of this triad is here reversed, so that Samgha comes first and Buddha last. It is hoped that thereby a clearer indication may emerge of the progress that devotees and aspirants, the ariyan disciples, ought to make.

Beginning as monks and nuns, in a regulated 'homeless life', they are disciplined from without and within by the authoritative rules and sanctions of the *Samgha* (monastic Order or Confraternity) to respond less and less to the demands of their sense-experiences. They can then strive the more ardently to acquire both a growing understanding and knowledge of Dharma and greater ease and success in practising it; thus they will become what they ought to be, in order finally to reach the Further Shore beyond the Rivers of Life and Death where they will stand on dry land, on the Isle of Nirvana, safe and secure in the plenitude of Wisdom. They are now Arahants, those who have done all there was to be done, and are perfectly 'finished'.

In order to represent *Dharma*, only one classification and one statement have been chosen from among the numerous classifications and statements found in the Pali Canon: the Five Faculties, which include not only faith but also concentration and wisdom; and, secondly, the essential formula of Conditioned Genesis or Dependent Origination, a teaching on the mean or middle way for the eradication of ill, suffering, insufficiency and anguish. "Precisely this do I teach, now as formerly: ill and the stopping of ill" (M. I. 140). Some of the ways of passing from the bonds and fetters of the Not-Beyond to the Freedom of the Beyond, the ways of Arahants and Buddhas, together with a small selection of the reasons for doing so, may be found in the chapter headed 'The Object of Wisdom'. The fundamental object was to *get free*—free from all undesirable conditions and mental objects, free also from the more desirable ones. And to be free in the Highest: "As the great ocean has but one taste, that of salt, so has this Dharma and Discipline but one taste, the taste of Freedom" (Vin. ii. 239; A. iv. 203; Ud. 56). Since this taste of Freedom permeates the whole of the teaching, no individual extracts have been included as a separate category.

The third division of the extracts concerns the *Buddha* who, although born a man, as Tathagata is inconnumerable, "beyond all ways of telling" (Sn. 1076). For, released from the world, freed from the denotation of the five skandhas, he is no longer to be reckoned, either as the man so-and-so, or as one about whom, after the dissolution of his body, the statement could be made in truth and in fact that he is, is not, both is and is not, neither is nor is not. Because his is Wisdom as seen and known from the Further Shore, he speaks and acts from this Wisdom and not from desire or volition; hence all that he does is karmically inoperative. Therefore he is trackless and untraceable. "They call him, by whom attachment and aversion and ignorance have been discarded: one of developed self, Brahman-become, Tathagata, Buddha, who has passed by fear and dread, and put away everything" (It. p. 57).

We now turn to the second section. For the *Mahayana* we

possess already an excellent Anthology, compiled by Santideva in the 8th century, under the title 'The Compendium of Training' (Sikshasamuccaya). An English translation appeared in 1922, but it is very carelessly done. The Sanskrit originals of many of Santideva's extracts are now lost, and his successors will have to draw heavily on his work. Among the doctrinal texts the Prajnaparamita Sutras are of outstanding importance, and therefore amply represented in Dr. Conze's selection. Most of them have not been translated before. With the Mahayana it is not the scarcity of sources which causes difficulties but their abundance. It was necessary to concentrate on a few of them, in a work which does not aim at giving a survey of the literary genres and sources but at illustrating the development of basic ideas.

The arrangement of the extracts, following fairly closely chapters V–VII of Dr. Conze's book on Buddhism, is simple and self-explanatory. The translation aims at being strictly literal; sometimes violence had to be done to English idioms. There are also occasional neologisms, as when *jñāna* is rendered by 'cognition', *carati* and *caryā* by 'course', or *manyanā* by 'mindings'. Buddhist style has many peculiarities of its own and, though other translators have thought differently, Dr. Conze believes that some of them should be reproduced in translation. Only readable extracts have been chosen, though the rule broke down in the case of the Yogacarins. Their vast literature is so permeated with scholasticism that it makes difficult reading everywhere. Nearly all the extracts are directly translated from the Sanskrit; there are, however, two exceptions: no. 148 has been rendered from the Chinese of Yüan-tsang by Arthur Waley. Yüan-tsang had before him a recension which is more interesting than the one we find in the Sanskrit and Tibetan. In this case also all the repetitions of the text have been left in, to give the reader an idea of how these texts were actually meant to be recited. No Sanskrit original exists for no. 184, and Prof. Lamotte's French translation from the Tibetan has been the main source here. We felt, however, the text to be sufficiently important to excuse this departure from the standard otherwise observed in this book.

In the third part, dealing with the *Tantras*, Dr. Snellgrove has attempted to illustrate the main themes of the followers of

the Tantras: their repudiation of all other practices, their conviction that the truth was but a matter for inner realization,
and that this was not to be found by fleeing from a world of
which man is essentially a part, but by comprehending it in its
true condition and by continuing to live in it. This is what is
meant by the unity of Samsara and Nirvana, which was for
them the limit of perfection. Philosophically this unity is expressed in terms of the unity of Wisdom, which is perfect
tranquillity, and Compassion, which is altruistic activity, also
known as Means. Cosmologically this unity is expressed in
terms of the continuing evolution and involution of phenomenal
existence, which was a universal Indian conception. Thus the
final stage of bliss and perfect self-realization is the state of
'two-in-one'. The Means of realization of this state involved
a ritual, an expression of the idea, which is therefore itself
symbolic of the twofold unity, for it is both expression and
idea, action and realization, Samsara and Nirvana. As such the
rite of the union of the yogin and the yogini was conceived. But
for its effectiveness it depended entirely upon the bestowing
of power (*adhishṭhāna*) by a qualified master. This involved
submission to his guidance and learning from him to begin
with the truth of the true nature of existence.

For this two chief means were employed, meditation upon
the Mandala and meditation upon divine forms. The intention
was always the same, namely to identify phenomenal existence
with these imagined forms and so to realize its complete non-
substantiality. The effectiveness of the ritual depended entirely upon the holding of these 'right views'. But this ritual
was also practised as an internal act and the two coefficients
are envisaged as two veins to the right and left of the human
body.[1]

A full discussion of all these ideas is clearly impossible here.
For further information the reader may refer to *An Introduction to Tantric Buddhism*, by S. B. Dasgupta, Calcutta, 1950,
and to Dr. Snellgrove's edition of the Hevajra-tantra, shortly
to be published.

A few words may be added about some of the works translated in Part III. Saraha's Treasury of Songs (no. 188) was
written, probably in the 9th century, by one of the chiefs of

[1] See p. 227, note 1.

the 84 Perfect Ones (Siddhas), to whom the beginnings of the Tantras are traditionally ascribed. It is written in Apabhramsa, an Eastern dialect of India, but the text is corrupt and obscure, and for interpretation we depend largely on the Tibetan translation. The work has been included in full because it gives a resumé of the basic Tantric ideas in an agreeable form.

Ananghavajra, another of the Perfect Ones, wrote 'The Attainment of the Realization of Wisdom and Means' (no. 189), of which the first three chapters have been translated (omitting vv. 11–23 of ch. 2). The first chapter provides a brief philosophical introduction. The second and third chapters serve to illustrate the relationship of master and pupil, and refer to the actual rite of union.

No. 190 describes briefly the five Tathagatas and their significance. It is preceded by a short note on the *Mandala*, to which it directly refers, and which is one of the pupil's means of meditation. No. 191, finally, illustrates the stages of internal reintegration. Readers may note how the words themselves have acquired a purely symbolic meaning, and how the four Buddha-bodies are conceived as existing within the human body. This whole meditation is an actualization of the doctrine that the whole truth exists within (see vv. 48 and 89 of Saraha's songs).

As to the fourth part, which contains a selection from the Chinese and Japanese sources, a special introduction by Dr. Arthur Waley will be found on p. 271.

February 1953   THE EDITORS

Note: Diacritical signs have been omitted, except in the notes and quotation of sources.

First Part

THE TEACHING OF THE ELDERS

by

I. B. Horner

THE SAMGHA

THE ORDER OF MONKS AND NUNS

1. *'Conversion' of Anathapindika and Gift of the Jeta Grove*

The householder Anathapindika, who was the husband of a sister of a banker in Rajagaha, went there on some business at a time when the Order with the Buddha at its head had been invited for the morrow by the banker. And the banker enjoined his slaves and servants to get up early in the morning and cook conjeys, rice, curries and vegetables. So the householder Anathapindika thought to himself: "Formerly, when I used to arrive here this householder put aside all his duties and did nothing but exchange greetings with me, but now he seems excited and is enjoining his slaves and servants to get up early tomorrow and cook various things. Can it be that there is a wedding on foot, or has a great oblation been arranged, or is King Seniya Bimbisara of Magadha invited for the morrow with his troops?" And he asked the banker what was going forward.

"There is neither a wedding, householder, nor has King Seniya Bimbisara been invited with his troops. But a great oblation has been arranged by me: the Order has been invited for the morrow with the Buddha at its head."

"Householder, did you say *Buddha*?"

"*Buddha* I did say, householder."

"Householder, did you say *Buddha*?"

"*Buddha* I did say, householder."

"Householder, did you say *Buddha*?"

"*Buddha* I did say, householder."

"Even this sound, *Buddha, Buddha* is hard to come by in the world. Could I go and see this Lord, Arahant, perfect Buddha?"

"Not now, but tomorrow early."

So the householder Anathapindika lay down with mind-fulness so much directed towards the Buddha that he got up three times during the night thinking it was daybreak. As he approached the gateway to the Cool Grove non-human beings opened it. But as he was going out from the town, light vanished, darkness appeared; and such fear, consternation, terror arose in him that he wanted to turn back from there. But the yakkha Sivaka, invisible, made this sound heard:

"A hundred elephants, horses or chariots with she-mules,
A hundred thousand maidens adorned with jewelled ear-
    rings—
These are not worth a sixteenth part of one length of stride.
Advance, householder; advance, householder.
Advance is better for you, not retreat."

Then the darkness vanished, light appeared so that Anatha-pindika's fear, consternation and terror subsided.

He then approached the Cool Grove and as the Lord was pacing up and down in the open air he saw him and, stepping down from the place where he had been pacing up and down, he addressed Anathapindika, saying: "Come, Sudatta." He thinking: "The Lord addressed me by name",[1] inclined his head at the Lord's feet and said he hoped that the Lord was living at ease. The Lord answered:

"Yes, always at ease he lives, the Brahmin, attained to
    nirvana,
Who is not stained by lusts, cooled, without 'basis',[2]
Having rent all clingings, having averted heart's care,
Tranquil he lives at ease, having won to peace of mind."[3]

Then the Lord talked a talk on various things to the house-holder Anathapindika, that is to say talk on giving, on moral habit and on heaven; he explained the peril, the vanity, the depravity of pleasures of the senses, the advantage in renounc-ing them. When the Lord knew that the mind of the house-

---

[1] Anāthapiṇḍika thought that, although the leaders of other sects, such as Pūraṇa Kassapa, claimed to be Buddhas, if this teacher was veritably the Buddha he would address him by his kuladattika name, i.e. the name given to him in his family, and known to none but himself.

[2] upadhi, a remaining substrate of clinging—to rebirth.

[3] Verse also at S. i. 212; A. i. 138.

holder Anathapindika was ready, malleable, devoid of the hindrances, uplifted, pleased, then he explained to him that teaching on Dhamma which the Buddhas have themselves discovered: ill, uprising, stopping, the Way. And as a clean cloth without black specks will easily take dye, even so as he was sitting on that very seat, Dhamma-vision, dustless, stainless, arose to the householder Anathapindika, that "whatever is liable to origination all that is liable to stopping". Then, having seen Dhamma, attained Dhamma, known Dhamma, plunged into Dhamma, having crossed over doubt, put away uncertainty and attained without another's help to full confidence in the Teacher's instruction, Anathapindika spoke thus to the Lord:

"It is excellent, Lord. Even as one might set upright what has been upset, or uncover what was concealed, or show the way to one who is astray, or bring an oil lamp into the darkness thinking that those with vision might see forms, even so is Dhamma explained in many a figure by the Lord. I myself, Lord, am going to the Lord for refuge, to Dhamma and to the Order of monks. May the Lord accept me as a lay disciple going for refuge from this day forth for as long as my life lasts. And, Lord, may the Lord consent to a meal with me on the morrow together with the Order of monks." The Lord consented by becoming silent. . . .

Then the householder Anathapindika, having concluded his business in Rajagaha, set out for Savatthi. On the way he enjoined people, saying: "Masters, build monasteries, prepare dwelling-places, furnish gifts; a Buddha has arisen in the world, and this Lord, invited by me, will come along this road." The people did so. And when the householder Anathapindika had arrived at Savatthi he looked all round it thinking:

"Now, where could the Lord stay that would be neither too far from a village nor too near, suitable for coming and going, accessible to people whenever they want, not crowded by day, having little noise at night, little sound, without folks' breath, secluded from people, fitting for meditation?"

Then the householder Anathapindika saw Prince Jeta's pleasure grove, neither too far from a village . . . fitting for meditation, and he approached Prince Jeta and said: "Young master, give me the pleasure grove to make a monastery."

"The pleasure grove cannot be given away, householder, even for the price of a hundred thousand (coins[1])."

"The monastery has been bought, young master."

"The monastery has not been bought, householder." They asked the chief ministers of justice whether it had been bought or not, and they said: "When the price was fixed by you, young master, the monastery was bought." So the householder Anathapindika, having gold coins brought out in wagons, spread the Jeta Grove with the price of a hundred thousand. But the gold coins that were brought out the first time were not enough to cover a small open space near the porch. So the householder Anathapindika enjoined the people, saying: "Go back, good people, bring (more) gold coins; I will spread this open space (with them)."

Then Prince Jeta thought to himself: "Now, this can be no ordinary matter inasmuch as this householder bestows so many gold coins", and he spoke thus to Anathapindika:

"Please, householder, let me spread this open space; give it to me, it will be my gift."

Then the householder Anathapindika thinking: "This Prince Jeta is a distinguished, well-known man; surely the faith in this Dhamma and Discipline of well-known men like this is very efficacious", made over that open space to Prince Jeta. And Prince Jeta built a porch on that open space. The householder Anathapindika had dwelling-places made and cells, porches, attendance-halls, fire halls, huts for what is allowable, privies, places for pacing up and down in, wells, bathrooms, lotus ponds and sheds.

Vinaya-piṭaka II, 154–59 (condensed)

2. ' Conversion' of General Siha and Meat-eating

The General Siha, a disciple of the Jains, was once sitting among some distinguished Licchavis who were speaking praise of the Buddha, Dhamma and the Order; and Siha con-

---

[1] kahāpaṇa is probably to be understood here. This medium of exchange is perhaps the one most often mentioned in Pali texts. But we do not know exactly what it or its value was at any given time or place; see BD. i, pp. 29, 71, notes.

ceived a strong aspiration to see the Lord. At last he went without asking the Jains' permission, and told the Lord various things he had heard of his teaching and asked whether such things were true or misrepresentations, for, "Indeed we, O Lord, do not wish to misrepresent the Lord." Gotama then told Siha the ways in which these assertions about his teachings would be true, for example that it is true he teaches the non-doing of wrong conduct in body, speech and thought, the detestation of it, the burning up of it, the doing of right conduct in these three ways, the averting of passion, hatred and confusion, the annihilation of them, the avoidance of recurrent becoming, and that he teaches a doctrine of confidence and in this trains disciples.

When he had spoken thus, General Siha spoke thus to the Lord: "It is excellent, Lord. . . . May the Lord accept me as a lay disciple going for refuge from this day forth for as long as life lasts."

"Now, Siha, make a proper investigation, for it is good that well-known men like you should do so."

"I am glad and satisfied that the Lord says this to me. If members of other sects had secured me as a disciple they would have paraded a banner all round Vesali announcing that I had become one of their disciples. But the Lord told me to make a proper investigation. So for a second time I, Lord, go to the Lord for refuge and to Dhamma and to the Order of monks. May the Lord accept me as a lay disciple going for refuge from this day forth for as long as life lasts."

"For a long time, Siha, your family has been a well-spring to the Jains. You will bethink to give alms to those who approach you? "

"I am glad and satisfied that the Lord says this to me. For I had heard that the recluse Gotama had said that gifts should be given to himself and his disciples only, not to others, and that only such gifts would be of great fruit, not gifts given to others. But now the Lord has urged me to give to the Jains too. Indeed, Lord, we shall know the right time for that. So for a third time I, Lord, go to the Lord for refuge and to Dhamma and the Order of monks. May the Lord accept me as a lay disciple going for refuge from this day forth for as long as life lasts."

Then the Lord talked on various things to General Siha.[1]
And when he had seen, attained, known Dhamma and plunged
into it, had crossed over doubt, put away uncertainty, and had
attained without another's help to full confidence in the
Teacher's instruction, he invited the Lord to a meal with him
on the morrow together with the Order of monks. And the
Lord consented by becoming silent. So General Siha asked a
man to go and find out if there was meat to hand[2] and during
the night had sumptuous solid and soft food prepared. In the
morning he told Gotama that the meal was ready, and together
with the Order of monks he went to Siha's dwelling and sat
down on the appointed seat.

Now at that time many Jains, waving their arms, were
moaning from carriage-road to carriage-road, from cross-road
to cross-road in Vesali: "Today a fat beast, killed by General
Siha, has been made into a meal for the recluse Gotama and he
has made use of this meat, knowing that it was killed on purpose for him, that the deed was done for his sake." A certain
man whispered these reports into General Siha's ear.
"Enough," he replied. "For a long time now these venerable
ones have been desiring dispraise of the Buddha, Dhamma
and the Order. But, vain, bad, lying as they are, they do
not harm this Lord because they are misrepresenting him
with what is not fact. Why, even we, for the sake of our
livelihood, would not intentionally deprive a living thing of
life."

Then General Siha, having with his own hand served and
satisfied the Order of monks with the Buddha at its head, sat
down at a respectful distance after the Lord had eaten and had
withdrawn his hand from the bowl. And when the Lord had
roused, rejoiced, gladdened, delighted General Siha with talk
on Dhamma, he departed. Having given reasoned talk on this
occasion, he then addressed the monks, saying:

"Monks, one should not knowingly make use of meat killed
on purpose for one. Whoever should make use of it, there is an
offence of wrong-doing. I allow you, monks, fish and meat that

[1] Insertion to be made here as in the case of the progressive talk to
Anāthapiṇḍika, see above, pp. 18–19.

[2] pavattamaṁsa, i.e. what had been already killed, but not killed on
purpose or specially for a meal for a monk, *uddissakataro*.

are quite pure in these three respects: if they have not been seen, heard or suspected (to have been killed on purpose for a monk)."

Vinaya-pitaka I, 236-38

3. *Ordination of Pajapati the Great*

At one time the Buddha, the Lord, was staying among the Sakyans at Kapilavatthu in the Banyan monastery. Then the Gotamid, Pajapati the Great, approached and greeted the Lord and, standing at a respectful distance, spoke thus to him:

"Lord, it were well that women should obtain the going forth from home into homelessness in this Dhamma and Discipline proclaimed by the Tathagata."

"Be careful, Gotami, of the going forth of women from home into homelessness in this Dhamma and Discipline proclaimed by the Tathagata."

A second and a third time both uttered these words. And Pajapati, thinking that the Lord did not allow the going forth of women, afflicted, grieved, with tearful face and crying, greeted the Lord and departed keeping her right side towards him.

Then the Lord set out for Vesali. And Pajapati too, having had her hair cut off and having donned saffron robes, set out for Vesali with several Sakyan women. Arrived at the Gabled Hall, she stood outside the porch, her feet swollen, her limbs covered with dust, with tearful face and crying. The venerable Ananda saw her, and hearing from her the reason for her distress, told her to wait a moment while he asked the Lord for the going forth of women from home into homelessness. But the Lord answered him as he had answered Pajapati. So Ananda thought: "Suppose that I should now ask the Lord by some other method?" and he spoke thus to the Lord:

"Now, Lord, are women, having gone forth from home into homelessness in this Dhamma and Discipline proclaimed by the Tathagata, able to realize the fruits of stream-winning, of once-returning and of non-returning, and arahantship?"

"Yes, Ananda."

"If so, Lord—and, Lord, the Gotamid, Pajapati the Great, was of great service: she was the Lord's aunt, foster-mother, nurse, giver of milk, for when the Lord's mother passed away she suckled him—it were well, Lord, that women should obtain the going forth from home into homelessness."

"If, Ananda, the Gotamid, Pajapati the Great, accepts these eight important rules, that may be ordination for her:

"A nun who has been ordained even for a century must greet respectfully, rise up from her seat, salute with joined palms and do proper homage to a monk ordained but that very day.

"A nun must not spend the rains in a residence where there is no monk.

"Every half month a nun should require two things from the Order of monks: the date of the Observance day, and the coming for the exhortation.

"After the rains a nun must 'invite' before both Orders[1] in respect of three matters: what has been seen, heard and suspected (to be an offence).

"A nun, offending against an important rule, must undergo *manatta*[2] discipline for a fortnight before both Orders.

"When, as a probationer, she has trained in the six rules for two years,[3] she should seek ordination from both Orders.

---

[1] That of the monks and that of the nuns.

[2] Information as to the nature of this penalty may be found at Vin. ii, 35–37. Briefly, a monk (or nun) on whom mānatta has been imposed should not consent to receive greetings or the proper duties from regular monks; he should not ordain, or exercise any of the various privileges of regular monks; he should announce that he is undergoing mānatta on various occasions, such as entering a monastery, and also daily; and a number of rulings govern his visits to other monasteries including staying in them. In short, he is temporarily suspended from leading the normal life of a monk. Mānatta is the third of the four parts that together compose the penalty for infringing any of the rules known as Sanghadisesa together with its termination by rehabilitating the offender to his former status: the Order imposes a probationary period, sends the offender back to the beginning (of the training), imposes mānatta, and then rehabilitates.

[3] The probationer, always a woman, undertakes for two years not to transgress her resolve to abstain from onslaught on creatures, from

"A monk must not be abused or reviled in any way by a nun.

"From today admonition of monks by nuns is forbidden, admonition of nuns by monks is not forbidden.

"Each of these rules is to be honoured, respected, revered, venerated, and is never to be transgressed by a nun during her life. If, Ananda, Pajapati accepts these eight important rules, that shall be ordination for her."

When Ananda had told Pajapati this matter, she said:

"Even, Ananda, as a woman or a man when young, of tender years and fond of ornaments, having washed his head, having obtained a garland of lotus or jasmine flowers or of some sweet-scented creeper, should take it in both hands and place it on top of his head—even so do I, honoured Ananda, accept these eight important rules, never to be transgressed during my life."

Then Pajapati approached the Lord and asked him what line of conduct she should follow in regard to the Sakyan women. When the Lord had rejoiced and delighted her with talk on Dhamma, she departed; and the Lord said to the monks: "I allow, monks, nuns to be ordained by monks."

These nuns said to Pajapati: "The lady is not ordained, neither are we ordained, for it was laid down by the Lord that nuns should be ordained by monks." Pajapati told the venerable Ananda who told the Lord. He said: "At the time, Ananda, when the eight important rules were accepted by Pajapati, that was her ordination."

Then Pajapati approached the Lord herself and, standing at a respectful distance, said to him:

"Lord, what line of conduct should we follow in regard to those rules of training for nuns which are in common with those for monks?"[1]

"As the monks train themselves, so should you train yourselves in these rules of training."

stealing, unchastity, lying, slothfulness due to drinking intoxicants, and from eating at the wrong time (i.e. after noon one day until sunrise the next).

[1] There were more rules for nuns than for monks; see BD. iii, Intr. p. xxxii f., xxxvii f.

"And what line of conduct should we follow in regard to those rules of training for nuns which are not in common with those for monks?"

"You should train yourselves in these rules of training according as they are laid down."

Vinaya-piṭaka II, 253 ff.

4. *Visakha, the Laywoman Supporter*

After Visakha, Migara's mother, had been roused, rejoiced, gladdened, delighted by the Lord with talk on Dhamma, she asked him to consent to accept a meal from her on the morrow together with the Order of monks. The Lord consented by becoming silent. Then towards the end of that night heavy rain poured over the four 'continents', and the Lord said to the monks: "Monks, even as it is raining in the Jeta Grove, so it is raining over the four continents. Let your bodies get wet with the rain, this is the last great cloud over the four continents."[1]

When the time for the meal had come, Visakha sent a servant woman to the monastery to announce the time. She saw the monks, their robes laid aside, letting their bodies get wet with the rain, but she thought they were Naked Ascetics,[2] not monks. Then the Lord addressed the monks, saying: "Monks, arrange your bowls and robes, it is time for the meal." —When Visakha had served and satisfied the Order of monks with the Buddha at its head with sumptuous food, solid and soft, she sat down at a respectful distance, and spoke thus to the Lord:

"Lord, I ask for eight boons from the Lord."

"Visakha, Tathagatas are beyond granting boons."

"Lord, they are allowable and blameless."

"Speak on, Visakha."

"I, Lord, for life want to give to the Order cloths for the rains, food for those coming in (to monasteries), food for those going out, food for the sick, food for those who nurse them,

[1] I.e. the end of the rains.
[2] Ājīvikas, an important sect contemporary with the Buddha.

medicine for the sick, a constant supply of conjey, and bathing-cloths for the Order of nuns."

"But, having what special reason in mind do you, Visakha, ask the Tathagata for the eight boons?"

"Lord, my servant woman told me there were no monks in the monastery, but Naked Ascetics were letting their bodies get wet with the rain. Impure, Lord, is nakedness, it is objectionable. It is for this special reason that for life I want to give the Order cloths for the rains.

"And again, an in-coming monk, not accustomed to the roads or resorts for alms, still walks for alms when he is tired. But if he eats my food for those coming in, then when he is accustomed to the roads and resorts for alms he will walk for alms without getting tired.

"And again, an out-going monk, while looking about for food for himself, might get left behind by the caravan, or, setting out tired on a journey, might arrive at the wrong time [1] at the habitation where he wants to go. But if he eats my food for those going out, these things will not happen to him.

"And again, Lord, if an ill monk does not obtain suitable meals, either his disease will get very much worse or he will pass away. But not if he eats my food for the sick.

"And again, Lord, a monk who nurses the sick, looking about for food for himself, will bring back food for the sick after the sun is right up and so he will miss his meal. But, having eaten my food for those who nurse the sick, he will bring back food for the sick during the right time and so he will not miss his meal.

"And again, Lord, if an ill monk does not obtain suitable medicines, either his disease will get very much worse or he will pass away. But this will not happen if he can use my medicine for the sick.

"And again, Lord, conjey was allowed by the Lord at Andhakavinda when he had its ten advantages in mind.[2] I, Lord, having this special reason in mind, want to give for life a constant supply of conjey to the Order.

"There was a case where nuns bathed naked together with

---

[1] The wrong time for eating is after noon until sunrise the next day.

[2] Enumerated at Vin. i, 221. Conjey also allowed to monks at Vin. i, 222.

prostitutes at the same ford of the river Aciravati, and the prostitutes made fun of them, saying: 'Why on earth, ladies, is the Brahma-faring led by you when you are still young? Surely sense-pleasures should be enjoyed? When you are old you can fare the Brahma-faring; and so will you experience both extremes.'[1] The nuns were ashamed. Impure, Lord, is nakedness for women, it is abhorrent and objectionable. I, Lord, having this special reason in mind, want to give for life bathing-cloths for the Order of nuns."

"It is very good that you, Visakha, are asking the Tathagata for these eight boons. I allow you, Visakha, these eight boons." Then the Lord, on this occasion, having given reasoned talk, addressed the monks, saying: "I allow, monks, cloths for the rains, food for those coming in, for those going out, for the sick, for those who nurse them, medicines for the sick, a constant supply of conjey, bathing-cloths for the Order of nuns."

Vinaya-piṭaka I, 290–94 (condensed)

5. Schism

As Devadatta was meditating in private a reasoning arose in his mind thus: "Whom could I now please so that, because he is pleased with me, much gain and honour would accrue to me?" And he thought of Prince Ajatasattu. Throwing off his own form and assuming that of a young boy clad in a girdle of snakes, he became manifest in the Prince's lap. Terrified, he asked who he was.

"I am Devadatta."

"If that is really so, please become manifest in your own form." And Devadatta, throwing off the young boy's form stood, wearing his outer cloak and his robes and carrying his bowl, before Prince Ajatasattu. Greatly pleased with this wonder of psychic power, morning and evening he went to wait on him with five hundred chariots, bringing five hundred offerings of rice cooked in milk as a gift of food. And in Devadatta, overcome by the gains, honours and fame, his mind obsessed by them, there arose the longing to be the one to lead

---

[1] This passage occurs again in Nuns' Pācittiya 21, where it is made an offence for nuns to bathe naked.

the Order of monks.[1] But at its very occurrence Devadatta declined in his psychic power.

At that time Kakudha the Koliyan had just died and had arisen in a mind-made body as a young deva. He approached the venerable Moggallana, whose attendant he had been, and warned him of Devadatta's longing. Moggallana then warned the Lord. He replied:

"Moggallana, this foolish man of himself will now betray himself. These five teachers are found in the world: the teacher who is not pure in moral habit, or in mode of livelihood, or in teaching Dhamma, or in the exposition, or in the vision of knowledge. But in each case he pretends that he is pure, and that his moral habit and so on are pure, clean, untarnished. Although disciples know this about him, they think: 'If we should tell this to householders, he would not like it, and how could we speak about what he would not like?' Moreover, he consents to accept the requisites of robes, almsfood, lodgings and medicines for the sick (thus conferring merit on the donors). Whatever anyone shall do, by that he shall be known.' Moggallana, disciples protect such a teacher and such a teacher expects protection from them.

"But I, Moggallana, am pure in moral habit, in mode of livelihood, in teaching Dhamma, the exposition and the vision of knowledge. And I acknowledge that I am pure, and that my moral habit and so on are pure, clean, untarnished. Disciples do not protect me and I do not expect protection from them."

Some monks then sat down near the Lord and told him how Prince Ajatasattu went morning and evening with the five hundred chariots to wait on Devadatta, bringing as a gift of food five hundred offerings of rice cooked in milk.

"Do not, monks, envy Devadatta's gains, honours and fame. For as long as Prince Ajatasattu goes to him morning and evening, Devadatta's wholesome mental states may be expected to decline, not to grow, just as a fierce dog would become much fiercer if a bladder were thrown at its nose. Devadatta's gains, honours and fame bring about his own hurt and destruction, just as a plaintain or bamboo or reed bears

[1] At D. ii, 100 Gotama is recorded to tell Ānanda that such a thought does not occur to a Tathāgata.

fruit or as a she-mule conceives to her own hurt and destruction.

> Truly its fruit the plaintain does destroy,
> Its fruit the bamboo, its fruit the reed;
> So honour does destroy the fool,
> Just as its embryo the mule."

Now at that time the Lord was sitting down teaching Dhamma surrounded by a large company which included a king. And Devadatta got up, saluted the Lord and spoke thus to him: "Lord, the Lord is now old, stricken in years and at the close of his life. Let him be content to abide in ease here and now, and hand over the Order of monks to me. It is I who will lead the Order of monks."

"Enough, Devadatta, please do not lead the Order of monks. I would not hand over the Order even to Sariputta and Moggallana. How then to you, a wretched one to be vomited up like spittle?"

And Devadatta, angry and displeased at having been disparaged, went away. The Lord addressed the Order of monks, saying: "Let the Order carry out a formal act of Information against Devadatta, to the effect that whereas Devadatta's nature was formerly of one kind, now it is of another; and that whatever he should do by gesture or by voice, in that neither the Buddha nor Dhamma nor the Order is to be seen, but only Devadatta."

Devadatta then asked Prince Ajatasattu to command his men to deprive the recluse Gotama of life. Sixteen men were sent out, but all, on seeing Gotama, admitted that they had transgressed in coming to him with their minds malignant and set on murder, and they asked to become lay followers for as long as their life lasted. On hearing the news Devadatta said that he himself would deprive the recluse Gotama of life. He saw the Lord pacing up and down in the shade of Mount Vulture Peak, and having climbed it he hurled down a great stone. But two mountain peaks, meeting, crushed it and only a fragment fell down; but it drew blood on the Lord's foot. Looking upwards he said to Devadatta: "You have produced much demerit, foolish man, in that you, with your mind malignant and set on murder, drew the Tathagata's blood."

And to the monks he said: "This is the first deed whose fruit is immediate that has been accumulated by Devadatta since, with his mind malignant and set on murder, he drew the Tathagata's blood."

On hearing that Devadatta had schemed to murder the Lord, the monks paced up and down on every side of his dwelling-place doing their studies together with a loud and great noise for his protection, defence and warding. The Lord sent Ananda to summon them to his presence, and said to them: "It is impossible, monks, it cannot come to pass that anyone could deprive a Tathagata of life by aggression. Tathagatas do not attain final Nirvana because of an attack. Go, monks, to your own dwelling-places. Tathagatas do not need to be protected."

Now at that time there was a fierce elephant in Rajagaha, a man-slayer, called Nalagiri. Devadatta went to Rajagaha, entered the elephant stable, and said to the mahouts: "We, my good fellows, are relations of the king, and are able to put in high positions those occupying lowly ones and to bring about an increase in food and wages. When the recluse Gotama is coming along this carriage road, release Nalagiri and bring him down the carriage road." When the mahouts saw the Lord coming in the distance they released the elephant. Raising his trunk, he rushed towards the Lord, his ears and tail erect. But the Lord suffused him with loving-kindness of mind. He put down his trunk and stood before the Lord who stroked his forehead with his right hand and spoke some verses. And the elephant, having taken the dust of the Lord's feet with his trunk and scattered it over his head, moved back bowing while he gazed upon the Lord and then returned to his stable. It was in this way that he became tamed.

Then Devadatta appealed to some friends of his saying: "Come, your reverences, we will approach the Lord and ask for five items, saying: 'Lord, the Lord in many a figure speaks in praise of desiring little, of being contented, of expunging evil, of being punctilious, of what is gracious, of decreasing the defilements, of putting forth energy. Lord, these following five items conduce thereto: It were good, Lord, if for as long as life lasted the monks might be forest dwellers; whoever should betake himself to a village, sin would besmirch him. For as long as life lasts let them be beggars for alms; whoever should accept an invitation to a meal, sin would besmirch him. For as long as life lasts, let them be rag-robe wearers; whoever should accept a robe given by a householder, sin would besmirch him. For as long as life lasts, let them dwell at the root of a tree; whoever should go under cover, sin would besmirch him. For as long as life lasts, let them not eat fish and flesh; whoever should eat fish and flesh, sin would besmirch him.' The recluse Gotama will not allow these five items, but we will win people over to them."

Devadatta's friends replied: "It is possible, with these five items, to make a schism in the recluse Gotama's Order, a breaking of the concord. For, your reverence, people esteem austerity."

So Devadatta and his friends approached the Lord, and put the matter of the five items before him.

"Enough, Devadatta," he said. "Whoever wishes, let him be a forest-dweller, whoever wishes, let him stay near a village; whoever wishes, let him be a beggar for alms, whoever wishes let him accept an invitation; whoever wishes, let him be a rag-robe wearer, whoever wishes, let him accept robes given by a householder. For eight months, Devadatta, lodging at the root of a tree is permitted by me.[1] Fish and flesh are quite pure[2] in respect of three points: if they are not seen, heard or suspected to have been killed on purpose for a monk."

Devadatta was joyful and elated that the Lord did not permit these five items. He entered Rajagaha and taught them to the people, and such people as were of little faith thought that Devadatta and his friends were punctilious while Gotama was striving after abundance. But the people who had faith and were believing complained to the monks that Devadatta was creating a schism, and the monks told the Lord. He said to Devadatta, who acknowledged the truth of the complaint:

"Do not let there be a schism in the Order, for a schism in the Order is a serious matter, Devadatta. He who splits an Order that is united sets up demerit that endures for an aeon

---

[1] For the four months of the rains monks have to live in a rains-residence.

[2] I.e. are permitted food if they conform to the three points; see above, p. 23.

and he is boiled in hell for an aeon. But he who unites an Order
that is split sets up sublime merit[1] and rejoices in heaven for
an aeon."

Vinaya-piṭaka II, 184–198 (condensed)

SKILL IN MEANS

6.

This consciousness (citta) is luminous, but it is defiled by
adventitious defilements. The uninstructed average person
does not understand this as it really is. Therefore I say that for
him there is no mental development.

This consciousness is luminous, and it is freed from adventitious defilements. The instructed ariyan disciple understands
this as it really is. Therefore I say that for him there is mental
development.

Anguttara-nikāya I, 10

7.

I, monks, am freed from all snares, both those of devas and
those of men. And you, monks, are freed from all snares,
both those of devas and those of men. Walk, monks, on tour
for the blessing of the manyfolk, for the happiness of the manyfolk, out of compassion for the world, for the welfare, the
blessing, the happiness of devas and men. Let not two of you
go by the same way. Monks, teach Dhamma that is lovely at
the beginning, lovely in the middle and lovely at the ending.
Explain with the spirit and the letter the Brahma-faring completely fulfilled and utterly pure. There are beings with little
dust in their eyes who, not hearing Dhamma, are decaying, but
if they are learners of Dhamma they will grow. And I, monks,
will go along to Uruvela, the Camp township, in order to teach
Dhamma.

Vinaya-piṭaka I, 20–21

[1] brahma puñña.

8.

A village headman spoke thus to the Lord:

"Is a Tathagata compassionate towards all living breathing creatures?"

"Yes, headman," answered the Lord.

"But does the Lord teach Dhamma in full to some, but not likewise to others?"

"Now, what do you think, headman? Suppose a farmer had three fields, one excellent, one mediocre, and one poor with bad soil. When he wanted to sow the seed, which field would he sow first?"

"He would sow the excellent one, then the mediocre one. When he had done that, he might or might not sow the poor one with the bad soil. And why? Because it might do if only for cattle-fodder."

"In the same way, headman, my monks and nuns are like the excellent field. It is to these that I teach Dhamma that is lovely at the beginning, lovely in the middle and lovely at the ending, with the spirit and the letter, and to whom I make known the Brahma-faring completely fulfilled, utterly pure. And why? It is these that dwell with me for light, me for shelter, me for stronghold, me for refuge.

"Then my men and women lay followers are like the mediocre field. To these too I teach Dhamma . . . and make known the Brahma-faring completely fulfilled, utterly pure. For they dwell with me for light, me for shelter, me for stronghold, me for refuge.

"Then recluses, Brahmins and wanderers of other sects than mine are like the poor field with the bad soil. To these too I teach Dhamma . . . and make known the Brahma-faring completely fulfilled, utterly pure. And why? Because if they were to understand even a single sentence, that would be a happiness and a blessing for them for a long time."

Samyutta-nikāya IV, 314–16

9.

Dhamma has been taught by me without making a distinction between esoteric and exoteric. For the Tathagata has not the closed fist of a teacher in respect of mental states.

Dīgha-nikāya II, 100

10.

The Lord said to the venerable Nanda[1]: "You admit it is true that without zest you fare the Brahma-faring, that you cannot endure it, and that, throwing off the training, you will return to the low life. How is this?"

"Revered sir, when I left my home a Sakyan girl, the fairest in the land, with hair half combed, looked back at me and said: 'May you soon be back again, young master.' Revered sir, as I am always thinking of that, I have no zest for the Brahma-faring, can't endure it, and, throwing off the training, will return to the low life."

Then the Lord, taking the venerable Nanda by the arm, as a strong man might stretch out his bent arm or might bend back his outstretched arm, vanishing from the Jeta Grove, appeared among the Devas of the Thirty-Three. At that time as many as five hundred nymphs were come to minister to Sakka, the lord of devas, and they were called 'dove-footed'. The Lord asked the venerable Nanda which he thought the more lovely, worth looking at and charming, the Sakyan girl, the fairest in the land, or these five hundred nymphs called 'dove-footed'.

"O, revered sir, just as if she were a mutilated monkey with ears and nose cut off, even so the Sakyan girl, the fairest in the land, if set beside these five hundred nymphs called 'dove-footed', is not worth a fraction of them, cannot be compared with them. Why, these five hundred nymphs are far more lovely, worth looking at and charming."

Thereupon the Lord, taking the venerable Nanda by the arm, vanished from the Devas of the Thirty-Three and reappeared in the Jeta Grove. Monks heard it said that the

[1] Gotama's cousin.

venerable Nanda was faring the Brahma-faring for the sake of
nymphs and that the Lord had assured him of getting five
hundred nymphs called 'dove-footed'. And the monks who
were his comrades called him 'hireling' and 'menial'. Thus
worried, humiliated and disgusted, the venerable Nanda, living
alone, aloof, diligent, ardent, self-resolute, soon realizing by
his own super-knowledge that incomparable goal of the
Brahma-faring for the sake of which young men of family
rightly go forth from home into homelessness, abided in it, and
he knew: "Destroyed is birth, brought to a close the Brahma-
faring, done is what was to be done, there is no more of being
such or such." Thus the venerable Nanda was one of the
arahants.

Udāna, 22–23

II.

In the Himalaya, monks, there is a region that is rough and
hard to cross, the range of neither monkeys nor human
beings. There is a similar region which is the range of monkeys
but not of human beings. Again, there are level and delightful
tracts of country, the range of both monkeys and human
beings. It is here, monks, that a hunter sets a trap of pitch in
the monkeys' tracks so as to catch them. Now, those monkeys
that are not stupid and greedy, on seeing that pitch-trap, keep
far away from it. But a stupid, greedy monkey comes up to the
pitch and handles it with one of his paws, and his paw sticks
fast in it. Then thinking to free his paw, he lays hold of it with
the other paw—but that too sticks fast. To free both paws he
lays hold of them with one foot, but that too sticks fast. To
free both paws and one foot he lays hold of them with the
other foot, but that too sticks fast. To free both paws and both
feet he lays hold of them with his muzzle, but that too sticks
fast.

So that monkey, thus trapped in five ways, lies down and
howls, thus fallen on misfortune and ruin, a prey for the hunter
to work his will on him. The hunter spits him and prepares him
for eating then and there over a charcoal fire and goes off at
his pleasure.

Even so it is with one that goes in wrong pastures, the beat of others. Therefore, monks, do not you so walk. To those that do, Mara gets access, Mara gets a chance over them. And what, monks, is the wrong pasture, the beat of others? It is the fivefold set of pleasures of the senses. What are the five? Material shapes cognizable by the eye, sounds cognizable by the ear, scents cognizable by the nose, tastes cognizable by the tongue, objects cognizable by the body, desirable, delightful, pleasant, dear, passion-fraught, inciting to lust. This, monks, is the wrong pasture, the beat of others. Go, monks, in a pasture that is your own native beat, for to those that so go Mara gets no access, Mara gets no chance over them. And what is a monk's pasture, his own native beat? It is the four applications of mindfulness.[1]

Samyutta-nikāya V, 148–49

12.

The Brahmin Sangarava spoke thus to the Lord:

"Let me tell you, good Gotama, that Brahmins offer sacrifice and get others to do so. All these are following a course of merit, due to sacrifice, that benefits many people. But whoever from this or that family has gone forth from home into homelessness, he tames but one self, calms but one self, makes but one self attain final Nirvana. Thus, due to his going forth, he is following a course of merit that benefits only one person."

"Well, Brahmin, I will ask you a question in return. What do you think? A Tathagata arises here in the world, an Arahant, a perfect Buddha, endowed with knowledge and right conduct, well-farer, knower of the world(s), incomparable charioteer of men to be tamed, teachers of devas and mankind, a Buddha, a Lord. He speaks thus: 'Come, this is the Way, this is the course I have followed until, having realized by my own super-knowledge the matchless plunge into the Brahma-faring, I have made it known. Come you too, follow likewise, so that you also, having realized by your own super-knowledge the matchless plunge into the Brahma-faring, may abide in it.' It is thus that the Teacher himself teaches Dhamma, and others

[1] See below, no. 32.

follow for the sake of Suchness. And moreover these number many hundreds, many thousands, many hundreds of thousands. So, as this is the case, do you think that the course of merit that is due to going forth benefits one person or many?"

"As this is the case, good Gotama, the course of merit that is due to going forth benefits many persons."

Anguttara-nikāya I, 168–69

13.

O nce upon a time when Brahmadatta was reigning in Benares, the Bodhisatta was reborn as a peacock. The shell of the egg that contained him was as golden in colour as a kanikara bud. After he had broken the shell, on issuing forth he was golden coloured, lovely and charming, and among his feathers were beautiful red streaks. To protect his own life, he traversed three mountain ranges and took up his abode on a fourth, on a plateau of a golden mountain called Dandaka. As the night was waning, he used to sit on the mountain peak watching the sun rise and he composed a mantra to Brahma beginning, 'There he rises', so as to preserve himself from difficulties in his own feeding-ground:

> There he rises, the visioned king of all,
> Golden coloured, splendour of the earth.
> Him I honour, the golden coloured, splendour of the earth,
> That today I may be protected by him all through the day.

After the Bodhisatta had honoured the sun with this verse, in a second verse he honoured the former Buddhas who had attained Nirvana as well as every excellence:

> Those Brahmins, deep in knowledge of all things,
> My honour is for these that they may guard me.
> Let there be honour for the Buddhas, honour for enlightenment ;
> Let there be honour for the freed, honour for freedom.

When he had composed this charm, the peacock used to roam about seeking (his food). After he had roamed about all day

he used to sit on the mountain peak in the evening watching
the sun and, reflecting on the excellences of the Buddhas, he
composed a mantra to Brahma beginning, 'There he sets', so
as to preserve himself from difficulties in his roosting-place:

There he sets, the visioned king of all,
Golden coloured, splendour of the earth.
Him I honour, the golden coloured, splendour of the earth,
That today I may be protected by him all through the night.
Those Brahmins, deep in knowledge of all things,
My honour is for these that they may guard me.
Let there be honour for the Buddhas, honour for enlighten-
ment;
Let there be honour for the freed, honour for freedom.

When he had made this charm the peacock used to lie down to
sleep.

Now there was a hunter who lived in a hunters' village near
Benares. Wandering about the Himalayan region, he saw the
Bodhisatta sitting on a peak of the golden mountain called
Dandaka. He went back home and told his son. Then one day
Khema, the queen of the king of Benares, saw in a dream a
golden peacock teaching Dhamma. She told the king, saying:
"I, sire, want to hear a golden peacock's Dhamma." The king
asked his ministers who said that the Brahmins would know.
And the Brahmins said: "Yes, there are golden peacocks." On
being asked where these were they replied that the hunters
would know. So the king called the hunters together and asked
them. That hunter's son said: "Yes, your majesty, there is a
golden mountain called Dandaka, and a golden peacock is
living there."

"Very well, capture that peacock without killing it and
bring it here."

The hunter went off and set snares in its feeding-ground.
But the snare, even when the peacock stepped on it, did not
close. The hunter, after wandering about for seven years without being able to catch it, died there. And queen Khema died
too without getting her wish. The king was wroth, thinking:
"My queen died on account of a peacock", and he had it
inscribed on a golden tablet which he placed in a golden casket
that: "There is a golden mountain called Dandaka in the

Himalayan region, and a golden peacock lives there; those who
eat his flesh are unageing and undying."

After he had died, another king, on coming to the throne,
heard tell of the golden tablet; and thinking: "I will be unageing, undying", he sent out another hunter. But he too,
being unable to catch the Bodhisatta after he had got there,
died there. In this way six reigns passed.

When the seventh king came to the throne he too sent out a
hunter. He went off and, knowing that the snare did not close
when the Bodhisatta stepped on it and also that he made a
charm for himself on going to his feeding-ground, went down
to a neighbouring place and caught a peahen. When he had
trained her to dance to the clapping of his hands and to utter
her call when he snapped his fingers, he then took her with him.
And early one morning, before the peacock had made his
charm, he drove in the stakes for the snare, set it, and made the
peahen utter her call. The peacock, hearing the unusual note of
the female, being affected by the defilements and unable to
make a charm, went along quickly and was caught in the
snare.[1] Then the hunter took hold of him, went back and
presented him to the king of Benares.

The king, delighted at the sight of his beauty, had a seat
offered to him. The Bodhisatta, sitting on the appointed seat,
asked why the king had had him caught. The king said: "They
say that those who eat your flesh are unageing and undying.
Because *I* want to be unageing and undying once I've eaten
your flesh, I therefore had you caught."

"Your majesty, only so long as they eat my flesh will they
be unageing and undying. But *I* will die."

"Yes, you will die."

"But with me dead and my flesh eaten up, what can I do so
that they will not die?"

"You are golden;[2] therefore it is said that those who eat
your flesh will be unageing and undying."

---

[1] Miln. 152–3 says that the fame of this story has spread throughout
the world: of how the hunters were unable to catch the peacock for
700 years, but the very day he failed to make the charm he fell into
the snare.

[2] Gold, hence yellow, saffron, etc., is the traditional colour-symbol
of light and immortality.

"Your majesty, not without reason was I born golden, for formerly, being a wheel-turning king in this very town, I guarded the five moral habits myself and made the inhabitants of the whole world guard them. When I died I was reborn in the Abode of the Thirty-Three. When I had stayed there for the length of my life-span, then deceasing thence I was, as the karmic result of a certain unskill, reborn as a peacock, but golden in colour through the power of my ancient moral habit."

"What, you a wheel-turner, keeping the moral habits, and as their fruit being born golden! How can we believe this? There is no witness."

"There is, your majesty."

"What is it called?"

"Your majesty, when I was a wheel-turner, sitting in a chariot made of jewels, I used to drive about the firmament. I had that chariot buried in the ground under the royal lake. If it is raised from the royal lake it will be my witness."

"Very well," the king answered in assent. And when he had had the water drained from the royal lake and the chariot drawn out, he believed the Bodhisatta. The Bodhisatta said:

"Your majesty, except for the great Nirvana of deathlessness, every other thing, being compounded, must perish, it is impermanent and subject to extinction and decay." And having said this, he taught Dhamma to the king and established him in the five moral habits.

The king, believing, honoured the Bodhisatta with his kingdom and paid him the greatest respect. The Bodhisatta, having given back the kingdom and staying on for a few days, exhorted the king, saying: "Be diligent, your majesty", and then, rising up into the firmament, he came back to the golden mountain called Dandaka. The king too, established in the Bodhisatta's exhortation, making meritorious gifts and so forth, went on according to his deeds.

Identifying this birth, the Teacher said: "At that time Ananda was the king, and I myself was the golden peacock."

Jātaka II, 33–38

ARAHANTS

14.

Ah, happy indeed the Arahants! In them no craving's found.
The 'I am' conceit is rooted out; confusion's net is burst.
Lust-free they have attained; translucent is the mind of them.
Unspotted in the world are they, Brahma-become, with out-
flows none.
Comprehending the five groups, pasturing in their seven own
mental states,[1]
Worthy of praise, the true men, own sons of the Buddha.
Endowed with the sevenfold gem,[2] trained in the three
trainings,[3]
These great heroes follow on, fear and dread overcome.
Endowed with the ten factors,[4] great beings concentrated,
Indeed they are best in the world; no craving's found in them.
Possessed of the adept's knowledge, this compound is their
last.
In that pith of the Brahma-faring[5] they depend not on others.
Unshaken by the triple modes,[6] well freed from again-
becoming,
Attained to the stage of 'tamed', they are victorious in the
world.
Above, across, below, no lure in them is found.
They roar the lion's roar: 'Incomparable are Buddhas in the
world.'

Samyutta-nikāya III, 83–84

15.

At one time when the Lord was staying at Rajagaha the
venerable Godhika was staying at Black Rock on Mount
Isigili. And abiding diligent, ardent, self-resolute, he attained

1 Faith, shame, fear of blame, truth, the output of vigour, mindfulness, wisdom.
2 The seven limbs of enlightenment.
3 Morality, concentration and wisdom.
4 The ten powers: of a Tathāgata, see below, no. 116.
5 At M. i, 197 this pith is called unshakable freedom of mind.
6 'I am better, equal, worse', in comparison with another person.

the freedom of mind that is temporary. But although he won this freedom of mind six times, six times he fell away from it. Then having won it for the seventh time, he thought: "Up to six times have I fallen away from this freedom of mind. What if I were to stab myself?"

But Mara, the Malign One, knowing the reasoning in the venerable Godhika's mind, approached the Lord and spoke these verses:

"Great Hero, Great Wisdom, radiant in glory and psychic power,
Who has passed all hatred and fear, O Visioned One, I salute thy feet.

Thy disciple, Great Hero, though he has overcome death,
Yet desires and strives for death. Dissuade him, O Light-bringer.

For how, Lord, can a disciple, delighting in your dispensation,
A learner, his wishes not yet fulfilled, take his life, O Renowned among men?"

At that moment the venerable Godhika stabbed himself. And the Lord, discerning that it was Mara, the Malign One, who had spoken, spoke this verse to him:

"Yes, so do the steadfast act, they do not yearn for life.
Tearing out craving with its root, Godhika has attained complete Nirvana."

Then the Lord, accompanied by the monks, went to the Black Rock where Godhika had stabbed himself. And they arrived there precisely as a smokiness, a murkiness was going towards the east, west, north and south, going aloft, downwards and towards the intervening points. The Lord asked the monks if they saw this smokiness going in all directions and explained that it was Mara, the Malign One, searching for Godhika's consciousness and wondering where it had a foothold. "But, monks, Godhika, the young man of family, has attained complete Nirvana without any foothold for (his) consciousness . . .

> That steadfast one, endowed with steadfastness,
> A meditator delighting ever in meditation,
> Practising it by day and night, not longing for life,
> Having conquered Death's host,
> Not coming to again-becoming,
> Tearing out craving with its root—
> Godhika has attained complete Nirvana."

Samyutta-nikāya I, 122–23

16.

A synonym for the Arahant is "the Brahmin who, crossed over, gone beyond, stands on dry land."

Ibid. IV, 175

17.

The Arahant is he who, the outflows extinguished, is unfettered from the bond of the sense-pleasures and the bond of becoming . . .

> And those who have cut off doubt,
> Their pride [1] in recurrent becoming extinguished,
> These in the world are truly goers beyond
> Who have won extinction of the outflows.

Itivuttaka, p. 95–96

18.

Wrath must ye slay and utterly abandon pride,
And all the fetters must ye overcome,
For sorrows follow not the man-of-naught
Who not to these in mind-and-body clings.

[1] māna, pride, conceit, arrogance, is a fetter.

He got rid of 'reckoning',[1] came not to a mansion,[2]
He cut off craving here for mind-and-body.
Him that has cut the bonds, unconcerned, desireless,
Neither devas nor men, searching here or beyond,
Do find in the heavens or any habitation.

Samyutta-nikāya I, 23

19.

He whose outflows are utterly extinguished
And who is independent of 'basis' (for rebirth),
Whose pasture is emptiness,
The signless and freedom—
His track is as difficult to know
As that of birds in the sky.

Dhammapada, 93

THE BUDDHIST APOCALYPSE

20.

The discourses spoken by the Tathagata are profound, of profound significance, dealing with the other world and bound up with the emptiness of this world. But the time will come when they will no longer be regarded as things to be studied and mastered; on the contrary, it is those discourses that are made by poets in the poetical style, with embellished sounds, overlaid with ornament, and spoken by profane auditors, that will be considered worthy of study and the others will disappear.[3] Wherefore, monks, you must train yourselves thus: We will listen, lend ear, and bring a mind set on gnosis to the discourses spoken by the Tathagata.

Samyutta-nikāya II, 267

[1] 'Reckoned as so-and-so' no longer applies, for all ways of telling who or what he was or is have been removed; cf. Sn. 1076.

[2] vimāna is rather an unusual word for rebirth.

[3] Above translation closely follows that of A. K. Coomaraswamy in *Some Pali Words*, HJAS., July 1939, p. 179.

21.

There is no disappearing of the true Dhamma until a counter-feit dhamma arises in the world. Once a counterfeit dhamma arises then there is a disappearing of the true Dhamma. It is when foolish persons arise here that they make this true Dhamma to disappear. But five things conduce to its maintenance, clarity and non-disappearance—that monks and nuns, laymen and laywomen live with reverence and deference for the Teacher, for Dhamma, for the Order, for the training and for concentration.

Samyutta-nikāya II, 224

22.

Praise to that Lord, Arahant, perfect Buddha.

Thus have I heard: At one time the Lord was staying near Kapilavatthu in the Banyan monastery on the bank of the river Rohani. Then the venerable Sariputta questioned the Lord about the future Conqueror:

"The Hero that shall follow you,
The Buddha—of what sort will he be?
I want to hear of him in full.
Let the Visioned One describe him."

When he had heard the Elder's speech
The Lord spoke thus:
"I will tell you, Sariputta,
Listen to my speech.

"In this auspicious aeon
Three leaders have there been:
Kakusandha, Konagamana
And the leader Kassapa too.

"I am now the perfect Buddha;
And there will be Metteyya too
Before this same auspicious aeon
Runs to the end of its years.

"The perfect Buddha, Metteyya
By name, supreme of men."

(Then follows a history of the previous existence of Metteyya
. . . and then the description of the gradual decline of the
religion:)
"How will it occur? After my decease there will first be five
disappearances.[1] What five? The disappearance of attainment[2] (in the Dispensation), the disappearance of proper conduct,[3] the disappearance of learning,[4] the disappearance of the
outward form,[5] the disappearance of the relics.[6] There will be
these five disappearances.

"Here attainment means that for a thousand years only
after the Lord's complete Nirvana will monks be able to
practise analytical insights. As time goes on and on these
disciples of mine are non-returners and once-returners and
stream-winners. There will be no disappearance of attainment
for these. But with the extinction of the last stream-winner's
life, attainment will have disappeared.

"This, Sariputta, is the disappearance of attainment.

"The disappearance of proper conduct means that, being
unable to practise jhana, insight, the Ways and the fruits, they
will guard no more the four entire purities of moral habit.[7] As
time goes on and on they will only guard the four offences entailing defeat.[8] While there are even a hundred or a thousand

---

[1] Cf. AA. i, 87 for these five disappearances.

[2] Cf. Miln. 133–134, 162–164. Adhigama, attainment, is explained
at AA. i. 87 as the four Ways, the four fruits, the four analytical
insights, the three knowledges, the six super-knowledges.

[3] paṭipatti. Cf. Miln. 133–134; AA. i. 87. MA. iv. 115, VbhA. 431–
432 give three disappearances: (1) pariyatti, meaning the three
Piṭakas, (2) paṭivedha, meaning penetration of truth, (3) paṭipatti,
meaning paṭipadā, the course or practice.

[4] pariyatti. VbhA. 432 says that while learning lasts the Dispensation
lasts (or stands firm).

[5] linga. Cf. Miln. 133–134.   [6] dhātu.

[7] These four purities refer to the morality that consists of 1. Restraint or Control in regard to the Patimokkha (rules of conduct for
monks and nuns); 2. Restraint or Control of the sense-organs; 3. Purity
of livelihood; 4. Morality in regard to the four requisites (robe-material,
almsfood, lodgings and medicines for the sick).

[8] These pārājika offences (four for monks, eight for nuns) constitute
the first and most important class of offence. For monks they are

monks who guard and bear in mind the four offences entailing defeat, there will be no disappearance of proper conduct. With the breaking of moral habit by the last monk or on the extinction of his life, proper conduct will have disappeared.

"This, Sariputta, is the disappearance of proper conduct.

"The disappearance of learning means that as long as there stand firm the texts with the commentaries pertaining to the word of the Buddha in the three Pitakas, for so long there will be no disappearance of learning. As time goes on and on there will be base-born kings, not Dhamma-men; their ministers and so on will not be Dhamma-men, and consequently the inhabitants of the kingdom and so on will not be Dhamma-men. Because they are not Dhamma-men it will not rain properly. Therefore the crops will not flourish well, and in consequence the donors of requisites to the community of monks will not be able to give them the requisites. Not receiving the requisites the monks will not receive pupils. As time goes on and on learning will decay. In this decay the Great Patthana itself will decay first. In this decay also (there will be) Yamaka, Kathavatthu, Puggalapannatti, Dhatukatha, Vibhanga and Dhammasangani. When the Abhidhamma Pitaka decays the Suttanta Pitaka will decay. When the Suttantas decay the Anguttara will decay first. When it decays the Samyutta Nikaya, the Majjhima Nikaya, the Digha Nikaya and the Khuddaka-Nikaya will decay. They will simply remember the Jataka together with the Vinaya-Pitaka. But only the conscientious (monks) will remember the Vinaya-Pitaka. As time goes on and on, being unable to remember even the Jataka, the Vessantara-jataka will decay first. When that decays the Apannaka-jataka will decay. When the Jatakas decay they will remember only the Vinaya-Pitaka. As time goes on and on the Vinaya-Pitaka will decay. While a four-line stanza still continues to exist among men, there will not be a disappearance of learning. When a king who has faith has had a purse containing a thousand (coins) placed in a golden casket on an elephant's back, and has had the drum (of proclamation)

offences of unchastity, stealing, murder and lying in the particular sense of claiming to have advanced further in mental and spiritual attainment than is really so. The penalty for committing any of these offences is expulsion from the Order with no possibility of reordination.

sounded in the city up to the second or third time, to the effect that: 'Whoever knows a stanza uttered by the Buddhas, let him take these thousand coins together with the royal elephant'—but yet finding no one knowing a four-line stanza, the purse containing the thousand (coins) must be taken back into the palace again—then will be the disappearance of learning.

"This, Sariputta, is the disappearance of learning.

"As time goes on and on each of the last monks, carrying his robe, bowl and tooth-pick like Jain recluses, having taken a bottle-gourd and turned it into a bowl for almsfood, will wander about with it in his fore-arms or hands or hanging from a piece of string. As time goes on and on, thinking: 'What's the good of this yellow robe?' and cutting off a small piece of one and sticking it on his nose or ear or in his hair, he will wander about supporting wife and children by agriculture, trade and the like. Then he will give a gift to the Southern community for those (of bad moral habit [1]). I say that he will then acquire an incalculable fruit of the gift. As time goes on and on, thinking: 'What's the good of this to us?', having thrown away the piece of yellow robe, he will harry beasts and birds in the forest. At this time the outward form will have disappeared.

"This, Sariputta, is called the disappearance of the outward form.

"Then, when the Dispensation of the Perfect Buddha is 5000 years old, the relics, not receiving reverence and honour, will go to places where they can receive them. As time goes on and on there will not be reverence and honour for them in every place. At the time when the Dispensation is falling into (oblivion), all the relics, coming from every place: from the abode of serpents and the deva-world and the Brahma-world, having gathered together in the space round the great Bo-tree, having made a Buddha-image, and having performed a 'miracle' like the Twin-miracle, will teach Dhamma. No human being will be found at that place. All the devas of the ten-thousand world system, gathered together, will hear Dhamma and many thousands of them will attain to Dhamma. And these will cry aloud, saying: 'Behold, devatas, a week from

[1] Addition from AA. i. 90.

today our One of the Ten Powers will attain complete Nirvana.'
They will weep, saying: 'Henceforth there will be darkness for
us.' Then the relics, producing the condition of heat, will burn
up that image[1] leaving no remainder.

"This, Sariputta, is called the disappearance of the relics."

Anāgatavamsa

[1] tam sarīram, that Buddha-image?

THE DHAMMA

THE FIVE FACULTIES COLLECTIVELY

23.

And of what sort, monks, is the faculty of faith? Herein an ariyan disciple has faith: he has faith in the enlightenment of the Tathagata, thus: "He is indeed the Lord, Arahant, perfect Buddha, endowed with knowledge and right conduct, wellfarer, knower of the world(s), incomparable charioteer of men to be tamed, teacher of devas and mankind, a Buddha, a Lord." This is called the faculty of faith.

And what is the faculty of vigour? It is the vigour that one lays hold of in practising the four right efforts.[1]

And what is the faculty of mindfulness? It is the mindfulness one lays hold of in practising the four applications of mindfulness.[2]

And what is the faculty of concentration? Herein the ariyan disciple, having made relinquishing the object of meditation, attains concentration, attains one-pointedness of mind.

And what is the faculty of wisdom? Herein the ariyan disciple has wisdom. He is endowed with wisdom leading to the knowledge of rise and fall, ariyan, piercing, leading rightly to the extinction of suffering. This, monks, is called the faculty of wisdom.

Samyutta-nikāya V, 199–200

24.

I do not say that the attainment of gnosis comes straightaway, but that it comes by a gradual training, a gradual practice, a gradual course. How is this? One having faith draws near;

[1] Those of controlling, getting rid of, developing and maintaining; the first two refer to unwholesome states of mind, and the second two to wholesome ones. See below no. 29.

[2] See below, no. 32.

he gives ear and hears Dhamma and tests the meaning of the things he has borne in mind, and they please him; mindfulness and zeal are produced in him; weighing it all up, he strives; being self-resolute he realizes the highest truth itself and sees it in all its detail by means of wisdom.

Majjhima-nikāya I, 479–80 (condensed)

THE FIVE FACULTIES SEPARATELY

Faith

25.

By faith you shall be free and go beyond the realm of death.

Suttanipāta, 1146

26.

Faith is the wealth here best for man—by faith the flood is crossed.

Ibid., 182, 184

27.

And what, monks, are the defilements of the mind? Greed and covetousness,[1] malevolence, anger, malice, hypocrisy, spite, envy, stinginess, deceit, treachery, obstinacy, impetuosity, arrogance, pride, conceit, indolence. If a monk thinks and knows that these are defilements of the mind and gets rid of them, he becomes possessed of unwavering confidence in the Buddha and thinks: "Thus indeed is he the Lord, Arahant, perfect Buddha . . . (as in no. 23) . . . a Buddha, a Lord." And he becomes possessed of unwavering confidence in Dhamma and thinks: "Dhamma is well taught by the Lord, it is thoroughly seen here and now, it is timeless,[2] inviting all to

[1] MA. i. 169 says greed is the passion of delight for one's own possessions, covetousness that for another's possessions.

[2] akālika, not belonging to time. The meaning is that the fruit is immediately followed by the Way without any interval of time. See Vism. 198–221.

come-and-see, leading onwards,[1] to be understood by the wise each for himself." And he becomes possessed of unwavering confidence in the Order and thinks: "The Lord's Order of disciples is of good conduct, upright, of wise conduct, of dutiful conduct, that is to say the four pairs of men, the eight persons.[2] This Order of the Lord's disciples is worthy of alms, hospitality, offerings and reverence, it is a matchless field of merit for the world."

At this stage[3] there is for him giving up, renouncing, rejecting, getting rid of, forsaking. When he thinks that he has unwavering confidence in the Buddha, Dhamma and the Order, he acquires knowledge of Dhamma and the delight connected with Dhamma; rapture is born from that delight; being rapturous, his body is impassible; this being so, joy is felt, and in consequence the mind is well concentrated.

Majjhima-nikāya I, 36–38 (condensed)

28.

The king said to Nagasena:
"How, revered sir, is aspiration the distinguishing mark of faith?"

"As, sire, an earnest student of yoga (yogavacara), on seeing that the minds of others are freed, jumps (as it were) into the fruit of stream-winning or of once-returning or of non-returning or into arahantship and practises yoga for the attainment of the unattained, the mastery of the unmastered, the realization of the unrealized—even so, sire, is aspiration the distinguishing mark of faith."

"Give an illustration."

"As, sire, when a great cloud pours down rain on a hill-slope, after the water, in flowing along according to the slope, had filled the clefts, fissures and gullies of the hill-slope, it would fill the river so that it would course along overflowing

[1] To Nirvana.
[2] Those on the four stages of the Way, and those who have attained the fruits of these four stages.
[3] yathodi, i.e. he is now a non-returner.

its banks; and then suppose that a great crowd of people were
to come, but, knowing neither the width nor the depth of the
river, were to stand afraid and hesitating on the bank. But
then suppose a knowledgeable man were to come and who, on
recognizing his own strength and power, should tie on his loin-
cloth firmly and, jumping, should cross over. When the great
crowd of people had seen him crossed over they too would cross
over. This is the way, sire, that an earnest student of yoga, on
seeing that the minds of others are freed, jumps (as it were)
into the fruit of stream-winning and so on and practises
yoga for the aims mentioned already. And this, sire, was said
by the Lord in the Samyutta Nikaya: [1]

> By faith the flood is crossed,
> By diligence the sea;
> By vigour ill is passed;
> By wisdom cleansed is he."

Milindapañha, 35–36

Vigour

29.

These are the four right efforts: a monk generates desire,
endeavours, stirs up vigour, exerts his mind and strives
that 1. evil unwholesome mental states that have not arisen
should not arise, 2. evil unwholesome mental states that have
arisen should be got rid of, 3. wholesome mental states that
have not arisen should arise, 4. wholesome mental states that
have arisen should be maintained, preserved, increased,
matured, developed and brought to completion. Herein many
of my disciples have reached full perfection[2] through super-
knowledge.

Dīgha-nikāya III, 221

[1] S. i. 214; also at Sn. 184, translated as above in E. M. Hare, *Woven Cadences.*

[2] pāramī. This last sentence occurs only at M. ii. 11.

30.

Sona Kolivisa, a merchant's son, received his going forth in the Lord's presence, he received ordination. Because of his great output of vigour while pacing up and down, his feet split and the place for pacing up and down in became stained with blood as though cattle had been slaughtered there. As the venerable Sona was meditating in private he thought: "The Lord's disciples, of whom I am one, dwell putting forth vigour; but even so my mind is not freed from the outflows with no (further) clinging, and moreover there are my family's possessions. Suppose I were to return to the low life, enjoy the possessions and do good?"

The Lord knew by mind the thoughts in the venerable Sona's mind. He approached him and said: "Sona, formerly when you were a householder were you clever at the lute's stringed music?"

"Yes, Lord."

"When the strings of the lute were too taut, was it tuneful and fit for playing?"

"Certainly not, Lord."

"And when they were too slack, was the lute tuneful and fit for playing?"

"No, Lord."

"But when the strings were neither too taut nor too slack but were keyed to an even pitch, was your lute tuneful and fit for playing?"

"Yes, Lord."

"Even so, Sona, does too much output of vigour conduce to restlessness and too feeble a vigour to slothfulness. Therefore, Sona, determine on evenness in vigour."

Vinaya-piṭaka I, 181–82

31.

Dhamma being well declared by me, made manifest, disclosed, brought to light, stripped of swathings, it is enough for the young man of family who has gone forth through faith to stir up vigour and think: "Gladly would I be reduced to skin and sinew and bones and let my body's flesh and blood dry up if there came to be a vortex of vigour so that which is not yet won might be won by human strength, by human vigour, by human striving."

Sadly lives the man of sloth, involved in evil unwholesome mental states, and great is the goal itself that he fails to win. But he of stirred up vigour lives happily, aloof from evil unwholesome mental states, and great is the goal itself that he makes perfect. Not through what is low comes the attainment of the highest, but through what is high comes the attainment of the highest. This Brahma-faring is worthy of praise. The Teacher has come (to us) face to face. Wherefore stir up vigour for the attainment of the unattained, for the mastery of the unmastered, for the realization of the unrealized. Thus will your going forth be not barren, but a fruitful and growing thing.

Samyutta-nikāya II, 28–29

Mindfulness

32.

There is this one way, monks, for the purification of beings, for the overcoming of sorrows and griefs, for the going down of sufferings and miseries, for winning the right path, for realizing Nirvana, that is to say the four applications of mindfulness. What are the four? Herein, monks, a monk lives contemplating the body in the body, ardent, clearly comprehending it and mindful of it; likewise the feelings in the feelings; likewise mind in the mind; likewise mental states in mental states so as control the coveting and dejection in the world.

And how does a monk live contemplating the body in the body? Herein, monks, a monk who has gone to a forest or the root of a tree or to an empty place, sits down cross-legged, holding his back erect, and arouses mindfulness in front of him. Mindful he breathes in, mindful he breathes out. Whether he is breathing in a long or a short breath, he comprehends that he is breathing in a long or a short breath. Similarly when he is

breathing out. He trains himself, thinking: "I shall breathe in,
I shall breathe out, clearly perceiving the whole (breath-)
body; I shall breathe in, breathe out, tranquillizing the activity
of the body." It is like a clever turner or a turner's apprentice
who, when he is making a long turn or a short turn comprehends exactly what he is doing. For in breathing in or out a
long or a short breath the monk comprehends that he is doing
so. . . . . Or, thinking: "There is body", his mindfulness is
established precisely to the extent necessary just for knowledge, just for remembrance, and he lives independently of and
not grasping anything in the world. It is thus too that a monk
lives contemplating the body in the body.

And again, when he is walking, standing still, sitting down
or lying down he comprehends that he is doing so. So that,
however his body is disposed, he comprehends that it is like
that. . . . Or, thinking: "There is body" . . . not grasping anything in the world (*as above*).

And again, when a monk is setting out (on his begging
round) or returning, looking in front or around, has bent in or
stretched out his arm, is carrying his outer cloak, bowl or
robe, is eating or drinking and so forth, is walking or standing
still and so forth, he is one acting in a clearly conscious way. . . .
It is thus too that he lives contemplating the body in the body.

And again, monks, a monk reflects precisely on this body
itself, encased in skin and full of various impurities, from the
soles of the feet upward and from the crown of the head
downward, that: "There is connected with this body hair of
the head, hair of the body, nails, teeth, skin, flesh, sinews,
bones, marrow, kidneys, heart, liver, membranes, spleen, lungs,
intestines, mesentery, stomach, excrement,[1] bile, phlegm, pus,
blood, sweat, fat, tears, serum, saliva, mucus, synovic fluid,
urine." Monks, it is like a double-mouthed provision bag, full
of such various grains as hill-paddy, paddy, kidney beans,
sesamum and rice, each of which would be recognized by a
keen-eyed man if he were to pour them out. For even so does a
monk reflect precisely on this body itself. . . .

And again, monks, a monk reflects on this body according to
how it is placed or disposed in respect of the elements, thinking: "In this body are the elements of earth, water, heat and

[1] The Commentaries here add 'brain'.

wind.[1] It is like a skilled cattle-butcher or his apprentice who, having slaughtered a cow, might sit displaying its carcase at cross-roads. For even so does a monk reflect precisely on this body itself according to how it is placed or disposed. . . ."

And again, monks, a monk might see a body in various stages of decomposition in a cemetery. He then draws along this body itself for comparison, thinking: "This body (of mine) is also of such a nature and constitution, it has not overpassed this state of things." . . . It is thus that he lives contemplating the body in the body.

And how does a monk live contemplating the feelings in the feelings? When he is experiencing a pleasant or a painful feeling or one that is neither painful nor pleasant, either in regard to what is temporal or spiritual, he comprehends that he is doing so.

And how does a monk live contemplating the mind in the mind? He comprehends the mind which has passion and that which has none as such, which has hatred and that which has none as such, which has confusion and that which has none as such; he comprehends the collected mind, the distracted mind as such; the mind which has become great and that which has not as such; the mind which has some other or no other (mental state) superior to it; the mind which is concentrated or that which is not as such; he comprehends the mind which is freed or that which is not freed as such. . . . It is thus that a monk lives contemplating the mind in the mind.[2]

And how does a monk live contemplating mental states in mental states?   In the first place he does so from the point of view of the five hindrances. He comprehends that he either has or has not an inward desire for sense-pleasures; also any desire that he has not had for them before; likewise the getting rid of a desire for them that has arisen; and if there is no future uprising of desire for them, he comprehends that. When ill-will is inwardly present in him, or sloth and torpor, or restless-

[1] paṭhavī, āpo, tejo, vāyo are the four 'elements' of which all bodies are composed; philosophically to be regarded as 1. the solid element of extension, 2. the liquid element of cohesion, 3. the heating element of radiation, 4. the mobile element of motion. If the words extension, cohesion, radiation and motion are found below, they are translations of paṭhavī, āpo, tejo and vāyo.

[2] For a later development of this method see no. 151.

ness and worry, or doubt, he comprehends that (as he comprehended the desire for sense-pleasures).

In the second place he lives contemplating mental states in mental states from the point of view of the five groups of grasping. As to this, he thinks: "Such is material shape, such its arising, such its setting", and he thinks likewise of feeling, perception, the impulses, consciousness.

Thirdly, he contemplates mental states in mental states from the point of view of the six inward-outward sense fields. As to this, he comprehends the eye and material shapes, and the fetter that arises dependent on both; and he comprehends the uprising of a fetter not arisen before, the getting rid of the fetter that has arisen, the non-uprising in the future of the fetter that has been got rid of. Similarly, he comprehends ear and sounds; nose and smells; tongue and tastes; body and tactile objects; mind and mental states and the corresponding fetter.

Fourthly, he contemplates mental states in mental states from the point of view of the seven limbs of enlightenment. When any of these limbs is present in him: mindfulness, investigation of mental states, vigour, tranquillity, rapture, concentration, even-mindedness—or when any is absent in him, he comprehends that. And in so far as there arises a limb of enlightenment that had not arisen before, he comprehends that. And in so far as there is completion by mental development of this uprisen limb, he comprehends that.

Fifthly, a monk lives contemplating mental states in mental states from the point of view of the four ariyan truths. He comprehends as it really is: "This is suffering, this its uprising, this its stopping, this the course leading to its stopping." It is thus that he lives contemplating mental states in mental states. . . . Or, thinking: "There are mental states", his mindfulness is established precisely to the extent necessary just for knowledge, just for remembrance, and he fares along independently of and not grasping anything in the world.

Whoever should thus develop these four applications of mindfulness for seven years . . . down to seven days, one of two fruits is to be expected for him: either gnosis here and now or, if there is any residue (for rebirth remaining), the state of no-return.

Majjhima-nikāya I, 55–63

Concentration

33.

"Brahmin, it is like a hen with eight or ten or twelve eggs on which she has sat properly, properly incubated and properly hatched; is that chick which should the first of all win forth safely, having pierced through the egg-shell with the point of the claw on its foot or with its beak, to be called the eldest or the youngest?"

"The eldest, good Gotama, for he is the eldest of these."

"Even so, Brahmin, I, having pierced through the shell of ignorance for the sake of creatures wrapped in ignorance, egg-born (as it were),[1] am unique in the world, utterly enlightened with unsurpassed enlightenment. I myself am the world's eldest and highest.[2]

"Unflinching vigour I have stirred up, clear mindfulness I have aroused, my body impassible, calm, my mind concentrated and one-pointed. Then I, Brahmin, aloof from pleasures of the senses, aloof from unwholesome states of mind, entered into and abided in the first jhana which is accompanied by initial thought and discursive thought, is born of aloofness and is rapturous and joyful. By allaying the initial and discursive thought, with the mind inwardly tranquillized and fixed on one point, I entered into and abided in the second jhana which is devoid of initial and discursive thought, is born of concentration and is rapturous and joyful. By the fading out of rapture, I dwelt with even-mindedness, mindful and clearly conscious; and I experienced with the body that joy of which the Ariyans say: 'Joyful lives he who is even-minded and joyful', and I entered into and abided in the third jhana. By getting rid of joy, by getting rid of suffering, by the dying down of my former pleasures and sorrows, I entered into and abided in the fourth jhana which has neither suffering nor joy, and is entirely purified by even-mindedness and mindfulness.

[1] AA. iv. 85 says that as beings born in eggs are called egg-born, so all men, born in the egg-shell of ignorance, are called egg-born.

[2] VinA. 140 says on account of being the first-born among the Ariyans. Ariyans are defined at VinA. 165 as Buddhas, Pacceka-buddhas and disciples of Buddhas.

"With the mind thus composed, quite purified, quite clari-
fied, without blemish, without defilement, grown soft and
workable, fixed, immovable, I directed my mind to the knowledge and recollection of former habitations. I remembered a
variety of former habitations, thus: one birth, two births . . .
or fifty or a hundred or a thousand or a hundred thousand
births; or many an aeon of integration, disintegration, integra-
tion-disintegration; such a one was I by name, having such and
such a clan, such and such a colour, so was I nourished, such
and such pleasant and painful experiences were mine, so did
the span of life end. Passing away from this, I came to be in
another state [1] where I was such a one by name . . . so did the
span of life end. Passing away from this, I arose here. [2] Thus I
remember divers former habitations in all their modes and
details. This, Brahmin, was the first knowledge attained by
me in the first watch of that night [3]; ignorance was dispelled,
knowledge arose, darkness was dispelled, light arose even as I
abided diligent, ardent, self-resolute. This, Brahmin, was my
first successful breaking forth, like a chick's from the egg-shell.

"With the mind thus composed . . . immovable, I directed
my mind to the knowledge of the deceasing (from one birth)
and arising (in another) of beings. With the purified deva-like
vision surpassing that of men, I saw beings as they were
deceasing and uprising; I comprehended that beings were
mean, excellent, comely, ugly, in a good bourn, in a bad bourn
according to the consequences of their karma. And I thought:
'Indeed these worthy beings who were possessed of mis-
conduct in body, speech and thought, scoffers at the Ariyans,
holding a wrong view, incurring karma consequent on a wrong
view—these at the breaking up of the body after dying have
arisen in a sorrowful state, a bad bourn, the abyss, Niraya Hell.
But these worthy beings who were possessed of right conduct
in body, speech and thought, who did not scoff at the Ariyans,

[1] MA. i. 125 says that this was the Tusita Abode (where the Bodhisatta passes his last 'birth' before being born for the final time, as a
man). Here he was a devaputta, and experienced deva-like happiness,
his painful experiences being only those connected with the samkhāras.

[2] MA. i. 126, 'here in the womb of the lady Mahāmāyā'.

[3] I.e. on the night of enlightenment. At Vin. i. 1 and Ud. i, the
Conditioned Genesis is said to have been mastered during the first
watch of this night.

holding a right view, incurring karma consequent on a right view—these at the breaking up of the body after dying have arisen in a good bourn, a heaven world. Thus with the purified deva-like vision . . . I comprehended that beings were mean, excellent . . . according to the consequences of their karma. This, Brahmin, was the second knowledge attained by me in the middle watch of that night; ignorance was dispelled . . . even as I abided diligent, ardent, self-resolute. This, Brahmin, was my second successful breaking forth, like a chick's from the egg-shell.

"With the mind thus composed . . . immovable, I directed my mind to the knowledge of the extinction of the outflows. I understood as it really is: This is suffering, this its arising, this its stopping, this the course leading to its stopping. I understood as it really is: These are the outflows, this their arising, this their stopping, this the course leading to their stopping. When this was known and seen thus by me, my mind was freed from the outflows of sense-pleasures, becoming, speculative view and ignorance.[1] In freedom the knowledge came to be: I am freed; and I comprehended that birth was destroyed, brought to a close the Brahma-faring, done what was to be done, and that there was no more of being such or such.[2] This, Brahmin, was the third knowledge attained by me in the third watch of that night; ignorance was dispelled, knowledge arose, darkness was dispelled, light arose even as I abided diligent, ardent, self-resolute. This, Brahmin, was my third successful breaking forth, like a chick's from the egg-shell."

Vinaya-piṭaka III, 3–6

34.

Ananda is speaking:

There is, householder, one thing (dhamma) pointed out by the Lord who knows and sees, Arahant, perfect Buddha, whereby if a monk abide diligent, ardent, self-resolute, his

---

[1] At M. i. 23, A. ii. 211, iv. 179 the outflow of false view is not mentioned.

[2] MA. i. 128 (cf. DA. 112, SA. i. 205) says that this is due either to the development of the Way or to the extinction of the defilements; or that there is no further continuity of the khandhas for, being thoroughly understood, they are like trees cut down at the roots.

mind, as yet unfreed, is freed; and the outflows, not yet extinguished, come to an end; and he attains the matchless security from the bonds. As to this, a monk abides in each of the jhanas,[1] and then he ponders thus: "This is just a higher product, belonging to the higher thought, and as such it is impermanent, liable to stopping." Established on that, he attains the extinction of the outflows; or if not, then by his attachment to Dhamma and his delight in it, by utterly extinguishing the five fetters binding to this lower shore, he is of spontaneous rebirth, attaining final Nirvana there, not liable to return from that world.

Then again, householder, the monk abides, having suffused the first quarter with a mind of friendliness, likewise the second, the third and the fourth; just so above, below, across he abides, having suffused the whole world everywhere, in every way with a mind of friendliness that is far-reaching, wide-spread, immeasurable, without enmity, without malevolence. He abides, having suffused the first quarter with a mind of compassion, then of sympathetic joy, then of even-mindedness, likewise the second, the third and the fourth; just so above, below, across he abides, having suffused the whole world everywhere, in every way with a mind of compassion, of sympathetic joy, of even-mindedness that is far-reaching, wide-spread, immeasurable, without enmity, without malevolence. In each case he reflects that the freedom of mind—whether it be of friendliness, compassion, sympathetic joy or even-mindedness—is a higher product, belonging to the higher thought, and as such is impermanent, liable to stopping. Established on that, he . . . is not liable to return from that world.

Then again, householder, a monk, by passing quite beyond all perceptions of material shapes, by the dying down of all perceptions of sensory reactions, by the non-attention to perceptions of difference, on thinking: "Ether is unending", enters into and abides in the plane of infinite ether.

By passing quite beyond the plane of infinite ether, on thinking: "Consciousness is unending", he enters into and abides in the plane of infinite consciousness.

By passing quite beyond the plane of infinite consciousness,

[1] Set out in detail, above, p. 60.

on thinking: "There is not anything", he enters into and abides in the plane of infinite no-thing-ness.

Of each of these attainments he ponders that it is just a higher product, belonging to the higher thought, and as such is impermanent, liable to stopping. Established on that, he attains . . . not liable to return from that world. Each one of the things mentioned has been pointed out by the Lord who knows and sees, Arahant, perfect Buddha, whereby if a monk abide diligent, ardent, self-resolute his mind, as yet unfreed, is freed; and the outflows, not yet extinguished, come to an end; and he attains the matchless security from the bonds.

Majjhima-nikāya I, 349–52

35.

But the monk can go further than that:

By passing quite beyond the plane of no-thing-ness, he enters into and abides in the plane of neither-perception-nor-non-perception. By passing quite beyond this plane, he enters into and abides in the stopping of feeling and perceiving. He has now crossed over the entanglement in the world, and is one who (as in the case of mastery in the four jhanas and the remaining four planes, ayatana), has made Mara blind and, blotting out his vision so that it has no range, goes unseen by the Malign One.

Majjhima-nikāya I, 160

Wisdom

36.

As, monks, the lion, king of beasts, is reckoned chief among animals, for his strength, speed and bravery, so is the faculty of wisdom reckoned chief among mental states helpful to enlightenment, for its enlightenment. And what are the mental states helpful to enlightenment? The faculty of faith, of vigour, of mindfulness, of concentration, of wisdom: each conduces to enlightenment.

Samyutta-nikāya V, 227

37·

What is the faculty of wisdom? Whatever is the wisdom that is comprehension, investigation, close investigation, investigation of mental states, discernment, discrimination, differentiation, cleverness, skill, subtlety, clear understanding, thought, examination, breadth (like the earth's, Asl. 147–48), sagacity, leading, insight, clear consciousness, which is as a goad, the wisdom that is wisdom as a faculty, as power, as sword,[1] as terraced heights, as light, effulgence, splendour, as a jewel; lack of confusion, investigation of mental states, right view—this is the faculty of wisdom.

Dhammasaṅgaṇi, 16

38.

What, sire, is the Lord's jewel of wisdom? It is that wisdom by which an ariyan disciple comprehends as it really is that this is wholesome, this unwholesome, that this is blameworthy, this blameless, that this is low, this excellent, that this is dark, this bright and that this is what participates in what is dark and bright[2]; and comprehends as it really is that this is suffering, this its arising, this its stopping, and this the course leading to its stopping.

Becoming[3] lasts not long for him garlanded with the jewel of wisdom;
Swiftly he attains the Deathless and delights not in becoming.[4]

Milindapañha, 337

CONDITIONED GENESIS COLLECTIVELY

39·

Who sees Conditioned Genesis sees Dhamma; who sees Dhamma sees Conditioned Genesis.

Majjhima-nikāya I, 190–91

[1] Cf. M. i. 144; 'weapon' is a synonym for the ariyan wisdom.
[2] The dark and the bright refer to kamma, see M. i. 389.
[3] bhava, probably equivalent to 'existence' here.
[4] The threefold becoming: kāma-, rūpa- and arūpa-bhava.

40.

This body, monks, is not yours, nor does it belong to others. It should be regarded (as the product of[1]) former karma, effected through what has been willed and felt. In regard to it, the instructed disciple of the Ariyans well and wisely reflects on Conditioned Genesis itself: If this is that comes to be; from the arising of this that arises; if this is not that does not come to be; from the stopping of this that is stopped. That is to say: ... (*continue as in next extract*).

Samyutta-nikāya II, 64–65

41.

Conditioned by ignorance are the karma-formations[2]; conditioned by the karma-formations is consciousness; conditioned by consciousness is mind-and-body; conditioned by mind-and-body are the six sense-fields; conditioned by the six sense-fields is impression; conditioned by impression is feeling; conditioned by feeling is craving; conditioned by craving is grasping; conditioned by grasping is becoming; conditioned by becoming is birth; conditioned by birth there come into being ageing and dying, grief, sorrow, suffering, lamentation and despair. Thus is the origin of this whole mass of suffering.

But from the stopping of ignorance is the stopping of the karma-formations; from the stopping of the karma-formations is the stopping of consciousness; from the stopping of consciousness is the stopping of mind-and-body; from the stopping of mind-and-body is the stopping of the six sense-fields; from the stopping of the six sense-fields is the stopping of impression; from the stopping of impression is the stopping of feeling; from the stopping of feeling is the stopping of craving; from the stopping of craving is the stopping of grasping; from the stopping of grasping is the stopping of becoming; from

[1] An addition from the Commentary, SA. ii. 70.

[2] The Saṁkhāra are karma-formations or karmical formations, in the sense of 'forming', as opposed to 'formed'. As such they may be said to represent the volitional activity (cetanā) of body (kāya), speech (vacī) and mind (mano).

the stopping of becoming is the stopping of birth; from the stopping of birth, ageing and dying, grief, sorrow, suffering, lamentation and despair are stopped. Thus is the stopping of this whole mass of suffering.

Vinaya-piṭaka I, 1

42.

From the arising of ignorance is the arising of the karma-formations; from the stopping of ignorance is the stopping of the karma-formations. This ariyan eightfold Way is itself the course leading to the stopping of the karma-formations, that is to say: right view, right thought, right speech, right action, right mode of livelihood, right endeavour, right mindfulness, right concentration.

When an ariyan disciple comprehends 'condition' thus, its arising, its stopping and the course leading to its stopping thus, he is called an ariyan disciple who is possessed of right view, of vision, one who has come into this true Dhamma, who sees this true Dhamma, who is endowed with the knowledge and lore of a learner, who has attained the stream of Dhamma, who is an Ariyan of penetrating wisdom, and who stands knocking at the door of the Deathless.

Samyutta-nikāya II, 43

43.

And what is ageing and dying? Whatever for this or that class of beings is ageing, decrepitude, breaking up, hoariness, wrinkling of the skin, dwindling of the life-span, overripeness of the sense-faculties: this is called ageing. Whatever for this or that being in this or that class of beings is the falling and deceasing, the breaking, the disappearance, the mortality and dying, the passing away, the breaking of the khandhas, the laying down of the body: this is called dying. This is called ageing and dying.

And what is birth? Whatever for this or that being in this or that class of beings is the conception, the birth, the descent, the production, the appearance of the khandhas, the acquiring of the sensory fields: this is called birth.

And what is becoming? There are these three becomings: sensuous becoming, fine-material becoming, immaterial becoming.

And what is grasping? There are four graspings: after sense-pleasures, after speculative view, after rite and custom, after the theory of self.

And what is craving? There are six classes of craving: for material shapes, sounds, smells, tastes, touches and mental objects.

And what is feeling? There are six classes of feeling: feeling due to visual, auditory, olfactory, gustatory, physical and mental impact.

And what is impression? There are six classes of impression: visual, auditory, olfactory, gustatory, physical and mental.

And what are the six sensory fields? The field of the eye, ear, nose, tongue, body, mind.

And what is mind-and-body? Feeling, perception, volition, impression, wise attention: this is called mind.[1] The four great elements[2] and the material shape derived from them: this is called body. Such is mind and such is body. This is called mind-and-body.

And what is consciousness? There are six classes of consciousness: visual, auditory, olfactory, gustatory, physical and mental consciousness.

And what are the karma-formations? There are three: karma-formations of body, of speech, of thought.

And what is ignorance? Whatever is the unknowing in regard to suffering, its arising, its stopping and the course leading to its stopping—this is called ignorance.

Majjhima-nikāya I, 49–54

44.

" Is suffering wrought by oneself, good Gotama? "
  "No, Kassapa."
  "Then by another? "

---

[1] Cf. Dhs. §1309 and Vbh. 136: What is mind? The group of feeling, that of perception, that of the impulses, that of consciousness, and the uncompounded element: this is called mind.

[2] Earth, water, fire and air; see above, pp. 57–58.

"No."

"Then by both oneself and another?"

"No, Kassapa."

"Well then, has the suffering that has been wrought neither by myself nor by another come to me by chance?"

"No, Kassapa."

"Then, is there not suffering?"

"No, Kassapa, it is not that there is not suffering. For there *is* suffering."

"Well then, the good Gotama neither knows nor sees suffering."

"It is not that I do not know suffering, do not see it. I know it, I see it."

"To all my questions, good Gotama, you have answered 'No', and you have said that you know suffering and see it. Lord, let the Lord explain suffering to me, let him teach me suffering."

"Whoso says, 'He who does (a deed) is he who experiences (its result)', is thereby saying that from the being's beginning suffering was wrought by (the being) himself—this amounts to the Eternity-view. Whoso says, 'One does (a deed), another experiences (the result)', is thereby saying that when a being is smitten by feeling the suffering was wrought by another— this amounts to the Annihilation-view.

"Avoiding both these dead-ends, Kassapa, the Tathagata teaches Dhamma by the mean: conditioned by ignorance are the karma-formations . . . *and so on*. Thus is the origin of this whole mass of suffering. By the utter stopping of that very ignorance is the stopping of the karma-formations . . . *and so on*. Thus is the stopping of this whole mass of suffering."

Samyutta-nikāya II, 19–21

45

Once when the Lord was staying among the Kurus, the venerable Ananda approached him and said: "It is wonderful, Lord, that while Conditioned Genesis is so deep and looks so deep, to me it seems perfectly clear."

"Do not speak like that, Ananda. For this Conditioned

Genesis is deep and looks deep too. It is from not awakening
to this Dhamma,[1] Ananda, from not penetrating it, that this
generation, become tangled like a ball of thread, covered as
with blight, twisted up like a grass-rope, cannot overpass the
sorrowful state, the bad bourn, the abyss, the circling on
(samsara).

Dīgha-nikāya II, 55

CONDITIONED GENESIS SEPARATELY

Ignorance

46.

I see no other single hindrance such as this hindrance of
ignorance, obstructed by which mankind for a long long time
runs on and circles on.

Itivuttaka, p. 8

47.

An uninstructed ordinary person does not comprehend as it
really is that material shape, feeling, perception, the impulses, consciousness are of the nature to originate, to decay,
and both to originate and decay; nor does he comprehend as it
really is the satisfaction and peril in them or the escape from
them.

Samyutta-nikāya III, 170–76 (condensed)

Consciousness

48.

That which we will and that which we intend to do and that
with which we are occupied, this is an object for the
support of consciousness. If there is an object there is a foothold for consciousness. With consciousness growing in this

[1] Cf. M. i. 190–91 (above, p. 65).

foothold there is rebirth and recurrent becoming in the future. If there is rebirth and recurrent becoming in the future, ageing and dying, grief, sorrow, suffering, lamentation and despair come into being in the future. Thus is the arising of this whole mass of suffering.

But if we neither will nor intend to do but are still occupied with something, the same sequence occurs.

But if we neither will nor intend to do and are not occupied with something, there is no object for the support of consciousness; hence no foothold for it; with consciousness having no foothold or growth, there is no rebirth or recurrent becoming in the future. In their absence birth, ageing and dying, grief, sorrow, suffering, lamentation and despair in the future are stopped. Thus is the stopping of this whole mass of suffering.

That which we will and that which we intend to do and that with which we are occupied is an object for the support of consciousness. If there is an object there is a foothold for consciousness. With consciousness growing in this foothold there is a descent of mind-and-body.

Conditioned by mind-and-body are the six sense-fields. Conditioned by these is impression. . . . Thus is the origin of this whole mass of suffering.

But if we neither will nor intend to do nor are occupied with something, there is no object for the support of consciousness; hence there is no foothold for it. With consciousness having no foothold or growth, there is no descent of mind-and-body. From the stopping of mind-and-body is the stopping of the six sensory fields. . . . Thus is the stopping of this whole mass of suffering.

Samyutta-nikāya II, 65–66

49.

Once upon a time a conch-blower, taking his conch, came to a border district and, standing in a village, blew on his conch three times, laid it aside and sat down. The people wondered who had made that lovely and charming sound, and they asked the conch-blower. He told them it was the conch and that was its lovely and charming sound. They laid the conch on its back and said: "Speak, conch, speak." But it gave never a sound. So they laid it curving downwards, then on one side, then on the other, and they stood it upright and topsy-turvy and they struck it on all its sides with their hands, with clods of earth, sticks and knives, saying: "Speak, conch, speak." But it gave never a sound. The conch-blower thought these border people were too stupid to see the conch's sound in such senseless ways. And while they watched he picked it up, blew on it three times and went away with it. Then these border people thought: "So long as this conch is accompanied by a man and by exertion and by wind it makes a sound. But so long as it is accompanied neither by a man nor by exertion nor by wind it makes no sound."

Even so, so long as this body is accompanied by life and heat and consciousness, so long does it walk backwards and forwards, stand still and sit and lie down, see, hear, smell, taste, touch and discern (vijanati) mental states with the mind. But so long as this body is accompanied neither by life nor heat nor consciousness, it does none of these things.

Dīgha-nikāya II, 337–38

Feeling

50.

If one[1] experiences a feeling that is pleasant, painful or neither painful nor pleasant, he comprehends that it is impermanent, not coveted, not welcomed,—and unfettered he experiences these feelings. If it is a feeling limited to the body or one limited to the life-principle, he comprehends that he is feeling such a feeling. And he comprehends that, at the breaking up of the body at the end of his life-time, all that has been felt here, but not delighting him, will become cool.

Majjhima-nikāya III, 244

[1] Now an Arahant.

Craving

51.

Who, knowing both (dead-)ends, by insight sticks not fast in the middle—him I call 'great man' that here has passed the sempstress [1] by.

Suttanipāta, 1042

52.

Which is one dead-end, which the other, what is in the middle, who the sempstress? The monks answered severally as follows:

Impression is one dead-end, its arising the other, its stopping is in the middle, craving is the sempstress, for craving sews one to the production of this or that becoming.

The past is one dead-end, the future the other, the present is in the middle, craving is the sempstress, for craving sews one . . .

Pleasant feeling is one dead-end, painful feeling the other, feeling that is neither painful nor pleasant is in the middle, craving is the sempstress, for craving sews one . . .

Mind is one dead-end, body the other, consciousness [2] is in the middle, craving is the sempstress, for craving sews one . . .

The six inner sense-fields are one dead-end, the six outer the other, consciousness [3] is in the middle, craving is the sempstress, for craving sews one . . .

Own body is one dead-end, own body's arising is the other, own body's stopping is in the middle, craving is the sempstress, for craving sews one to the production of this or that becoming.

Anguttara-nikāya III, 399–401 (condensed)

[1] sibbanī is the sempstress or spinster rather than the sewing.
[2] AA. iii. 404 says that this is paṭisandhi-viññāṇa, re-linking or re-instatement consciousness.
[3] AA. iii. 404 calls this kamma-viññāṇa, karma (karmical) consciousness,

Grasping

53.

An uninstructed ordinary person is not wisely reflecting if he thinks: "In the past was I, was I not, what was I, what was I like, having been what what was I?" Or if he thinks: "In the future will I be, will I not be, what will I be, what will I be like, having been what what will I be?" Or if he is subjectively doubtful now in the present and thinks: "Am I, am I not, what am I, what like, whence has this being come, where-going will it come to be?"

To one who is thus not wisely reflecting, one of six speculative views may arise as though it were real and true: "There is self for me[1]; there is not self for me; simply by self am I aware of self; simply by self am I aware of not-self; simply by not-self am I aware of self." Or he may have a speculative view such as this: "That self of mine that speaks and knows, which experiences now here, now there the results of karma that was lovely or evil, that self of mine is permanent, stable, eternal, it will stand fast like unto the eternal"—this is called speculative view, holding a speculative view, the wilds, wriggling, scuffling and fetter of speculative views. Fettered by this fetter, the ordinary uninstructed person is not freed from birth, from ageing and dying or from grief, sorrow, suffering, lamentation and despair. I say that he is not freed from suffering.

Majjhima-nikāya I, 8

54.

If one does not behold any self or anything of the nature of self in the five groups of grasping[2] (material shape, feeling, perception, the impulses, consciousness), one is an Arahant, the outflows extinguished.

Samyutta-nikāya III, 127-28

---

[1] An Eternalist view; the next is an Annihilationist view.
[2] See under 'Emptiness'.

55.

The instructed disciple of the Ariyans does not regard material shape as self, or self as having material shape, or material shape as being in the self, or the self as being in material shape. Nor does he regard feeling, perception, the impulses, or consciousness in any of these ways. He comprehends of each of these khandhas as it really is that it is impermanent, suffering, not-self, compounded, murderous. He does not approach them, grasp after them or determine 'Self for me'[1]—and this for a long time conduces to his welfare and happiness.

Samyutta-nikāya III, 114–15

56.

The instructed disciple of the Ariyans beholds of material shape and so on: "This is not mine, this am I not, this is not my self." So that when the material shape and so on change and become otherwise there arise not for him grief, sorrow, suffering, lamentation and despair.

Samyutta-nikāya III, 19 etc.

57.

Material shape and the other khandhas are impermanent; what is impermanent is suffering; what is suffering is not-self; what is not-self—this is not mine, this am I not, this is not my self. This should be seen by means of right wisdom as it really is.

Vinaya-piṭaka I, 14

58.

When ignorance has been got rid of and knowledge has arisen, one does not grasp after sense-pleasures, speculative views, rites and customs, the theory of self.

Majjhima-nikāya I, 67

[1] attā me, or 'my self'.

Birth, Ageing and Dying

59.

There are four kinds of descent into a womb: (1) that when someone,[1] not clearly conscious, descends into the mother's womb, stays in it, and issues forth from it (this is the conception of ordinary mundane people, DA. 885); (2) that when someone, clearly conscious, descends into the mother's womb, but, not clearly conscious, stays in it and issues forth from it (the conception of 80 great Elders, DA. 885); (3) that when someone, clearly conscious, descends into and stays in the mother's womb, but, not clearly conscious, issues forth from it (the conception of the two chief disciples and of Bodhisattas striving to become Buddhas of and for themselves[2]—they issue forth to great suffering, DA. 886); (4) that when someone, clearly conscious, descends into, stays in and issues forth from the mother's womb (the conception of the Bodhisattas striving for omniscience, DA. 886).

Dīgha-nikāya III, 103

60.

On the conjunction of three things there is descent into the womb. As to this, there must be coitus of the parents, it must be the mother's season, and the gandharva must be present. For so long there is conception.

Majjhima-nikāya I, 265

61.

Gandharva (gandhabba) means: the being who is coming into the womb . . . the being about to enter the womb (tatrupakasatta). Should be present means: it is not that (he) remains nearby observing the union of the parents, but that a

---

[1] ekacco, not explained in the Commentary.
[2] This term, pacceka-bodhisatta, is of rare occurrence in the Pali texts.

certain being is about to be born in that situation, being driven on by the mechanism of karma[1]—this is the meaning here.

Papañcasūdanī II, 310

62.

Gotama is recounting to Assalayana, a learned young Brahmin, a story from the past in which Asita Devala had defeated in argument seven Brahmin seers who held views like Assalayana's.

"Then, Assalayana, the seven Brahmin seers approached the seer Asita Devala in order to honour him, and he spoke thus to them: 'I have heard that while the seven Brahmin seers were living in leaf-huts in a stretch of forest a false view like this arose to them: Only Brahmins form the best caste, the fair caste, all other castes are low and dark; only Brahmins are pure, not non-Brahmins; only Brahmins are own sons of Brahma, born of his mouth, born of Brahma, formed by Brahma, heirs to Brahma.'"

"That is so, sir."

"But do you know whether their mothers consorted only with Brahmins, not with non-Brahmins? Or whether their mothers' mothers, back through seven generations, consorted only with Brahmins, not with non-Brahmins? And do you know whether their fathers consorted only with Brahmin women, not with non-Brahmins? And whether their fathers' fathers, back through seven generations, did likewise?"

"We don't know, sir."

"But do you know how there is descent into the womb?"

"We know this, sir. Here there must be coitus of the parents, it must be the mother's season, and the gandharva must be present. If there is conjunction of three things thus, there is descent into the womb."

---

[1] For this translation I am indebted to O. H. de A. Wijesekera, *Vedic Gandharva and Pali Gandhabba*, University of Ceylon Review, vol. III, No. 1, April, 1945, p. 88. He suggests that gandhabba means "a (samsāric) being in the intermediate stage (between death and birth)".—See below, no. 205.

"But do you know, good sirs, whether that gandharva is a noble warrior or a Brahmin or a merchant-trader or a low-class worker[1]? "
"We do not know that."
"That being so, good sirs, do you know who you are? "
"That being so, sir, we do not know who we are."

Majjhima-nikāya II, 156–57

63.

Revered Nagasena, this was said by the Lord:

"When there is the conjunction of three things there is conception . . ." (M. i. 265). This is an exhaustive and unreserved statement. But there is conception on the conjunction of two things: the female (here Parika, a female ascetic) must be having her season, and the male must touch her navel with his right hand. Therefore what the Lord said was wrong, for both the boy Sama and the brahman youth Mandavya were born by the conjunction of these two things. . . .

But, sire, at the invitation of Sakka, the lord of devas, on the day when these two things occurred a devaputta (a young deva) was also present there. Thus there were these three conjunctions (of circumstances). . . .

Sire, there is conception of beings by four modes: by karma, by womb, by category (kula), by invitation. But all beings are produced by karma, arise from karma . . . And how is there conception of beings according to category? The four cate-

---

[1] O. H. de A. Wijesekera, op. cit., p. 89, says: "Here the text is unequivocal and leaves no doubt as to the real nature of gandhabba which clearly must refer in the context to the 'spirit' of a previously dead kṣatriya, brāhmana, vaiśya or śūdra, a sense which the term had already assumed in the pre-Buddhist period. It is not surprising therefore to find Buddhaghosa maintaining discreet silence . . . for the implied *identity* of the 'gandhabba' with any previous person cannot be palatable to him. . . . That the meaning of the term in the above contexts is 'a (saṁsāric) being in the intermediate state (between death and rebirth)' is supported by Amarakośa . . . and seems to preserve a genuine tradition."

gories, sire, are called egg-born, womb-born, moisture-born, and of spontaneous uprising. If the gandharva is there, having come from where-so-ever, and arises in an egg-born, womb-born, moisture-born category or in that of spontaneous uprising, it is there egg-born, womb-born, moisture-born or of spontaneous uprising respectively. For, sire, whatever gandharva, having come from where-so-ever, and arising in an egg-born, womb-born, moisture-born womb or in a womb of spontaneous uprising, having shed its own kind of nature (sabhavavanna), becomes egg-born and so on respectively. Thus is there conception of creatures according to category.

And how is there conception of beings by means of invitation? Here there is a family that is childless, with faith and believing; and there is a young devaputta with abundant root for skill, liable to decease (from the devaloka). Out of compassion for that family, Sakka, the lord of devas, asks him to direct himself to the womb of the chief wife in that family. And because he is invited, he directs himself to that family. . . . Prince Sama, sire, invited by Sakka, the lord of devas, descended into the womb of Parika, the female ascetic.

Milindapañha, 123–29 (condensed)

64.

Countless are the births wherein I have circled and run seeking, but not finding, the builder of the house; ill is birth again and again.

Now thou art seen, thou builder of the house; never again shalt thou build (me) a house. All thy rafters are broken, shattered the roof-plate; my thought is divested of the samkharas; the extinction of craving has been won.

Dhammapada, 153–54

65.

Few are the beings born again among men; more numerous are those born elsewhere than among men.

Anguttara-nikāya I, 35

66.

By whom was wrought this puppet?[1]
Where is the puppet's maker?
And where does the puppet arise?
Where is the puppet stopped?

Not made by self is this puppet,
Nor is this misfortune made by others.
Conditioned by cause it comes to be,
By breaking of cause is it stopped.

. . . .

By whom was wrought this being?
Where is the being's maker?
Where does the being arise?
Where is the being stopped?

Why do you harp on 'being'?
It is a false view for you.
A mere heap of samkharas, this—
Here no 'being' is got at.

For as when the parts are rightly set
We utter the word 'chariot',
So when there are the khandhas—
By convention, 'there is a being' we say.

For it is simply suffering that comes to be,
Suffering that perishes and wanes,
Not other than suffering comes to be,
Naught else than suffering is stopped.

Samyutta-nikāya I, 134–35

67.

The being is bound to samsara,[2] karma is his (means for)
going beyond.

Samyutta-nikāya I, 38

[1] bimba, doll.

[2] Or, produces samsāra. Cf. Maitrī Upanishad, 6. 34: "Samsāra is
just (one's own) thought", cittam-eva samsāram.

68.

By getting rid of three mental states: passion, aversion and confusion, one is able to get rid of birth, ageing and dying. By getting rid of three mental states: false view as to 'own body', doubt and dependence on rite and custom, one is able to get rid of passion, aversion and confusion. By getting rid of three mental states: unwise reflection, treading the wrong way and mental laziness, one is able to get rid of false view as to 'own body', doubt and dependence on rite and custom.

Anguttara-nikāya V, 147

69.

Mara: In what do you, nun, take no pleasure?

Cala, the nun: I take no pleasure in birth.

Mara: And why not? He who is born delights in sense-pleasures. Who made you accept this: "Do not take pleasure in birth"?

The Nun: Dying is for the born; he that is born sees ills: bonds, miseries and calamities. Therefore I take no pleasure in birth. The Buddha taught Dhamma for overpassing birth, for getting rid of all suffering—*he* established me in Truth.

Those beings who have gone to fine-materiality[1]
And those who remain in immateriality,[1]
Not comprehending cessation
Are returners to again-becoming.

Samyutta-nikāya I, 132–33

70.

But they who know fine-materiality,
Not remaining in immateriality,
They who are freed by cessation—
These are the folk that leave death behind.

[1] rūpa and arūpa are two of the three modes of becoming, bhava.

Having in his person attained the
Deathless element which has no 'basis',
By making real the casting out of 'basis',
The Perfect Buddha, of no outflows,
Teaches the griefless, stainless state.

Itivuttaka p. 62

71.

Gotama says:

This itself is the whole of the Brahma-faring: friendship,
association and intimacy with the Lovely. Because of my
friendship with the Lovely, beings liable to birth are freed
from birth, beings liable to ageing, decaying and dying are
freed therefrom. Thus must you train: I will become a friend,
associate and intimate of the Lovely. In order to do so this one
thing must be closely observed, namely diligence among
wholesome mental states.

Samyutta-nikāya I, 88–89

THE OBJECT OF WISDOM

72. *Crossing Over by Bridge and Ship*

People said:

"Revered Sumedha,[1] do you not know that Dipankara, Him
of the Ten Powers, and who, after attaining perfect
Buddhahood set rolling the excellent wheel of Dhamma, is
walking on tour and has arrived in our town and is staying in
the great monastery Sudassana? We have invited that Lord,
and we are adorning the way by which this Buddha, this Lord
must come."

The ascetic Sumedha thought: "Even the sound *Buddha* is
difficult to meet with in the world, how much more the arising
of a Buddha. I too will set to work together with these men
preparing the way for Him of the Ten Powers." And he asked
the men to give him just one place so that, with them, he
could adorn the way. They gave him a swampy part knowing
him to be of psychic power. Sumedha, having caught the

[1] This was the Bodhisatta's name at the time of Dīpankara, the first
Buddha, and under whom he took his vow one day to become a Buddha.

rapture that is founded on a Buddha, thought: "I can adorn this place by means of psychic power; but if I did so I should not be satisfied. Today I must do menial tasks." And fetching earth he threw it on that spot.

But before it was adorned, Dipankara, Him of the Ten Powers, surrounded by a hundred thousand sixfold-knowledge men who were of great majesty, their outflows extinguished, being honoured by devatas and men . . . came along that adorned and bedeckt way with the infinite grace of a Buddha, like a lion arousing on a flat rocky platform.[1] The ascetic Sumedha, opening his eyes and regarding Him of the Ten Powers . . . exclaimed:

"Do not let the Lord step in the mire but, with the four hundred thousand whose outflows are extinguished, let him go trampling on my back, as though stepping on a bridge of jewelled planks, and for long that will be for my welfare and happiness."

And having loosened his hair, and spread his black antelope skin, his matted locks and his cloths of bark over the dark mire, he lay down on the mire like a bridge of jewelled planks. . . . And while he was lying on the mire, opening his eyes and again beholding the Buddha-splendour of Dipankara, Him of the Ten Powers, he thought:

"Suppose that I, like Dipankara, Him of the Ten Powers, having reached supreme self-enlightenment, having embarked in the ship of Dhamma, having helped the great populace across the ocean of samsara, should afterwards attain final Nirvana?[2] This is fitting for me."

As I lay upon the earth, this was my thought:
So wishing, I could today destroy my defilements.
But why should I, unknown, realize Dhamma here?

[1] manosilātala means a platform where a seat for the Buddha is placed and whence he roars his lion's roar.

[2] By this Act of Renunciation the Bodhisatta gave up his immediate entry into Nirvana, and chose instead to endure ages of hard trials during which to master fully the pāramitās, goings beyond or perfections, accomplishment in which is necessary and preliminary to winning Buddhahood with its concomitant powers to become free from the samsaric ocean by crossing over to the safe and secure Farther Shore beyond. In other traditions the Farther Shore is called the Waters of Life.

Having won omniscience, I will become a Buddha for (the
world) with the devas.
Why should I, a man perceiving steadfastness, cross over
alone?
Having won omniscience, I will help (the world) with the
devas across.
By this resolution of mine, a man perceiving steadfastness,
I will attain omniscience and help the great populace across.
Having cut through samsara's stream, having extirpated the
three becomings,
Embarking in the ship of Dhamma, I will help (the world)
with the devas across.

Jātaka I, 12–14 (condensed)

73. Crossing over by Bridge

Once upon a time the Bodhisatta was born a monkey.
When he grew up he lived in the Himalayan region with
80,000 monkeys. There was a splendid mango tree near the
Ganges, and the monkeys, led by the Bodhisatta, used to eat
its fruit, although he feared danger would come from eating
the fruit of a great branch that overhung the Ganges. In spite
of all precautions, a ripe mango that had been concealed by
an ants' nest fell from this branch into the river and was
hauled in by some fishermen. They showed it to the King who
then tasted mango for the first time, and so enraptured was he
by its sweet flavour that he decided to visit the mango tree.
Travelling upstream by boat with his retinue, he pitched camp
at the root of the tree but was wakened in the night by the
herd of monkeys as they moved from branch to branch and ate
the mangoes. So he roused his archers and ordered them to
shoot the monkeys: "Tomorrow we shall eat both mangoes and
monkey-flesh." The monkeys, seeing the archers surrounding
the tree, were stricken with the fear of death and, unable to
run away, asked the Great Being what they should do.

The Bodhisatta said: "Do not fear, I will give you life." And
while comforting the monkeys he climbed on to the branch
that stretched towards the river, and leaping from its end and
covering as much as a hundred bow-lengths,[1] he alighted on

[1] An incident illustrated in the Bharhut Stūpa.

top of a thicket on the river bank. On coming down, he measured the space, thinking: "This much will be the distance I have come", and cutting off a rattan-rope at the root and stripping it, he thought: "So much will go round the tree, so much will be in the air", but in determining these two lengths he did not think of the part to be tied round his own waist. He took the rattan-rope, bound one end round the tree and the other round his waist, and cleared the space of the hundred bow-lengths with the speed of a cloud rent by the winds. But because he had not thought of the part bound round his waist, he could not reach the tree. So taking the mango branch firmly in both hands, he beckoned to the herd of monkeys and said: "Trampling on my back, go quickly to safety along the rattan-rope."

The 80,000 monkeys, having saluted the Great Being, apologizing[1] to him, went as he had told them.

At that time Devadatta was a monkey[2] among that herd. He thought: "This is the time for me to see the back of my enemy", and climbing on to a high branch he put forth speed and fell on the Great Being's back. The Bodhisatta's heart was broken and anguished feelings beset him. But he who had caused that pain went away. The Great Being was as though alone. The King, being awake, saw all that was done by the monkeys and the Great Being, and he thought: "This animal, not recking of his own life, gave safety to his company." And as the night waned, he further thought: "It is not right to destroy this monkey king. By some means I will get him down and look after him." So, turning a raft downstream and building a platform there, he made the Great Being come down gently[3], spread yellow garments[4] over his back, had him bathed with Ganges water, offered him sugared water to drink,

[1] Or, saying goodbye.

[2] See Jā. no. 404. This incident of Devadatta's malice is not mentioned in the Jātakamāla.

[3] The Bodhisatta naturally came down on *this* shore or bank, *this* side of the river (symbolic of the River of Death that has to be crossed in order to find Deathlessness on its Farther Shore), for as yet, and not until he became the Buddha, did he stand safely and securely on that Farther Shore. But in this story he is shown in his capacity of Wayfinder, finding the Way for others to follow, helping them across.

[4] On gold and yellow, as colour, see above, p. 40.

had his body cleansed and anointed with highly refined oil, and having an oiled skin spread over a bed he made him lie down there, and himself sitting on a low seat,[1] he spoke the first stanza:

> "Having made of yourself a causeway
> You helped them across to safety.
> What are you then to them,
> And what they to you, great monkey?"
>
> *Jātaka III, 370–73, no. 407 (condensed)*

Crossing over by Boat

74.

The man who plunges in the spate,
  Flooding and turgid, swift of flow,
He, borne along the current's way,
How can he others help to cross? . . .

As one who boards a sturdy boat
With oars and rudder well equipt,
May many others help to cross—
Sure, skilful knower of the means:

So the self-quickened lore-adept,
Listener imperturbable,
By knowledge may help others muse,
The eager-eared adventurers.[2]

Suttanipāta, 319, 321–22

75.

Hence, ever-watchful, man
  Should pleasures shun; thus rid,
Their vessels baling out,
Yon-farers cross the flood.[2]

Suttanipāta, 771

[1] A mark of respect.
[2] Translation as in E. M. Hare, *Woven Cadences*.

76.

Bale out this boat, monk; baled out
'Twill lightly go along for you;
When passion and hatred have been cut off
So forward to Nirvana will you go.

Dhammapada, 369

77. *Crossing over by Raft*

"Monks, I will teach you Dhamma—the Parable of the Raft—for crossing over, not for retaining. Listen to it, attend carefully, and I will speak.

"A man going along a high-road might see a great stretch of water, the hither bank dangerous and frightening, the farther bank secure, not frightening. But if there were no boat for crossing by or a bridge across for going from the not-beyond to the beyond, he might think: 'If I were to collect sticks, grass, branches, foliage and to tie a raft, then, depending on the raft and striving with my hands and feet, I might cross over safely to the beyond.' If he carried out his purpose, then, crossed over, gone beyond, it might occur to him: 'Now, this raft has been very useful to me. Depending on it and striving with my hands and feet, I have crossed over safely to the beyond. Suppose now, having put this raft on my head or lifted it on to my shoulder, I should proceed as I desire?' Now, monks, in doing this is that man doing what should be done with that raft?"

"No, Lord."

"But, monks, it might occur to him after he has crossed over and gone beyond: 'Now, this raft has been very useful to me. Depending on it and striving with my hands and feet, I have crossed over safely to the beyond. Suppose now, having beached this raft on the dry ground or having submerged it in the water, I should proceed as I desire?' In doing this, monks, that man would be doing what should be done with that raft. Even so is the Parable of the Raft Dhamma taught by me for crossing over, not for retaining. You, monks, by understanding the Parable of the Raft, should get rid even of (wholesome) mental states,[1] all the more of unwholesome ones."[2]

Majjhima-nikāya I, 134–35

78. *Crossing over by Ford and Swimming*

Thus have I heard: At one time the Lord was staying among the Vajjis at Ukkacela on the banks of the river Ganges. While he was there, the Lord addressed the monks, saying: "Monks." "Revered One," these monks answered the Lord in assent.

"Once upon a time, monks, an incompetent herdsman of Magadha in the last month of the rains at harvest time, without considering either the hither or the farther bank of the river Ganges, drove his cattle across to the farther bank in Suvideha at a place where there was no ford. Then, monks, the cattle, huddled together in the middle of the stream of the river Ganges, got into difficulties and misfortune there. Even so, monks, whoever think they should listen to and put their trust in those recluses and brahmans who are unskilled about this world, the world beyond, Mara's realm,[3] what is not Mara's realm,[4] Death's realm, what is not Death's realm, that will be for a long time for their woe and anguish.

"Once upon a time, monks, a competent herdsman of Magadha in the last month of the rains at harvest time, having considered both the hither and the farther bank of the river Ganges, drove his cattle across to the farther bank in Suvideha at a place where there was a ford. First of all he drove across those bulls who were the sires and leaders of the herd, next the sturdy bullocks and young steers, then the half-grown bull-calves and heifers, and then the weaker calves. All cut across

---

[1] MA. ii. 109 refers to M. i. 456: "I speak of getting rid of the plane of neither-perception-nor-non-perception—this is to get rid of the desire for calm and vision." And it refers to M. i. 260: "Even if this view of yours is purified thus, do not cling to it."

[2] Such as Ariṭṭha's perverted view.

[3] The threefold becoming: kāma, rūpa, arūpa, MA. ii. 266.

[4] The nine other worldly things, MA. ii. 266. These are the four ways, the four fruits and Nirvana.

the stream of the Ganges and went safely beyond. At that time there was a young new-born calf which, by following the lowing of its mother, also cut across the stream of the Ganges and went safely beyond. Even so, monks, whoever think they should listen to and put their faith in those recluses and brahmans who are skilled about this world, the world beyond, Mara's realm, what is not Mara's realm, Death's realm, what is not Death's realm, that will be for a long time for their welfare and happiness.

"Monks, like unto those bulls who were the sires and leaders of the herd and who, having cut across the stream of the Ganges, went safely beyond, are those monks who are arahants, the outflows extinguished, who have lived the life, done what was to be done, laid down the burden, attained their own goal, the fetters of becoming utterly extinguished, freed by perfect gnosis. For these, having cut across Mara's stream,[1] have gone safely beyond.[2]

"Monks, like unto those sturdy bullocks and young steers who, having cut across the stream of the Ganges, went safely beyond, are those monks who, by utterly extinguishing the five fetters binding to this lower (shore), are of spontaneous uprising, and being ones who attain Nirvana there are not liable to return from that world. For these also, having cut across Mara's stream, will go safely beyond.

"Monks, like those half-grown bull-calves and heifers who, having cut across the stream of the Ganges, went safely beyond, are those monks who, by utterly extinguishing the three fetters, by reducing passion, aversion and confusion, are once-returners who, having come back again to this world once only, will make an end of suffering. For these also, having cut across Mara's stream, will go safely beyond.

"Monks, like unto those weaker calves who, having cut across the stream of the Ganges, went safely beyond, are those monks who, by utterly extinguishing the three fetters, are stream-winners, not liable for a sorrowful state, assured, bound for awakening. For these also, having cut across Mara's stream, will go safely beyond.

"Monks, like unto that young new-born calf which, by

[1] The stream of taṇhā, craving, MA. ii. 267.
[2] Beyond saṁsāra to Nirvana, MA. ii. 267.

following the lowing of its mother, also cut across the stream of the Ganges and went safely beyond, are those monks who are striving for Dhamma, striving for faith. For these also, having cut across Mara's stream, will go safely beyond.

"Now I, monks, am skilled about this world, the world beyond, Mara's realm, what is not Mara's realm, Death's realm, and what is not Death's realm. For those who think they should listen to me and place faith in me there will be welfare and happiness for a long time."

Thus spoke the Lord; the Well-farer having said this, the Teacher then spoke thus:

"This world, the world beyond are well explained by the one who knows,
    And what is accessible by Mara and what is not accessible by Death.
    By the Buddha, comprehending, thoroughly knowing every world,
    Opened is the door of the Deathless for reaching Nirvana-security.
    Cut across is the stream of the Malign One, shattered, destroyed;
    Let there be abundant rapture, monks, let security be reached."

Majjhima-nikāya I, 225–26 (condensed)

Emptiness

79.

As in the ocean's midmost depth no wave is born, but all is still, so let the monk be still, be motionless, and nowhere should he swell.[1]

Suttanipāta, 920

---

[1] Cf. E. Conze, *Buddhism*, p. 130: "something which looks 'swollen' from the outside is 'hollow' within".

80.

R egard the world as void; and e'er
  Alert, uproot false view of self.
Thus, Mogharajah, thou wouldst be
Death's crosser; and, regarding thus
The world, death's king doth see thee not.[1]

Suttanipāta, 119

81.

"To what extent is the world called 'empty', Lord?"
  "Because it is empty of self or of what belongs to self,
it is therefore said: 'The world is empty.' And what is empty of
self and what belongs to self? The eye, material shapes, visual
consciousness, impression on the eye—all these are empty of
self and of what belongs to self. So too are ear, nose, tongue,
body and mind (and their appropriate sense-data, appropriate
consciousness and the impression on them of their appropriate
sense-data—*as above*): they are all empty of self and of what
belongs to self. Also that feeling which arises, conditioned by
impression on the eye, ear, nose, tongue, body, mind, whether
it be pleasant or painful or neither painful nor pleasant—that
too is empty of self and of what belongs to self. Wherefore is
the world called empty because it is empty of self and of what
belongs to self."

Samyutta-nikāya IV, 54

82.

A nd what is the freedom of mind that is empty? As to this,
  a monk forest-gone or gone to the root of a tree or to an
empty place reflects thus: This is empty of self or of what
belongs to self. This is called the freedom of mind that is
empty. . . . To the extent that the freedoms of mind are
immeasurable, are of no-thing, are signless, of them all unshakable freedom of mind is pointed to as chief, for it is empty
of passion, empty of aversion, empty of confusion.

Majjhima-nikāya I, 297–98

[1] Translation by E. M. Hare, *Woven Cadences*. Cf. Dhp. 170.

83.

"By abiding in what (concept) are you now abiding in its fulness, Sariputta?"

"By abiding in (the concept of) emptiness am I now abiding in its fulness, Lord."

"This is the abiding of 'great men', Sariputta, that is to say (the concept of) emptiness."

Majjhima-nikāya III, 294

Nirvana

84.

The stopping of becoming is Nirvana.

Samyutta-nikāya II, 117

85.

It is called Nirvana because of the getting rid of craving.

Samyutta-nikāya I, 39

86.

The steadfast go out (nibbanti) like this lamp.

Suttanipāta, 235

87.

I will pull the wick right down (into the oil)—the going out (nibbana) of the lamp itself was deliverance of the mind.

Therīgātha, 116

88.

The going out of the flame itself was deliverance of the mind.

Dīgha-nikāya II, 157

89.

The Brahma-faring is lived for the plunge into Nirvana, for going beyond to Nirvana, for culmination in Nirvana.

Samyutta-nikāya III, 189

90.

That monk of wisdom here, devoid of desire and passion, attains to deathlessness, peace, the unchanging state of Nirvana.

Suttanipāta, 204

91.

For those who in mid-stream stay, in great peril in the flood —for those adventuring on ageing and dying—do I proclaim the Isle:

Where is no-thing, where naught is grasped, this is the Isle of No-beyond. Nirvana do I call it—the utter extinction of ageing and dying.

Suttanipāta, 1093–94

92.

"To what extent, Lord, is one a speaker of Dhamma?"

"Monk, if one teaches Dhamma for the turning away from material shape, from feeling, perception, the impulses, consciousness, for dispassion in regard to them, for their cessation, it is fitting to call him a monk who is a speaker of Dhamma. If he is himself faring along for the turning away from material shape and so on, for dispassion in regard to them, for their cessation, it is fitting to call him a monk who is faring along in accordance with Dhamma. Monk, if he is freed by this turning away, by dispassion in regard to these things, by their cessation, it is fitting to call him a monk who has attained Nirvana here and now."

Samyutta-nikāya III, 163–64

93.

A wanderer who ate rose-apples spoke thus to the venerable Sariputta:

"Reverend Sariputta, it is said: 'Nirvana, Nirvana.' Now, what, your reverence, is Nirvana?"

"Whatever, your reverence, is the extinction of passion, of aversion, of confusion, this is called Nirvana."

"Is there a way, your reverence, is there a course for the realization of this Nirvana?"

"There is, your reverence."

"What is it, your reverence?"

"This ariyan eightfold Way itself is for the realization of Nirvana, that is to say right view, right thought, right speech, right action, right mode of livelihood, right endeavour, right mindfulness, right concentration."

"Goodly, your reverence, is the Way, goodly the course for the realization of this Nirvana. But for certain it needs diligence."

Samyutta-nikāya IV, 251–52

94.

A s to this, Ananda, he perceives thus: This is the real, this the excellent, namely the calm of all the impulses, the casting out of all 'basis', the extinction of craving, dispassion, stopping, Nirvana.

Anguttara-nikāya V, 322

95.

There is, monks, that plane where there is neither extension nor . . . motion [1] nor the plane of infinite ether . . . nor that of neither-perception-nor-non-perception,[2] neither this world nor another, neither the moon nor the sun. Here, monks, I say that there is no coming or going or remaining or deceasing or uprising, for this is itself [3] without support,[4] without con-

---

[1] cf. p. 58 n. 1.   [2] cf. pp. 63–64.

[3] UdA. 392 says "this plane itself is called Nirvana".

[4] Being uncompounded.

tinuance,[1] without mental object—this is itself the end of suffering.

There is, monks, an unborn, not become, not made, un-compounded,[2] and were it not, monks, for this unborn, not become, not made, uncompounded, no escape could be shown here for what is born, has become, is made, is compounded. But because there is, monks, an unborn, not become, not made, uncompounded, therefore an escape can be shown for what is born, has become, is made, is compounded.

Udāna, 80–81

96.

" Ananda, when Sariputta attained final Nirvana did he take with him either the body of moral habit, of concentration, of wisdom, of freedom, of the knowledge and insight of freedom? "

"No, Lord. . . ."

"Have I not aforetime, Ananda, pointed out that in all that is dear and beloved there is the nature of diversity, separation and alteration? That one could say in reference to what has been born, has become, is compounded and liable to dissolution: 'O let not that be dissolved'—this situation does not exist. As, Ananda, one of the larger boughs of a great, stable and pithy tree might rot away, so out of the great, stable and pithy Order of monks, Sariputta has attained final Nirvana. Wherefore, Ananda, dwell having self for island, self for refuge and no other refuge; having Dhamma for island, Dhamma for refuge and no other refuge. And how does one do this?

"As to this, Ananda, a monk lives contemplating the body in the body, ardent, clearly comprehending it and mindful of it; likewise the feelings in the feelings, the mind in the mind, and mental states in mental states, so as to control the coveting and dejection in the world."[3]

Samyutta-nikāya V, 162–63

[1] In saṁsāra.

[2] UdA. 395 says that all these four words are synonyms and refer to the uncompounded (or unconstructed or unconditioned) nature of Nirvana. Their opposites are the compounded things of nāma-rūpa, mind-and-body.

[3] See above, p. 56.

97.

Monks, there are these two elements of Nirvana: the
Nirvana-element with the groups of existence still remaining,[1]
and the Nirvana-element without these groups remaining.[2]
Of what kind is the former? As to this, monks, a monk is an
Arahant whose outflows are extinguished, who has lived the
life, done what was to be done, laid down the burden, attained
his own goal, the fetter of becoming utterly extinguished,
released by perfect gnosis. In him the five sense-organs still
remain; and as they have not yet departed he experiences
through them what is pleasing and displeasing and undergoes
happiness and suffering. Whatever is his extinction of passion,
of aversion, of confusion, this, monks, is called the Nirvana-
element with the groups of existence still remaining.

And what, monks, is the Nirvana-element without the
groups of existence still remaining? As to this, monks, a monk
is an Arahant, whose outflows are extinguished, who has lived
the life, done what was to be done, laid down the burden,
attained his own goal, the fetter of becoming utterly extinguished, released by perfect gnosis. Here itself, monks, all that
has been felt, but not delighting him, will become cool. This,
monks, is called the Nirvana-element that is without the
groups of existence still remaining.

The Lord gave this meaning, regarding which it is said:

These two Nirvana-elements are shown by the Visioned One,
   independent, and who is 'such'.[3]
The one element here belongs to the here-now—that which
   still has the groups—although becoming's conduit is
   destroyed.

[1] sa-upādi-sesa-nibbāna. This is the same as kilesa-nibbāna, the
burning up or putting out of the defilements. Upādi denotes the five
khandhas.

[2] anupādi-sesa-nibbāna. This is khandha-nibbāna, the putting out
of the groups of existence (through the extinction of grasping or
clinging, upādi).

[3] tādin, an epithet of the Tathāgata, see below, no. 112. His evenness
of mind in the six sensory spheres is such that to him both desirable
and undesirable things are as but one, ItA. i. 167.

But that without the groups remaining belongs to the future
—herein are all becomings stopped.

Whoever, by knowing this uncompounded state, their minds
released by the extinction of becoming's conduit—

They, delighting in extinction,[1] reach the pith of mental
states.[2]

Those who are 'such' get rid of all becomings.

Itivuttaka, p. 38–39

98.

"Revered Nagasena, things produced of karma are seen in
the world, things produced of cause are seen, things
produced of nature[3] are seen. Tell me what in the world is born
not of karma, not of cause, not of nature."

"These two, sire, in the world are born not of karma, not of
cause, not of nature. Which two? Ether, sire, and Nirvana."

"Do not, revered Nagasena, corrupt the Conqueror's words
and answer the question ignorantly."

"What did I say, sire, that you speak thus to me?"

"Revered Nagasena, what you said about ether—that it is
born not of karma nor of cause nor of nature—is right. But
with many a hundred reasons did the Lord, revered Nagasena,
point out to disciples the Way to the realization of Nirvana—
and then *you* speak thus: 'Nirvana is born of no cause.'"

"It is true, sire, that with many a hundred reasons did the
Lord point out to disciples the Way to the realization of

[1] I.e. of passion, aversion and confusion, and which is Nirvana,
ItA. i. 167.

[2] dhammasāra. ItA. i. 167 says that this means: because of the pith
(core, heartwood, sāra) of freedom obtained by reaching Arahantship,
the pith of mental objects (dhammesu sārabhūtassa) in this Dhamma
and Discipline. . . . Or, saying: the pith of mental states (dhammesu)
because of the existence of permanence, of the best, the pith of mental
states (dhammasāra), Nirvana. This has been said: "Dispassion is the
best of mental states, of these dispassion is shown to be the chief" (A.
iii. 35).

[3] utu. This is the creative power of physical nature, or simply
physical nature itself. Called at Comp. p. 161 'physical change', with a
note calling it 'temperature', to which, as the manifestation of
radiation (tejo), every change in physical nature is attributed.

Nirvana; but he did not point out a cause for the production of Nirvana."

"Here we, revered Nagasena, are entering from darkness into greater darkness, from a jungle into a deeper jungle, from a thicket into a denser thicket, inasmuch as there is indeed a cause for the realization of Nirvana, but no cause for the production of that thing.[1] If, revered Nagasena, there is a cause for the realization of Nirvana, well then, one would also require a cause for the production of Nirvana. For inasmuch, revered Nagasena, as there is a child's father, for that reason one would also require a father of the father; as there is a pupil's teacher, for that reason one would also require a teacher of the teacher; as there is a seed for a sprout, for that reason, one would also require a seed for the seed. Even so, revered Nagasena, if there is a cause for the realization of Nirvana, for that reason one would also require a cause for the production of Nirvana. Because there is a top to a tree or a creeper, for this reason there is also a middle, also the root. Even so, revered Nagasena, if there is a cause for the realization of Nirvana, for that reason one would also require a cause for the production of Nirvana."

"Nirvana, sire, is not to be produced; therefore a cause for Nirvana being produced is not pointed out."

"Please, revered Nagasena, giving me a reason, convince me by means of the reason, so that I may know: There is a cause for the realization of Nirvana; there is no cause for the production of Nirvana."

"Well then, sire, attend carefully, listen closely, and I will tell the reason as to this. Would a man, sire, with his natural strength be able to go from here up a high Himalayan mountain?"

"Yes, revered Nagasena."

"But would that man, sire, with his natural strength be able to bring a high Himalayan mountain here?"

"Certainly not, revered sir."

"Even so, sire, it is possible to point out the Way for the realization of Nirvana, but impossible to show a cause for the

---

[1] Dhamma. Everything is a dhamma, including the uncompounded Nirvana. Therefore when Dhp. 279 says 'everything is not-self', *sabbe dhammā anattā*, it means Nirvana as well.

production of Nirvana. Would it be possible, sire, for a man who, with his natural strength, has crossed over the great sea in a boat to reach the farther shore? "

"Yes, revered sir."

"But would it be possible, sire, for that man, with his natural strength, to bring the farther shore of the great sea here? "

"Certainly not, revered sir."

"Even so, sire, it is possible to point out the Way to the realization of Nirvana, but impossible to show a cause for the production of Nirvana. For what reason? It is because of the uncompounded nature of the thing."

"Revered Nagasena, is Nirvana uncompounded? "

"Yes, sire, Nirvana is uncompounded; it is made by nothing at all. Sire, one cannot say of Nirvana that it arises or that it does not arise or that it is to be produced or that it is past or future or present, or that it is cognizable by the eye, ear, nose, tongue or body."

"If, revered Nagasena, Nirvana neither arises nor does not arise and so on, as you say, well then, revered Nagasena, you indicate Nirvana as a thing that is not: Nirvana is not."

"Sire, Nirvana is; Nirvana is cognizable by mind; an ariyan disciple, faring along rightly with a mind that is purified, lofty, straight, without obstructions, without temporal desires, sees Nirvana."

"But what, revered sir, is that Nirvana like that can be illustrated by similes? Convince me with reasons according to which a thing that is can be illustrated by similes."

"Is there, sire, what is called wind? "

"Yes, revered sir."

"Please, sire, show the wind by its colour or configuration or as thin or thick or long or short."

"But it is not possible, revered Nagasena, for the wind to be shown; for the wind cannot be grasped in the hand or touched; but yet there is the wind."

"If, sire, it is not possible for the wind to be shown, well then, there is no wind."

"I, revered Nagasena, know that there is wind, I am convinced of it, but I am not able to show the wind."

"Even so, sire, there is Nirvana; but it is not possible to show Nirvana by colour or configuration."

"Very good, revered Nagasena, well shown is the simile, well seen the reason; thus it is and I accept it as you say: There is Nirvana."

Milindapañha, 268–71

99.

Dispassion is called the Way. It is said: "Through dispassion is one freed." Yet, in meaning, all these (words: stopping, renunciation, surrender, release, lack of clinging[1]) are synonyms for Nirvana. For according to ultimate meaning, Nirvana is the Ariyan Truth of the stopping of suffering. But because, when that (Nirvana) is reached, craving detaches itself, besides being stopped, it is therefore called Dispassion and it is called Stopping. And because, when it is reached, there is renunciation and so on, and there does not remain even one sensory pleasure that is clung to, it is therefore called Renunciation, Surrender, Release, Lack of Clinging.

Its distinguishing mark is peace; its flavour is unchangeable or its flavour is a means of comforting; its manifestation is the signless or its manifestation is unimpeded. Could it be said: "Indeed, there is not Nirvana. It is like the horn of a hare; it is not to be got at[2]"? No, (this could not be said) for it is to be got at by (a certain) means. It is to be got at by means of attainments suitable to it, as the other-worldly thought of others (is to be got at) by such cognition as encompasses the mind. Therefore it should not be said: "Because it is not to be got at (by more ordinary means) it is not", any more than it should be said that that is not which ignorant average persons do not get at. Moreover it could not be said: "There is not Nirvana." Why is this? Because the practice of Dhamma is not barren. For if Nirvana were not, there would be barrenness in regard to (spiritual) attainment in the three categories of

[1] These are the words found in the statement of the Third Truth, that of Stopping.

[2] I.e. it is inexistent; or the meaning may be that it is 'incomprehensible'.

Moral Habit and so on that begin with Right View.[1] But due to the attainment of Nirvana, there is not this barrenness. . . .

But according to what was said, beginning: "Whatever, your reverence, is the extinction of passion"[2]—(it might be asked): Is Nirvana extinction? No, because there is extinction also for arahantship, shown by such expressions as that just cited.

Furthermore, if Nirvana were of short duration and so on, it would be stained. Were this the case, one might conclude that Nirvana, short in duration, with 'compounded' as its distinguishing mark, would be attainable without any need for Right Endeavour.[3] But (it might be asked), as, after extinction there is no further procedure, is not that a stain on the existence of Nirvana? No, for extinction such as this does not exist. Even had it existed, it could not have transcended the stains we have spoken of. And belonging to the Ariyan Way is the finding of the existence of Nirvana. For the Ariyan Way extinguishes stains, and is therefore called Extinction. Further than that there is no procedure for stains. It is called Extinction because in a broad sense it is the sufficing condition of the extinction which is called stopping without rebirth. Why is it not called this explicitly? Because of its extreme subtlety. Its extreme subtlety is successful in bringing unconcernedness to the Lord and in being seen through ariyan vision.

This (Nirvana), attainable by one possessed of the Way, not shared with others, from having no earliest beginning is without source. But if it exists due to the existence of the Way, is it not without source? No, because it cannot be produced by means of the Way. It is only attainable by means of the Way—it cannot be produced by it. Therefore is it precisely without source. Because it is without source it is unageing and undying. Because there is no source, no ageing or dying, it is permanent. . . . Because it transcends material shape it is without material shape (formless or immaterial). Since for the Buddhas and so

[1] This is a reference to the eight parts of the Way (the first being Right View) and which are distributed between the three great categories of the whole training: Moral Habit, Concentration and Wisdom.

[2] S. iv. 251 (see no. 93 above).

[3] sammāvāyāma, the sixth factor in the Eightfold Way.

on there is no distinction of goal, "there is only one goal".[1]
Attained (by someone) through mind-development, it is called
(Nirvana) with the groups of existence still remaining. For
here, although his defilements are allayed, some groups of
existence (still) remain and grasping is (still) evident. But he
who, by getting rid of its arising, and with the last thought of
the fruit of karma extinguished, from the non-arising of the
'procedure' groups (of grasping) and from the disappearance
of those that have arisen—for him there is then the absence cf
the groups of existence. And for him, now without the groups
of existence remaining, it can be laid down: Here there is not a
group of existence remaining.

Because it is attainable by means of the special cognition
perfected by unfailing effort, because it was spoken of by the
Omniscient One, because it has existence in the ultimate
meaning, Nirvana is not non-existent. So this was said:
"There is, monks, an unborn, not become, not made, uncompounded."[2]

Visuddhimagga, 507–09

[1] M. i. 64.
[2] Ud. 80; It. p. 37 (see above, p. 95).

THE BUDDHA AND TATHAGATA

100.

In the Sakyan clan there was born
A Buddha, peerless among men,
Conqueror of all, repelling Mara—
The Visioned One sees all.
The extinction of all karma has he won,
And by removal of the 'basis' is he freed.

Samyutta-nikāya I, 134

101.

Now I know well that when I approached various large
assemblies, even before I had sat down there or had
spoken or begun to talk to them, whatever might have been
their sort I made myself of like sort, whatever their language
so was my language. And I rejoiced them with a talk on
Dhamma, made it acceptable to them, set them on fire,
gladdened them.

Dīgha-nikāya II, 109

102.

Monks, the Tathagata's body remains although he has cut
off the conduit for becoming. As long as his body remains
devas and men shall see him; but at the breaking up of his
body at the end of his life-time devas and men shall see him
not.

Dīgha-nikāya I, 46

103.

What is there, Vakkali, in seeing this vile body? Whoso
sees Dhamma sees me; whoso sees me sees Dhamma.
Seeing Dhamma, Vakkali, he sees me; seeing me, he sees
Dhamma.

Samyutta-nikāya III, 120

104.

Monks, you have not a mother or a father who might tend you. If you do not tend one another, who is there who will tend you? Whoever, monks, would tend me, he should tend the sick.

Vinaya-piṭaka I, 302

105.

At one time the Lord was journeying along the high-road between Ukkattha and Setabbya; so also was the Brahmin Dona. He saw on the Lord's footprints the wheels [1] with their thousand spokes, their rims and hubs and all their attributes complete, and he thought: "Indeed, how wonderful and marvellous—it cannot be that these are the footprints of a human being."

Then Dona, following the Lord's footprints, saw that he was sitting under a tree, comely, faith-inspiring, his sense-faculties and his mind peaceful, attained to the calm of uttermost control, restrained, tamed and guarded as to his sense-faculties. Seeing the 'elephant', [2] Dona approached the Lord and said:

"Is your reverence a deva?"

"No indeed, brahmin, I am not a deva."

"Then a gandharva?"

"No indeed, brahmin."

"A yakkha then?"

"No indeed, brahmin, I am not a yakkha."

"Then is your reverence a human being?"

"No indeed, brahman, I am not a human being."

"You answer No to all my questions. Who then is your reverence?"

[1] Wheels on the soles of the feet are among the 32 signs of a Great Man. "The Buddha's footprints are invisible, but on this occasion he purposely allowed the impressions to be seen by the Brahmin"—so AA. iii. 77–78.

[2] nāga, bull-elephant, cobra and great man, "a synonym for the monk whose outflows are extinguished" (M. i. 145).

"Brahmin, those outflows whereby, if they had not been extinguished, I might have been a deva, gandharva, yakkha or a human being—those outflows are extinguished in me, cut off at the root, made like a palm-tree stump that can come to no further existence in the future. Just as a blue, red or white lotus, although born in the water, grown up in the water, when it reaches the surface stands there unsoiled by the water—just so, brahmin, although born in the world, grown up in the world, having overcome the world, I abide unsoiled by the world. Take it that I am Buddha,[1] brahmin."

> The outflows whereby would be
> A deva-birth or airy sprite,
> Gandharva, or whereby myself
> Would reach the state of yakkhahood,
> Or go to birth in human womb—
> Those outflows now by myself
> Are slain, extinguished and rooted out.
>
> As a lotus, fair and lovely,
> By the water is not soiled,
> By the world am I not soiled:
> Therefore, brahmin, am I Buddha.[2]

Anguttara-nikāya II, 37–39

106.

I am not a Brahmin, rajah's son or merchant; nor am I any what[3]; I fare in the world a sage, of no-thing,[4] homeless, self completely gone out—it is inept to ask me of my lineage.

Suttanipāta, 455–56 (condensed)

[1] Buddha means awakened, hence The Wake or Awakened One.
[2] Following for the verses F. L. Woodward's translation at G.S. ii. 45.
[3] SnA. 402 draws attention to the passage which speaks of the rivers (=attainers) which, on reaching the sea (=nibbāna), lose their former names and identities.
[4] Without craving, SnA. 403.

107.

"If a fire were blazing in front of you, Vaccha, would you know that it was?"

"Yes, good Gotama."

"And would you know the reason for its blazing?"

"Yes, because it had a supply of grass and sticks."

"And would you know if it were to be put out (nibba-yeyya)?"

"Yes, good Gotama."

"And on its being put out, would you know the direction the fire had gone to from here—east, west, north, south?"

"This question does not apply, good Gotama. For the fire blazed because it had a supply of grass and sticks; but when it had consumed this and had no other fuel, then, being without fuel, it is reckoned as gone out."

"Even so, Vaccha, that material shape, that feeling, perception, those impulses, that consciousness by which one, in defining the Tathagata, might define him—all have been got rid of by the Tathagata, cut off at the root, made like a palm-tree stump that can come to no further existence in the future. Freed from reckoning by material shape, feeling, perception, the impulses, consciousness is the Tathagata; he is deep, immeasurable, unfathomable, as is the great ocean. 'Arises' does not apply, nor does 'does not arise', nor 'both arises and does not arise', nor 'neither arises nor does not arise'."

Majjhima-nikāya I, 487–88

108.

Since a Tathagata, even when actually present, is incomprehensible, it is inept to say of him—of the Uttermost Person, the Supernal Person, the Attainer of the Supernal—that after dying the Tathagata is, or is not, or both is and is not, or neither is nor is not.

Samyutta-nikāya III, 118,

109.

Whose victory is not turned to defeat,
to conquer whom no one one on earth sets out,
the Buddha, whose range is unending,
the trackless, by what track will you lead him?

In whom there is no entangling, embroiling craving
to lead him anywhere,
the Buddha, whose range is unending,
the trackless, by what track will you lead him?

Dhammapada, *179–80*

110.

When a monk's mind is freed by getting rid of ignorance,
of again-becoming and circling on in births, of craving,
of the five fetters binding to this lower shore, of the conceit
'I am', then the devas—those with Inda, those with Brahma,
those with Pajapati—do not succeed in their search if they
think, "This is the (discriminative) consciousness attached to
a Tathagata.[1]" What is the reason for this? I here and now
say that a Tathagata is untraceable.

Majjhima-nikāya I, 139

111.

At one time when he was staying near Savatthi the Lord
was delighting, arousing, setting on fire and gladdening the
monks with reasoned talk concerning Nirvana, and the monks
were listening attentively with their whole minds. It then
occurred to Mara, the Malign One: "Suppose I were to
approach this recluse Gotama as he is delighting the monks
with talk concerning Nirvana so as to make him perplexed?"
So Mara, the Malign One, having assumed the form of a
ploughman, shouldering a great plough, taking hold of a long

---

[1] MA. ii. 117 says here tathāgata means satta (being), the highest
person, whose outflows are extinguished. Cf. MA. iii. 141.

goad, his hair dishevelled, clothed in a coarse hempen tunic, his feet spattered with mud, approached the Lord and said:

"Recluse, did you see any oxen?"

"What have you, Malign One, to do with oxen?"[1]

"Mine, recluse, is the eye, mine are material shapes, mine is the field of visual consciousness. Where can you go, recluse, to escape from me? Precisely mine, recluse, are the ear, sounds, the field of auditory consciousness: the nose, scents, the field of olfactory consciousness; the tongue, tastes, the field of gustatory consciousness; the body, touches, the field of tactile consciousness; precisely mine, recluse is the mind, mine are mental states, mine is the field of mental consciousness."

"Precisely yours, Malign One, is all this. But where there is none of all this, there is no coming in for you."

Mara: "That which they call 'mine', and those who say 'mine',
　　　　　Here if you had mind for them, you would not, recluse, be free from me."

The Lord: "What they speak of is not 'mine', for those who speak there is no 'I'.
　　　　　Find it to be so, Malign One—you will not even see the path of me."

Samyutta-nikāya I, 114–16

112.

A Tathagata is a seer of what is to be seen, but he does not mind[2] the seen, the unseen, the seeable, the seer. So likewise with the heard, the sensed and the cognized: he thinks of none of these modes of theirs. Therefore among things seen, heard, sensed and cognized he is precisely 'such' (tadi). Moreover, than he who is 'such' there is no other 'such' further or more excellent.

Anguttara-nikāya II, 25

[1] At Vin. i. 23, when some young men asked Gotama whether he had seen a woman, he answered, "What have you to do with a woman? Is it not better to seek self?"

[2] This 'not thinking' or 'disregarding', na maññati, must contain an allusion to upek(k)hā, the even-mindedness where one is unaffected by sense-data although not unaware of them.

113.

In regard to things that are past, future and present the Tathagata is a speaker at a suitable time, a speaker of fact, on what has bearing, of Dhamma, of Discipline. Therefore is he called Tathagata.

Inasmuch as what is seen, heard, felt, cognized, achieved, sought, pondered in the mind by recluses and Brahmins, devas and men—inasmuch as it is all fully awakened to by the Tathagata is he therefore called Tathagata.

And from the night when the Tathagata fully awoke to the supreme self-Awakening to the night when he attained final Nirvana in the Nirvana-element without the groups of existence remaining—in that interval what he spoke, declared and explained, all that is exactly so and not otherwise. Therefore is he called Tathagata.

As the Tathagata speaks so he does, as he does so he speaks. Because he speaks as he does and does as he speaks, he is therefore called Tathagata.

In the world with its devas, Maras and Brahmas, amid living beings with recluses and Brahmins, devas and mankind, the Tathagata is the victor unvanquished, the absolute seer, self-controlled. Therefore is he called Tathagata.

Dīgha-nikāya III, 135

114.

Or the Lord (bhagava) is a partaker (bhagi) of the ten powers of a Tathagata, of the four confidences, of the four analytical insights, of the six super-knowledges, of the six Buddha-dhammas.

Niddesa I, 143

115.

There is no distinction between any of the Buddhas in physical beauty, moral habit, concentration, wisdom, freedom, cognition and insight of freedom, the four confidences, the ten powers of a Tathagata, the six special cognitions, the fourteen cognitions of Buddhas, the eighteen Buddha-dhammas,[1] in a word in all the dhammas of Buddhas, for all Buddhas are exactly the same as regards Buddha-dhammas.

Milindapañha, 285

116.

Now, Sariputta, there are these ten powers of a Tathagata, endowed with which a Tathagata claims the leader's place, roars a lion's roar in assemblies, and sets rolling the Brahma-wheel. What are the ten?

Herein, Sariputta, a Tathagata comprehends as they really are causal occasion as causal occasion, non-causal occasion as non-causal occasion.

And again, Sariputta, a Tathagata comprehends as it really is the result of the causal occasion, of the cause of taking on of karma, past, future and present.

And again, Sariputta, a Tathagata comprehends as it really is the course leading to all bourns.

And again, Sariputta, a Tathagata comprehends as it really is the world[2] with its manifold elements, its various elements.

And again, Sariputta, a Tathagata comprehends as they really are the various inclinations of beings.

And again, Sariputta, a Tathagata comprehends as it really is the state of the faculties (cardinal virtues, of faith and so on) of other beings, of other persons.

And again, Sariputta, a Tathagata comprehends as it really is the defilement of, the purification of,[3] the emergence from the attainments of the (four) jhanas, the (eight) deliverances, the (three) concentrations.[4]

[1] Enumerated at Mahāvastu i. 160. See no. 140.

[2] MA. ii. 29 says that here 'world' means the world of the khandhas, āyatanas and dhātus.

[3] But MA. ii. 30 says that 'defilement', sankilesa, is what conduces to decrease, and that 'purification', vodāna, is what conduces to progress, visesabhāgiyadhamma; and where visesa can also mean a specific idea in meditation.

[4] The numbers in brackets are taken from MA. ii. 30. For the four jhānas see above, p. 60; the eight deliverances are found at D. ii. 70; and the three concentrations are those on the signless, emptiness and non-desiring.

And again, Sariputta, a Tathagata remembers a variety of former habitations, thus: one birth . . .[1] Thus does he remember divers former habitations in all their mode and detail.

And again, Sariputta, a Tathagata with his purified deva-like vision surpassing that of men sees beings as they are deceasing and uprising . . .[2] and he comprehends that beings are mean, excellent, comely, ugly, in a good bourn, in a bad bourn according to the consequence of karma.

And again, Sariputta, a Tathagata, by the extinction of the outflows, having realized here and now the freedom of mind and the freedom through wisdom that have no outflows, entering thereon abides therein. That a Tathagata does this, Sariputta, is a Tathagata's power of a Tathagata owing to which he claims the leader's place, roars a lion's roar in assemblies, and sets rolling the Brahma-wheel. These, Sariputta, are a Tathagata's ten powers of a Tathagata endowed with which a Tathagata claims the leader's place, roars a lion's roar in assemblies, and sets rolling the Brahma-wheel.

Majjhima-nikāya I, 69–71

117.

Whoever, Sariputta, knowing that it is so of me, seeing that it is so, should speak thus: "There are no states of further-men, no excellent cognition and insight befitting the Ariyans in the recluse Gotama; the recluse Gotama teaches Dhamma on (a system of) his own devising beaten out by reasoning and based on investigation"—if he does not retract that speech, Sariputta, if he does not retract that thought, if he does not cast out that view, he is verily consigned to Niraya Hell according to his deserts. Even if it were a monk, Sariputta, endowed with moral habit, concentration and wisdom, who should here and now arrive at gnosis, I (still) say that this results thus: If he does not retract that speech and that thought, if he does not cast out that view, he is verily consigned to Niraya Hell according to his deserts.

Sariputta, there are these four confidences of a Tathagata,

---

[1] See above, p. 61.   [2] See above, p. 61.

endowed with which confidences a Tathagata claims the leader's place, roars a lion's roar in assemblies, and sets rolling the Brahma-wheel. What are the four?

If anyone says: "These mental states are not fully awakened to by you although you claim to be a perfect Buddha", I do not behold the ground, Sariputta, on which a recluse or a Brahmin or a deva or Mara or Brahma or anyone in the world can reprove me with rightness for that. As I do not behold this ground, Sariputta, I abide attained to security, fearlessness and confidence.

If anyone says: "These outflows are not utterly extinguished although you claim to be one whose outflows are extinguished", I do not behold the ground . . . I abide attained to . . . confidence.

If anyone says: "In following those mental states called stumbling-blocks by you there is no stumbling-block at all", I do not behold the ground . . . I abide attained to . . . confidence.

If anyone says: "Dhamma does not rightly lead onward to the extinction of suffering the doer of it for whose sake it was taught by you", I do not behold the ground, Sariputta, on which a recluse or a Brahmin or a deva or Mara or Brahma or anyone in the world can reprove me with rightness for that. As I do not behold this ground, Sariputta, I abide attained to security, fearlessness and confidence.

These, Sariputta, are the four confidences of a Tathagata, endowed with which confidences the Tathagata claims the leader's place, roars a lion's roar in assemblies, and sets rolling the Brahma-wheel.

Majjhima-nikāya I, 71–72

118.

The Lord is speaking:

He, Vasettha, whose faith in the Tathagata is settled, rooted, established, firm, a faith not to be shaken by a recluse or Brahmin or deva or by Mara or Brahma or by anyone in the world—he may say: "I am the Lord's own son, born of his mouth, born of Dhamma, formed by Dhamma, heir to

Dhamma." What is the reason for this? This, Vasettha, is a synonym for the Tathagata: Dhamma-body and again Brahma-body, and again Dhamma-become and again Brahma-become.

Dīgha-nikāya III, 84

119.

The king said: "Did you, revered Nagasena, see the Buddha?"

"No, sire."

"Then did your teachers see the Buddha?"

"No, sire."

"Well then, revered Nagasena, there is not a Buddha."

"But have you, sire, seen the Himalayan river Uha?"

"No, revered sir."

"Then did your father ever see it?"

"No, revered sir."

"Well then, sire, there is not a river Uha."

"There is, revered sir. Even if neither my father nor I have seen it, there is the river Uha all the same."

"Even so, sire, even if neither my teachers nor I have seen the Lord, there is the Lord all the same."

"Very good, revered Nagasena. But is the Buddha pre-eminent?"

"Yes, sire."

"But how do you know, revered Nagasena, when you have not seen in the past, that the Buddha is pre-eminent?"

"What do you think about this, sire? Could those who have not already seen the great ocean know that it is so mighty, deep, immeasurable, unfathomable,[1] that although these five great rivers—the Ganges, Jumna, Aciravati, Sarabhu and the Mahi—flow into it constantly and continually, yet is neither its emptiness nor its fulness affected thereby?[2]"

"Yes, they could know that, revered sir."

[1] At M. i. 488, S. iv. 376 the Tathāgata is said to be deep, immeasurable, unfathomable like the great ocean.

[2] This is one of the sea's eight characteristics—that to which Nirvana is compared at Vin. ii. 239, A. iv. 202; Ud. 56.

"Even so, sire, having seen great disciples who have attained Nirvana, I know that the Lord is pre-eminent."

"Very good, revered Nagasena. Is it then possible to know this?"

"Once upon a time, sire, the Elder named Tissa was a teacher of writing. Many years have passed since he died. How is it that he is known?"

"By his writing, revered sir."

"Even so, sire, he who sees Dhamma sees the Lord[1]; for Dhamma, sire, was taught by the Lord."

"Very good, revered Nagasena. Have you seen Dhamma?"

"Sire, disciples are to conduct themselves for as long as life lasts with the Buddha as conduit, with the Buddha as designation."

"Very good, revered Nagasena. But is there a Buddha?"

"Yes, sire, there is a Buddha."

"But is it possible, revered Nagasena, to point to the Buddha as being either here or there?"

"Sire, the Lord has attained Nirvana in the Nirvana-element that has no groups of existence still remaining. It is not possible to point to the Lord as being either here or there."

"Make a simile."

"What do you think about this, sire? When some flame in a great burning mass of fire goes out, is it possible to point to the flame as being either here or there?"

"No, revered sir. That flame has ceased to be, it has disappeared.[2]"

"Even so, sire, the Lord has attained Nirvana in the Nirvana-element that has no groups of existence still remaining. The Lord has gone home.[3] It is not possible to point to him as being here or there. But it is possible, sire, to point to the Lord by means of the Dhamma-body[4]; for Dhamma, sire, was taught by the Lord."

"Very good, revered Nagasena."

Milindapañha, 70–73

[1] Cf. no. 103.

[2] Or, cannot be designated; it has, literally, gone to non-designability, *appaññattim gata*.

[3] Or, who has 'set', *attham gato*, like the sun, whose Kinsman he was.

[4] See D. iii. 84 (above, p. 113).

120.

At all times (at the dissolution of a world cycle by water, fire or wind) one Buddha-field perishes. A Buddha-field is threefold: the field of his birth, the field of his authority, the field of his range. Of these, the field of his birth is bounded by the ten thousand world system, which quaked at the time of the Tathagata's reinstatement, and so forth.[1] The field of his authority is bounded by a myriad hundred thousand world systems where these protective spells have power: the Jewel Sutta,[2] the Khandha spell,[3] the Dhajjagga spell,[4] the Atanatiya spell,[5] the Peacock spell.[6] The field of his range is infinite, immeasurable. It has been said of this: "As far as he wishes", since whatever the Tathagata wishes, that he knows. Thus among these three Buddha-fields, the one—the field of authority—perishes. But when it perishes, the field of birth perishes too. Perishing, they perish together; persisting, they persist together.

Visuddhimagga, 414

[1] "And so forth" refers to the times when the Tathāgata descended into his mother's womb, issued from it, was self-awakened, turned the Dharma-wheel, and loosened the sankhāras at his final nirvana—MA. iv. 114; AA. ii. 9; VbhA. 430.

[2] Ratana-sutta, Sn. p. 39 ff.; Khp. VI; cf. Miln. 150.

[3] Vin. ii. 109 f.; A. ii. 72; Miln. 150.

[4] S. i. 218–20; Miln. 150–51.

[5] D. iii. 195 ff.; cf. Miln. 151.

[6] Ja. ii. 33 (and see p. 38, above).

Second Part

THE MAHAYANA

by
Edward Conze

BASIC NOTIONS

CRITICISM OF THE HINAYANA POSITION

121. *Bodhisattvas and Disciples*

The Lord: What do you think, Sariputra, does it occur to any of the Disciples and Pratyekabuddhas to think that "after we have known full enlightenment, we should lead all beings to Nirvana, into the realm of Nirvana which leaves nothing behind"? [1]

Sariputra: No indeed, O Lord.

The Lord: One should therefore know that this wisdom of the Disciples and Pratyekabuddhas bears no comparison with the wisdom of a Bodhisattva. What do you think, Sariputra, does it occur to any of the Disciples and Pratyekabuddhas that "after I have practised the six perfections, have brought beings to maturity, have purified the Buddha-field, have fully gained the ten powers of a Tathagata, his four grounds of self-confidence, the four analytical knowledges and the eighteen special dharmas of a Buddha, after I have known full enlightenment, I shall lead countless beings to Nirvana"?

Sariputra: No, O Lord.

The Lord: But such are the intentions of a Bodhisattva. A glowworm, or some other luminous animal, does not think that its light could illuminate the Continent of Jambudvipa, or radiate over it. Just so the Disciples and Pratyekabuddhas do not think that they should, after winning full enlightenment, lead all beings to Nirvana. But the sun, when it has risen, radiates its light over the whole of Jambudvipa. Just so a Bodhisattva, after he has accomplished the practices which lead to the full enlightenment of Buddhahood, leads countless beings to Nirvana.

Pañcaviṃśatisāhasrikā 40–41

---

[1] This is also translated as "Nirvana without any residue".

122. *The Conversion of Śāriputra*

Then the Venerable Sariputra, contented, elated, rejoicing, overjoyed, filled with zest and gladness, stretched his joined hands towards the Lord, and, looking upon the Lord he said to the Lord: "I am astonished and amazed, O Lord! I exult at hearing such a call from the Lord. For before I had heard this Dharma from the Lord, I used to see other Bodhisattvas, and heard that in a future period they would bear the name of Buddhas. I then was exceedingly grieved and ashamed to think that I had strayed away from this range of the cognition of the Tathagata, and from the vision of this cognition. And again and again, as I went to mountain caves, wood thickets, parks, rivers and the roots of trees to meditate in the open air, I was constantly preoccupied with the ever-recurring thought: 'The entrance into the Realm of Dharma is surely the same for all. But we have been dismissed by the Lord with an inferior vehicle.¹' At the same time, however, it occurred to me that this was our fault, and not the Lord's. For, if we had heeded the Lord at the time when he preached the lofty demonstration of dharma concerning this supreme enlightenment, then we would have gone forth in these dharmas. But, at the time when no Bodhisattvas were present (at the preaching), we did not understand what the Lord had said with a hidden meaning, and in our hurry we heard only the beginning of what the Tathagata demonstrated as dharma, learned only that, bore in mind and developed only that, reflected on only that, attended only to that. My days and nights, O Lord, I used increasingly to spend in self-reproach. But today, O Lord, I have attained Nirvana. Today I have entered Nirvana. Today I have won Arhatship. Now I am the Lord's eldest son, the son of his breast, born from his mouth, born from the Dharma, formed by the Dharma, a heir of the Dharma, accomplished in the Dharma. Now I am free from all mental anguish, O Lord, since I have heard this call from the Lord, this wonderful Dharma, which I had not heard before."

Thereupon the Venerable Sariputra on that occasion addressed the Lord with the following stanzas:

¹ Or 'career', hīna-yāna.

1. Struck with wonder, O great Leader,
   And amazed I heard your voice.
   All my perplexity has passed away,
   Fully ripe I am for this superior vehicle.

2. Truly wonderful is the voice of the Sugatas;
   Doubt and sorrow it removes from all that lives.
   My outflows became extinguished, all my sorrow quite left
     me,
   When I heard that voice.

3. Daily when walking in woody thickets and parks,
   Or going to the roots of trees,
   Or to mountain caves,
   I have again and again reflected to myself:

4. "Alas, by evil thoughts have I been quite deceived:
   Whereas the dharmas without outflows are all equal,
   Shall I not be one who demonstrates in a future period
   The supreme Dharma to the triple world?

5. I am excluded from the thirty-two marks,
   Excluded am I from the golden colour of the skin;
   All the (ten) powers and emancipations I have forgone;
   Alas, how deluded I have been about the dharmas being
     equal!

6. And also the minor marks of the great Sages,
   Fully eighty, excellent, and distinguished,
   And the eighteen special dharmas also,
   Excluded I am from them; O, how I have been deceived!

7. And when I had seen you, so benign and merciful towards
     the world,
   When, lonely, I took my daily walk,
   Then I reflected: "Alas, I have been cheated out of
   The inconceivable non-attached cognition."

8. Days and nights I spent, O Saviour,
   Reflecting always on this same thing.
   At last I will ask the Lord
   Whether I am excluded or whether I am not.

9. When I was thus reflecting, O Chief of Jinas,
   When thus I passed my days and nights,
   And when I had seen many other Bodhisattvas
   Praised by the Leader of the world,

10. And when I had heard this Buddha-dharma,
    I thought: "With a hidden sense this is surely preached.
    It is a cognition which is inscrutable, subtle, without out-
       flows,
    That the Jina has displayed on the terrace of enlighten-
       ment.

11. For in the past I have clung to false views,
    When I was a Wanderer, and of the same mind as the
       heretics.
    Thereafter the Saviour, when he saw my earnest intentions,
    Has taught me Nirvana, to free me from false views.

12. When from all those false views I had become free,
    And when I had experienced dharmas as empty,
    Then I thought: 'I am at Rest.'
    Yet this is not what is called Nirvana.

13. But when one becomes a Buddha, a supreme being,
    Honoured by men, Gods, Yakshas and Rakshasas,
    One who wears a body with the thirty-two marks,
    Then one has completely gone to Rest."

14. All my former cares have now been removed,
    Since I have heard your call. Now I have gone to Rest
    Since you predicted my supreme enlightenment
    In front of the world with its Gods.

15. At first I felt mightily afraid
    When I heard the Leader's words.
    I feared that it might be Mara, intent on harming me,
    Who had conjured up the guise of the Buddha.

16. But when the thousands of millions of arguments,
    Of reasons and examples had been shown
    And well established that supreme enlightenment of a
       Buddha,
    Then did I lose my doubts and knew I heard the Dharma.

17. And when you had proclaimed to me the thousands of
    millions of Buddhas,
    The Jinas of the past who have won the final Rest,
    And how they also have demonstrated this Dharma,
    Having firmly established it by (their) skill in means;

18. And the Buddhas of the future, and those who
    Just now stand in the world as seers of ultimate truth,
    How by hundreds of skilful devices they will expound
    Or do expound this Dharma;

19. And when further you celebrated your own course,
    Beginning with your leaving home,
    And how you became a Buddha who turns the wheel of
    Dharma,
    And how you demonstrated Dharma for a long time:

20. Then I knew for certain that "this was not Mara;
    It was the Saviour of the world who showed (me) the true
    course.
    For here the Maras are out of their element."
    So it was that for a while my heart knew doubts.

21. But then by the melodious, deep and sweet
    Voice of the Buddha I was gladdened:
    Shattered were all my hesitations,
    My doubts vanished, and I was established in gnosis.

22. Indubitably I shall be a Tathagata,
    Honoured by the world with its Gods.
    In a hidden way I shall teach this Buddha-enlightenment,
    Thereby arousing many Bodhisattvas.

Thereupon the Lord said to the Venerable Sariputra: "I
tell you, Sariputra, I announce to you, in front of the world
with its Devas, with its Maras, with its Brahmas, in front of
these people, including the ascetics and Brahmins, that you,
Sariputra, have been matured by me for the supreme enlightenment in the presence of twenty hundred thousands of
Nayutas of Kotis of Buddhas, and that you have been trained

by me for a long time. This my utterance has furnished you
with the Bodhisattva counsel and the Bodhisattva secret.
You, Sariputra, do not, through a Bodhisattva's sustaining
power, remember your former vow to practise (as a Bodhisattva), nor the Bodhisattva counsel or the Bodhisattva secret.
You think that you have won Nirvana. But in order to remind
you, Sariputra, of the vow you made in the past, I reveal to
the Disciples this discourse of doctrine, the 'Lotus of the
Good Dharma', a Sutra of great length, an instruction for the
Bodhisattvas, the property of all Buddhas.

"Moreover, Sariputra, in a future period, after innumerable,
inconceivable and immeasurable aeons, after you have borne
in mind the good Dharma of many hundreds of thousands of
Nayutas of Kotis of Tathagatas, and after you have done
manifold worship to them, and have quite fulfilled just this
course of a Bodhisattva,—you shall be a Tathagata in the
world, with the name of Padmaprabha, an Arhat, fully enlightened, endowed with knowledge and conduct, a Sugata,
knower of the world, unsurpassed, a tamer of men to be tamed,
a teacher of Gods and men, a Buddha, a Lord!"

Saddharmapuṇḍarīka III, 59–65

123. *The Provisional and the Final Nirvana*

59. Beings, because of their great ignorance, born blind,
  wander about;
  Because of their ignorance of the wheel of cause and effect,
  of the track of ill.

60. In the world, deluded by ignorance, the supreme all-
  knowing one,
  The Tathagata, the great physician, appears, full of compassion.

61. As a teacher, skilled in means, he demonstrates the good
  Dharma:
  To those most advanced he shows the supreme Buddha-
  enlightenment.

62. To those of medium wisdom the Leader reveals a medium
enlightenment.
Another enlightenment again he recommends to those who
are afraid of birth-and-death.

63. To the Disciple, who has escaped from the triple world, and
who is given to discrimination
It occurs: "Thus have I attained Nirvana, the blest and
immaculate."

64. But I now reveal to him that this is not what is called
Nirvana,
But that it is through the understanding of all dharmas
that deathless Nirvana can be attained.

65. To him the great Seers, committed to compassion, will say:
"Deluded you are, and you should not think that you have
won gnosis.

66. "When you are inside your room, enclosed by walls,
You do not know what takes place outside, so tiny is your
mental power.

67. "When you are inside your room, you do not know
What people outside are doing or not doing, so tiny is your
mental power.

68. "You cannot hear a sound five miles away,
How much less one that is still farther distant.

69. "Whether others are well or badly disposed towards you,
That you cannot know; how can you be so conceited?

70. "When you have to walk for only a Kos, you cannot do so
without a beaten track;
And what happened to you in your mother's womb, all that
you have quite forgotten.

71. "But one who has those five kinds of superknowledge,[1] he
is here called omniscient.
It would be mere delusion, however, to call yourself omniscient, when you know nothing.

[1] They correspond to vv. 66–70, and overcome the limitations
described there.

72. "If you wish to win omniscience, then you should aspire to
superknowledge,
And then reflect, in the forest, on the emission of the super-
knowledges,
The pure dharma, by which you will gain the super-
knowledges."

73. When he has grasped the meaning (of this advice), and
gone to the remote forest, he will reflect, well concentrated,
Before long he attains the five superknowledges, endowed
with virtues.

74. Just so with all the Disciples who have formed the notion
that they have attained Nirvana.
To them the Jina teaches This is a temporary repose, not
the final Nirvana.

75. As a device of the Buddhas it was introduced. But outside
this principle of all-knowledge,
They teach, there is no (final) Nirvana. Exert yourselves on
behalf of that!

76. The absolute cognition of the three periods of time, and the
six lovely perfections,
Emptiness, the Signless, the shedding of plans for the
future,

77. The thought of enlightenment, and all the other dharmas
which lead to Nirvana,
(Be they with or without outflows, tranquil and like empty
space,)

78. What has been taught as the four stations of Brahma,[1] and
as the (four) means of conversion,
All that the great Seers have proclaimed for the purpose of
disciplining beings.

79. And someone who discerns dharmas as in their own-being
like an illusion or a dream,
Without a core, like a plantain tree, or similar to an echo,

---

[1] I.e. Unlimited friendliness, compassion, sympathetic joy and even-
mindedness.

80. And who knows that the triple world, without exception, has such an own-being,
And is neither bound nor freed, he does not discern Nirvana (as separate from the triple world).

81. He knows that all dharmas are the same, empty, essentially without multiplicity.
He does not look towards them, and he does not discern any separate dharma.

82. Then, greatly wise, he sees the Dharma-body, completely.
There is no triad of vehicles, but here there is only one vehicle.

83. All dharmas are the same, all the same, always quite the same.
When one has cognized this, one understands Nirvana, the deathless and blest.

Saddharmapuṇḍarīka V, 59–83

THE BODHISATTVA

124. *The Bodhisattva's Friendliness and Compassion*

The Lord: Subhuti, that son or daughter of good family who, as a Bodhisattva, even for one single day remains attentive to the perfection of wisdom, begets a great heap of merit. For, as he goes on dwelling day and night in those mental activities, he becomes more and more worthy of the gifts bestowed on him by all beings. Because no other being has a mind so full of friendliness as he has, except for the Buddhas, the Lords. And the Tathagatas, of course, are matchless, unequalled, endowed with inconceivable dharmas.

How then does that son or daughter of good family at first aspire to that merit? He becomes endowed with that kind of wise insight which allows him to see all beings as on the way to their slaughter. Great compassion thereby takes hold of him. With his heavenly eye he surveys countless beings, and what he sees fills him with great agitation: so many carry the burden of a karma which will soon be punished in the hells, others have acquired unfortunate rebirths, which keep them away from the Buddha and his teachings, others are doomed soon to be killed, or they are enveloped in the net of false views, or fail to find the path, while others who had gained a rebirth favourable to their emancipation have lost it again.

And he radiates great friendliness and compassion over all those beings, and gives his attention to them, thinking: "I shall become a saviour to all those beings, I shall release them from all their sufferings!" But he does not make either this, or anything else, into a sign with which he becomes intimate. This also is the great light of a Bodhisattva's wisdom, which allows him to know full enlightenment. For, when they dwell in this dwelling, Bodhisattvas become worthy of the gifts of the whole world, and yet they do not turn back on full enlightenment. When their thoughts are well supported by perfect wisdom and when they are near to all-knowledge, then they purify the gifts of those who give them the requisites of life. Therefore a Bodhisattva should dwell in this mental work associated with perfect wisdom, if he does not want to consume his alms fruitlessly, if he wants to point out the path to all beings, to shed light over a wide range, to set free from birth-and-death all the beings who are subject to it, and to cleanse the organs of vision of all beings.

Ashṭasāhasrikā XXII, 402–04

125. *The Bodhisattva a compassionate Hero*

The Lord: Suppose, Subhuti, that there were a most excellent hero, very vigorous, of high social position, handsome, attractive and most fair to behold, of many virtues, in possession of all the finest virtues, of those virtues which spring from the very height of sovereignty, morality, learning, renunciation and so on. He is judicious, able to express himself, to formulate his views clearly, to substantiate his claims; one who always knows the suitable time, place and situation for everything. In archery he has gone as far as one can go, he is successful in warding off all manner of attack, most skilled in all arts, and foremost, through his fine achievements, in all crafts . . . He is versed in all the treatises, has many friends, is wealthy, strong of body, with large limbs, with all his faculties complete, generous to all, dear and pleasant to many. Any work he might undertake he manages to complete, he speaks methodically, shares his great riches with the many, honours what should be honoured, reveres what should be revered, worships what should be worshipped. Would such a person, Subhuti, feel ever-increasing joy and zest?

Subhuti: He would, O Lord.

The Lord: Now suppose, further, that this person, so greatly accomplished, should have taken his family with him on a journey, his mother and father, his sons and daughters. By some circumstance they find themselves in a great, wild forest. The foolish ones among them would feel fright, terror and hair-raising fear. He, however, would fearlessly say to his family: "Do not be afraid! I shall soon take you safely and securely out of this terrible and frightening forest. I shall soon set you free!" If then more and more hostile and inimical forces should rise up against him in that forest, would this heroic man decide to abandon his family, and to take himself alone out of that terrible and frightening forest—he who is not one to draw back, who is endowed with all the force of firmness and vigour, who is wise, exceedingly tender and compassionate, courageous and a master of many resources?

Subhuti: No, O Lord. For that person, who does not abandon his family, has at his disposal powerful resources, both within and without. On his side forces will arise in that wild forest which are quite a match for the hostile and inimical forces, and they will stand up for him and protect him. Those enemies and adversaries of his, who look for a weak spot, who seek for a weak spot, will not gain any hold over him. He is competent to deal with the situation, and is able, unhurt and uninjured, soon to take out of that forest, both his family and himself, and securely and safely will they reach a village, city or market town.

The Lord: Just so, Subhuti, is it with a Bodhisattva who is full of pity and concerned with the welfare of all beings, who dwells in friendliness, compassion, sympathetic joy and even-mindedness.

Ashtasāhasrikā XX, 371–73

126. *Description of a Bodhisattva*

69. Although the son of the Jina has penetrated to this im-
    mutable true nature of dharmas,
    Yet he appears like one of those who are blinded by
    ignorance, subject as he is to birth, and so on. That is
    truly wonderful.

70. It is through his compassionate skill in means for others
    that he is tied to the world,
    And that, though he has attained the state of a saint, yet
    he appears to be in the state of an ordinary person.

71. He has gone beyond all that is worldly, yet he has not
    moved out of the world;
    In the world he pursues his course for the world's weal, un-
    stained by worldly taints.

72. As a lotus flower, though it grows in water, is not polluted
    by the water,
    So he, though born in the world, is not polluted by worldly
    dharmas.

73. Like a fire his mind constantly blazes up into good works
    for others;
    At the same time he always remains merged in the calm of
    the trances and formless attainments.

74. Through the power of his previous penetration (into
    reality), and because he has left all discrimination behind,
    He again exerts no effort when he brings living things to
    maturity.

75. He knows exactly who is to be educated, how, and by what
    means,
    Whether by his teaching, his physical appearance, his
    practices, or his bearing.

76. Without turning towards anything, always unobstructed
    in his wisdom,
    He goes along, in the world of living beings, boundless as
    space, acting for the weal of beings.

77. When a Bodhisattva has reached this position, he is like
the Tathagatas,
Insofar as he is in the world for the sake of saving beings.

78. But as a grain of sand compares with the earth, or a puddle
in a cow's footprint with the ocean,
So great still is the distance of the Bodhisattvas from the
Buddha.

Ratnagotravibhāga I, vv. 69–78

127. *The Bodhisattva's infinite Compassion*

A Bodhisattva resolves: I take upon myself the burden of
all suffering, I am resolved to do so, I will endure it. I do
not turn or run away, do not tremble, am not terrified, nor
afraid, do not turn back or despond.

And why? At all costs I must bear the burdens of all beings,
In that I do not follow my own inclinations. I have made the
vow to save all beings. All beings I must set free. The whole
world of living beings I must rescue, from the terrors of birth,
of old age, of sickness, of death and rebirth, of all kinds of
moral offence, of all states of woe, of the whole cycle of birth-
and-death, of the jungle of false views, of the loss of wholesome dharmas, of the concomitants of ignorance,—from all
these terrors I must rescue all beings. . . . I walk so that the
kingdom of unsurpassed cognition is built up for all beings.
My endeavours do not merely aim at my own deliverance. For
with the help of the boat of the thought of all-knowledge, I
must rescue all these beings from the stream of Samsara,
which is so difficult to cross, I must pull them back from the
great precipice, I must free them from all calamities, I must
ferry them across the stream of Samsara. I myself must grapple
with the whole mass of suffering of all beings. To the limit of
my endurance I will experience in all the states of woe, found
in any world system, all the abodes of suffering. And I must
not cheat all beings out of my store of merit. I am resolved to
abide in each single state of woe for numberless aeons; and
so I will help all beings to freedom, in all the states of woe that
may be found in any world system whatsoever.

And why? Because it is surely better that I alone should be
in pain than that all these beings should fall into the states of
woe. There I must give myself away as a pawn through which
the whole world is redeemed from the terrors of the hells, of
animal birth, of the world of Yama, and with this my own
body I must experience, for the sake of all beings, the whole
mass of all painful feelings. And on behalf of all beings I give
surety for all beings, and in doing so I speak truthfully, am
trustworthy, and do not go back on my word. I must not
abandon all beings.

And why? There has arisen in me the will to win all-
knowledge, with all beings for its object, that is to say, for the
purpose of setting free the entire world of beings. And I have
not set out for the supreme enlightenment from a desire for
delights, not because I hope to experience the delights of the
five sense-qualities, or because I wish to indulge in the pleasures of the senses. And I do not pursue the course of a Bodhisattva in order to achieve the array of delights that can be
found in the various worlds of sense-desire.

And why? Truly no delights are all these delights of the
world. All this indulging in the pleasures of the senses belongs
to the sphere of Mara.

                                   Śikshāsamuccaya, 280–81 (*Vajradhvaja Sūtra*)

128. *The Dedication of Merit*

Subhuti: A Bodhisattva, a great being, considers the world
with its ten directions, in every direction, extending everywhere. He considers the world systems, quite immeasurable,
quite beyond reckoning, quite measureless, quite inconceivable, infinite and boundless.

He considers in the past period, in each single direction, in
each single world system, the Tathagatas, quite immeasurable,
quite beyond reckoning, quite measureless, quite inconceivable, infinite and boundless, who have won final Nirvana
in the realm of Nirvana which leaves nothing behind,—their
tracks cut off, their course cut off, their obstacles annulled,
guides through (the world of) becoming, their tears dried up,
with all their impediments crushed, their own burdens laid
down, with their own weal reached, in whom the fetters of

becoming are extinguished, whose thoughts are well freed by right understanding, and who have attained to the highest perfection in the control of their entire hearts.

He considers them, from where they began with the production of the thought of enlightenment, proceeding to the time when they won full enlightenment, until they finally entered Nirvana in the realm of Nirvana which leaves nothing behind, and the whole span of time up to the vanishing of the good Dharma (as preached by each one of these Tathagatas).

He considers the mass of morality, the mass of concentration, the mass of wisdom, the mass of emancipation, the mass of the vision and cognition of emancipation of those Buddhas and Lords.

In addition he considers the store of merit associated with the six perfections, with the achievement of the qualities of a Buddha, and with the perfections of self-confidence and of the powers; and also those associated with the perfection of the superknowledges, of comprehension, of the vows; and the store of merit associated with the accomplishment of the cognition of the all-knowing, with the solicitude for beings, the great friendliness and the great compassion, and the immeasurable and incalculable Buddha-qualities.

And also the full enlightenment and its happiness, and the perfection of the sovereignty over all dharmas, and the accomplishment of the measureless and unconquered supreme wonder-working power which has conquered all, and the power of the Tathagata's cognition of what is truly real, which is without covering, attachment or obstruction, unequalled, equal to the unequalled, incomparable, without measure, and the power of the Buddha-cognition pre-eminent among the powers, and the vision and cognition of a Buddha, the perfection of the ten powers, the obtainment of that supreme ease which results from the four grounds of self-confidence and the obtainment of Dharma through the realization of the ultimate reality of all dharmas.

He also considers the turning of the wheel of Dharma, the carrying of the torch of Dharma, the beating of the drum of Dharma, the filling up of the conch-shell of Dharma, the sounding of the conch-shell of Dharma, the wielding of the sword of Dharma, the pouring down of the rain of Dharma, the offering of the sacrifice of Dharma, the refreshment of all beings through the gift of Dharma, through its presentation to them. He further considers the store of merit of all those who are educated and trained by those demonstrations of Dharma,—whether they concern the dharmas of Buddhas, or those of Pratyekabuddhas, or of Disciples,—who believe in them, who are fixed on them, who are bound to end up in full enlightenment.

He also considers the store of merit, associated with the six perfections, of all those Bodhisattvas of whom those Buddhas and Lords have predicted full enlightenment. He considers the store of merit of all those persons who belong to the Pratyeka-buddha-vehicle, and of whom the enlightenment of a Pratyeka-buddha has been predicted. He considers the meritorious work founded on giving, morality and meditational development of those who belong to the Disciple-vehicle, and the roots of good with blemish,[1] of those who are still in training, as well as the unblemished[2] roots of good of the adepts.

He considers the roots of good which the common people have planted as a result of the teaching of those Tathagatas. He considers the meritorious work, founded on giving, morality and meditational development, of the four assemblies of those Buddhas and Lords, i.e. of the monks and nuns, the laymen and laywomen. He considers the roots of good planted during all that time by Gods, Nagas, Yakshas, Gandharvas, Asuras, Garudas, Kinnaras and Mahoragas, by men and ghosts, and also by animals, at the time when those Buddhas and Lords demonstrated the Dharma, and when they entered Parinirvana, and when they had entered Parinirvana—thanks to the Buddha, the Lord, thanks to the Dharma, thanks to the Samgha, and thanks to persons of right mind-culture. (In his meditation the Bodhisattva) piles up the roots of good of all those, all that quantity of merit without exception or remainder, rolls it into one lump, weighs it, and rejoices over it with the most excellent and sublime jubilation, the highest and utmost jubilation, with none above it, unequalled, equalling the unequalled. Having thus rejoiced, he would utter the remark: "I turn over into full enlightenment the meritorious

---

[1] Literally: with outflows. [2] Literally: without outflows.

work founded on jubilation. May it feed the full enlightenment, (of myself and of all beings)!"

Ashtasāhasrikā VI, 135–38

THE SIX PERFECTIONS

129. *The Six Perfections Defined*

Subhuti: What is a Bodhisattva's perfection of giving?

The Lord: Here a Bodhisattva, his thoughts associated with the knowledge of all modes, gives gifts, i.e. inward or outward things, and, having made them common to all beings, he dedicates them to supreme enlightenment; and also others he instigates thereto. But there is nowhere an apprehension of anything.

Subhuti: What is a Bodhisattva's perfection of morality?

The Lord: He himself lives under the obligation of the ten ways of wholesome acting, and also others he instigates thereto.

Subhuti: What is a Bodhisattva's perfection of patience?

The Lord: He himself becomes one who has achieved patience, and others also he instigates to patience.

Subhuti: What is a Bodhisattva's perfection of vigour?

The Lord: He dwells persistently in the five perfections, and also others he instigates to do likewise.

Subhuti: What is the Bodhisattva's perfection of concentration (or meditation)?

The Lord: He himself, through skill in means, enters into the trances, yet he is not reborn in the corresponding heavens of form as he could; and others also he instigates to do likewise.

Subhuti: What is a Bodhisattva's perfection of wisdom?

The Lord: He does not settle down in any dharma, he contemplates the essential original nature of all dharmas; and others also he instigates to the contemplation of all dharmas.

Pañcaviṃśatisāhasrikā, 194–95

130. *The Six Perfections and the Body*

This rejection and surrender of the body, this indifference to the body, that for him is the Perfection of Giving.

In that, even when his body is dismembered, he radiates good will towards all beings, and does not contract himself from the pain, that for him is the Perfection of Conduct.

In that, even when his body is dismembered, he remains patient for the sake of the deliverance even of those that dismember it, does them no injury even with his thoughts, and manifests the power of patience. That for him is the Perfection of Patience.

That vigour by which he refuses to give up the urge towards omniscience, and holds fast on to it, depending on the power of thought, that vigour by which he remains within the coming and going of birth-and-death (without entering Nirvana as he could), and continues to bring to maturity the roots of goodness, that for him is the Perfection of Vigour.

That, even when his body is dispersed, he does not become confused in his cultivation of the thought of omniscience which he has gained, has regard only for enlightenment, and takes care only of the peaceful calm of cessation, that for him is the Perfection of Concentration.

That, even when his body is dismembered, he looks upon the phantom and image of his body as upon so much straw, a log, or a wall; arrives at the conviction that his body has the nature of an illusion, and contemplates his body as in reality being impermanent, fraught with suffering, not his own, and at peace, that for him is the Perfection of Wisdom.

Śikshāsamuccaya, 187 (Sāgaramati Sūtra)

131. *The Perfection of Giving*

Sariputra: What is the worldly, and what is the supramundane perfection of giving?

Subhuti: The worldly perfection of giving consists in this: The Bodhisattva gives liberally to all those who ask, all the while thinking in terms of real things.[1] It occurs to him: "I

---

[1] Literally: leaning on something.

give, that one receives, this is the gift. I renounce all my possessions without stint. I act as one who knows the Buddha. I practise the perfection of giving. I, having made this gift into the common property of all beings, dedicate it to supreme enlightenment, and that without apprehending anything. By means of this gift, and its fruit may all beings in this very life be at their ease, and may they one day enter Nirvana!" Tied by three ties he gives a gift. Which three? A perception of self, a perception of others, a perception of the gift.

The supramundane perfection of giving, on the other hand, consists in the threefold purity. What is the threefold purity? Here a Bodhisattva gives a gift, and he does not apprehend a self, nor a recipient, nor a gift; also no reward of his giving. He surrenders that gift to all beings, but he apprehends neither beings nor self. He dedicates that gift to supreme enlightenment, but he does not apprehend any enlightenment. This is called the supramundane perfection of giving.

Pañcaviṃśatisāhasrikā, 263–64

132. *The Perfection of Patience*

The Lord: A Tathagata's perfection of patience is really no perfection. Because, Subhuti, when the king of Kalinga cut my flesh from every limb, at that time I had no notion of a self, or of a being, or of a soul, or of a person, nor had I any notion or non-notion. And why? If, Subhuti, at that time I had had a notion of self, I would also have had a notion of ill-will at that time. If I had had a notion of a being, of a soul, of a person, then I also would have had a notion of ill-will at that time. And why? By my superknowledge I know the past, five hundred births, and how I have been the Rishi, 'Preacher of Patience'. Then also I have had no notion of a self, or of a being, or a soul, or a person. Therefore then, Subhuti, a Bodhisattva, a great being should, after he has got rid of all notions, raise his thought to the supreme enlightenment. Unsupported by form a thought should be produced, unsupported by sounds, smells, tastes, touchables or mind-objects a thought should be produced, unsupported by dharma a thought should be produced, unsupported by no-dharma a thought should be produced, unsupported by anything a thought should be produced. And why? What is supported has no support.

Vajracchedikā, 14 e

133. *The Perfection of Meditation*

The Lord: When he practises the perfection of meditation for the sake of other beings his mind becomes undistracted. For he reflects that "even worldly meditation is hard to accomplish with distracted thoughts, how much more so is full enlightenment. Therefore I must remain undistracted until I have won full enlightenment." ... Moreover, Subhuti, a Bodhisattva, beginning with the first thought of enlightenment, practises the perfection of meditation. His mental activities are associated with the knowledge of all modes when he enters into meditation. When he has seen forms with his eye, he does not seize upon them as signs of realities which concern him, nor is he interested in the accessory details. He sets himself to restrain that which, if he does not restrain his organ of sight, might give occasion for covetousness, sadness or other evil and unwholesome dharmas to reach his heart. He watches over the organ of sight. And the same with the other five sense-organs,—ear, nose, tongue, body, mind.

Whether he walks or stands, sits or lies down, talks or remains silent, his concentration does not leave him. He does not fidget with his hands or feet, or twitch his face; he is not incoherent in his speech, confused in his senses, exalted or uplifted, fickle or idle, agitated in body or mind. Calm is his body, calm is his voice, calm is his mind. His demeanour shows contentment, both in private and public. ... He is frugal, easy to feed, easy to serve, of good life and habits; though in a crowd he dwells apart; even and unchanged, in gain and loss; not elated, not cast down. Thus in happiness and suffering, in praise and blame, in fame and disrepute, in life or death, he is the same unchanged, neither elated nor cast down. And so with foe or friend, with what is pleasant or unpleasant, with holy or unholy men, with noises or music, with forms that are dear or undear, he remains the same unchanged, neither elated nor cast down, neither gratified nor thwarted. And why? Because he sees all dharmas as empty of marks of their own, without true reality, incomplete and uncreated.

Śikshāsamuccaya, 202–03 (Prajñāpāramitā)

THE BUDDHA

134. *The Tathagata as a Rain-cloud*

1. The King of Dharma I am, who arose in the world to crush becoming;
   Dharma I teach to beings, after I have discerned their dispositions.

5. It is like a great cloud which rises above the earth,
   Which covers up everything and overshadows the firmament,

6. And this great cloud, filled with water, wreathed with lightning,
   Resounds with thunder, and refreshes all the creatures.

16. Just so, O Kasyapa, the Buddha also
    Arises in this world just like a rain-cloud.
    And when he has arisen, then the World's Saviour speaks,
    And shows the true course to all living beings.

17. And the great Seer announces,
    Honoured by the whole world with its Gods:
    "The Tathagata am I, the best of men, a Jina,
    Arisen in the world just like a rain-cloud.

18. I shall refresh all living beings,
    Whose bodies are withering away, who cling to the triple world,
    Who wither away in pain,—at ease I will place them,
    And pleasures I will give them and the final Rest.

21. With one and the same voice I preach to all the Dharma,
    I always make enlightenment its foundation.
    For this is the same for all, about it there is no partiality.
    I know no hatred and no love.

24. I refresh this entire world
    Like a cloud which releases its rain evenly for all;
    Equal is enlightenment for noble and mean alike,
    For those who are immoral and for moral ones,

25. For those who lead a depraved life,
    As well as for those whose conduct is good,
    For those who hold false views and unsound views,
    And for those who hold right views and pure views.

26. I preach the Dharma to beings whether their intellect
    Be inferior or superior, and their faculties weak or strong.
    Setting aside all tiredness,
    I rain down the rain of the Dharma.

36. When I rain down the rain of the Dharma,
    Then all this world is well refreshed.
    Each one according to their power take to heart
    This well-preached Dharma, one in taste."

37. As when it rains the shrubs and grasses,
    The bushes and the smaller plants,
    The trees and also the great woods
    Are all made splendid in the ten regions;

38. So the nature of Dharma always exists for the weal of the
       world,
    And it refreshes by this Dharma the entire world.
    And then, refreshed, just like the plants,
    The world will burst forth into blossoms.

Saddharmapuṇḍarīka V, vv. 1, 5, 16–18, 21, 24–26, 36–38

135. *The real Buddha*

The Lord said: As a result of my sustaining power this
world, with its Gods, men and Asuras, forms the notion
that recently the Lord Sakyamuni, after going forth from his
home among the Sakyas, has awoken to full enlightenment, on
the terrace of enlightenment, by the town of Gaya.

But one should not see it thus, sons of good family. In fact
it is many hundreds of thousands of myriads of Kotis of aeons

ago that I have awoken to full enlightenment. . . . Ever since,
during all that time I have demonstrated Dharma to beings in
this Saha world system, and also in hundreds of thousands of
Nayutas of Kotis of other world systems. But when I have
spoken of other Tathagatas, beginning with the Tathagata
Dipankara, and of the Nirvana of these Tathagatas, then that
has just been conjured up by me as an emission of the skill in
means by which I demonstrate Dharma.

Moreover, the Tathagata surveys the diversity in the
faculties and vigour of successive generations of beings. To
each generation he announces his name, declares that he has
entered Nirvana, and brings peace to beings by various discourses on Dharma. To beings who are of low[1] disposition,
whose store of merit is small, and whose depravities are many,
he says in that case: "I am young in years, monks, I have left
the home of my family, and but lately have I won full enlightenment." But when the Tathagata, although fully
enlightened for so long, declares that he has been fully enlightened but recently, then such discourses on Dharma have
been spoken for no other reason than to bring beings to
maturity and to save them. All these discourses on Dharma
have been taught by the Tathagata in order to discipline
beings.

And whatever the Tathagata says to educate beings, and
whatever the Tathagata utters,—whether he appears as himself or as another, whether under his own authority or another,
—all these discourses on dharma are taught as factually true
by the Tathagata, and there is no false speech in them on the
part of the Tathagata. For the Tathagata has seen the triple
world as it really is: It is not born, it dies not; there is no
decease or rebirth, no Samsara or Nirvana; it is not real, or
unreal, not existent, or non-existent, not such, or otherwise,
not false or not-false. Not in such a way has the Tathagata
seen the triple world as the foolish common people see it. The
Tathagata is face to face with the reality of dharmas; he can
therefore be under no delusion about them. Whatever words
the Tathagata may utter with regard to them, they are true,
not false, not otherwise.

He utters, however, different discourses on Dharma, which

[1] Read hīna- for nānā-.

differ in their objective basis, to beings who differ in their mode of life and their intentions, and who wander amidst discriminations and perceptions, in order to generate the roots of good in them. For a Tathagata performs a Tathagata's work. Fully enlightened for ever so long, the Tathagata has an endless span of life, he lasts for ever. Although the Tathagata has not entered Nirvana, he makes a show of entering Nirvana, for the sake of those who have to be educated. And even today my ancient course as a Bodhisattva is still incomplete, and my life span is not yet ended. From today onwards still twice as many hundreds of thousands of Nayutas of Kotis of aeons must elapse before my life-span is complete. Although therefore I do not at present enter into Nirvana (or extinction), nevertheless I announce my Nirvana. For by this method I bring beings to maturity. Because it might be that, if I stayed here too long and could be seen too often, beings who have performed no meritorious actions, who are without merit, a poorly lot, eager for sensuous pleasures, blind, and wrapped in the net of false views, would, in the knowledge that the Tathagata stays (here all the time), get the notion that life is a mere sport, and would not conceive the notion that the (sight of the) Tathagata is hard to obtain. In the conviction that the Tathagata is always at hand they would not exert their vigour for the purpose of escaping from the triple world, and they would not conceive of the Tathagata as hard to obtain.

Hence the Tathagata, in his skill in means, has uttered to those beings the saying that "Rarely, O monks, do Tathagatas appear in the world." Because, during many hundreds of thousands of Nayutas of Kotis of aeons those beings may have the sight of a Tathagata, or they may not. And therefore, basing my statement on this fact, I say that "Rarely, O monks, do Tathagatas appear in the world." To the extent that they understand the rarity of a Tathagata's appearance, to that extent they will wonder (at his appearance), and sorrow (at his disappearance), and when they do not see the Tathagata, they will long for the sight of him. The wholesome roots, which result from their turning their attention towards the Tathagata as towards an objective basis, will for a long time tend to their weal, benefit and happiness. Considering this, the Tathagata, although he does not actually enter Nirvana, announces his entering into Nirvana, for the sake of those to be educated. And that is a discourse on Dharma by the Tathagata himself. When he utters it, there is in it no false speech on the part of the Tathagata.

Saddharmapuṇḍarīka XV, 268–72

136. Coming and Going of Tathagatas

Dharmodgata: A man, scorched by the heat of the summer, during the last month of summer, at noon, might see a mirage floating along, and might run towards it, and think: "There I shall find water, there I shall find something to drink." What do you think, son of good family, has that water come from anywhere, or does that water go anywhere, to the Eastern great ocean, or the Southern, or the Western or the Northern?

Sadaprarudita: No water exists in that mirage. How could its coming or going be conceived? That man again is foolish and stupid if, on seeing the mirage, he forms the idea of water where there is no water. Water in its own-being certainly does not exist in that mirage.

Dharmodgata: Equally foolish are all those who adhere to the Tathagata through form and sound, and who in consequence imagine the coming or going of a Tathagata. For a Tathagata cannot be seen from his form-body. The Dharma-bodies are the Tathagatas.

Ashṭasāhasrikā XXXI, 512–13

The Dharma-Body

137.

Sakra: It is because the Lord has trained himself in just this perfection of wisdom that the Tathagata has acquired and known full enlightenment or all-knowledge.

The Lord: Therefore the Tathagata does not derive his name from the fact that he has acquired this physical personality, but from the fact that he has acquired all-knowledge.

And this all-knowledge of the Tathagata has come forth from the perfection of wisdom. The physical personality of the Tathagata, on the other hand, is the result of the skill in means of the perfection of wisdom. And that becomes a sure foundation for the acquisition of the cognition of the all-knowing by others. Supported by this foundation the revelation of the cognition of the all-knowing takes place, the revelation of the Buddha-body, of the Dharma-body, of the Samgha-body.

Ashṭasāhasrikā III, 58

138.

The Lord: Those who by my form did see me,
And those who followed me by my voice,
Wrong are the efforts they engaged in,
Me those people will not see.
From the Dharma one should see the Buddha,
For the Dharma-bodies are the guides.
Yet Dharmahood is not something one should
  become aware of,
Nor can one be made aware of it.

Vajracchedikā 26a, b

139. *Tathagata and Suchness*

The Lord: How, Manjusri, should the Tathagata be seen and honoured?

Manjusri: Through the mode of Suchness (tathata) do I see the Tathagata, through the mode of non-discrimination, in the manner of non-observation. I see him through the mode of non-production and non-existence. But Suchness does not attain full knowledge,—thus I see the Tathagata. Suchness does not become, does not cease to become,—thus do I see the Tathagata. Suchness does not stand at any point or spot,—thus do I see the Tathagata. Suchness is not past, future or present,—thus do I see the Tathagata. Suchness is neither brought about by duality nor by non-duality,—thus do I see the Tathagata. Suchness is neither defiled nor purified,—thus do I see the Tathagata. Suchness is neither produced nor stopped,—thus do I see the Tathagata. In this way the Tathagata is seen and honoured.

Saptaśatikā, 195

140. *The 18 special dharmas of a Buddha*

What are the eighteen special dharmas of a Buddha? From the night when the Tathagata knew full enlightenment, to the day when he becomes extinct in Nirvana, during all this time, the Tathagata 1. Does not stumble, 2. He is not rash or noisy in his speech, 3. He is never deprived of his mindfulness, 4. He has no perception of difference, 5. His thought is never unconcentrated, 6. His evenmindedness is not due to lack of consideration, 7. His zeal never fails, 8. His vigour never fails, 9. His mindfulness never fails, 10. His concentration never fails, 11. His wisdom never fails, 12. His deliverance never fails, 13. All the deeds of his body are preceded by cognition, and continue to conform to cognition, 14. All the deeds of his voice are preceded by cognition, and continue to conform to cognition, 15. All the deeds of his mind are preceded by cognition, and continue to conform to cognition, 16. His cognition and vision regarding the past period of time proceeds unobstructed and freely, 17. His cognition and vision regarding the future period of time proceeds unobstructed and freely, 18. His cognition and vision regarding the present period of time proceeds unobstructed and freely.

Śatasāhasrikā IX, 1449-50

THE NEW WISDOM SCHOOL

THE PERFECTION OF WISDOM

141. *The Praise of perfect Wisdom*

Sariputra: The perfection of wisdom, O Lord, is the accomplishment of the cognition of the all-knowing. The perfection of wisdom is the state of all-knowledge.

The Lord: So it is, Sariputra, as you say.

Sariputra: The perfection of wisdom gives light, O Lord. I pay homage to the perfection of wisdom! She is worthy of homage. She is unstained, and the entire world cannot stain her. She is a source of light, and from everyone in the triple world she removes darkness, and leads them away from the blinding darkness caused by defilements and wrong views. In her we can find shelter. Most excellent are her works. She makes us seek the safety of the wings of enlightenment. She brings light to the blind, so that all fear and distress may be forsaken. She has gained the five eyes, and she shows the path to all beings. She herself is an organ of vision. She disperses the gloom and darkness of delusion. She guides to the Path those who have strayed on to a bad road. She is identical with all-knowledge. She never produces any dharma, because she has forsaken the residues relating to both kinds of coverings, those produced by defilement and those produced by the cognizable. She does not stop any dharma. Herself unstopped and unproduced is the perfection of wisdom. She is the Mother of the Bodhisattvas, on account of the emptiness of own-marks. As the donor of the jewel of all the Buddha-dharmas she brings about the ten powers of a Tathagata. She cannot be crushed. She protects the unprotected, with the help of the four grounds of self-confidence. She is the antidote to birth-and-death. She has a clear knowledge of the own-being of all dharmas, for she does not stray away from it. The perfection of wisdom of the Buddhas, the Lords, sets in motion the wheel of Dharma.

Ashṭasāhasrikā VII, 170–71

RAHULABHADRA

Hymn to Perfect Wisdom

142.

1. Homage to Thee, Perfect Wisdom,
   Boundless, and transcending thought!
   All Thy limbs are without blemish,
   Faultless those who Thee discern.

2. Spotless, unobstructed, silent,
   Like the vast expanse of space;
   Who in truth does really see Thee
   The Tathagata perceives.

3. As the moonlight does not differ
   From the moon, so also Thou
   Who aboundst in holy virtues,
   And the Teacher of the world.

4. Those, all pity, who came to Thee,
   Buddha-dharmas heralding,
   They will win with ease, O Gracious!
   Majesty beyond compare.

5. Pure in heart, when once they duly
   Look upon Thee, surely then
   Their complete success is certain,—
   O Thou, fruitful to behold!

6. To all heroes who of others
   Have the welfare close at heart
   Thou a mother, who does nourish,
   Who gives birth, and who gives love.

7. Teachers of the world, the Buddhas
   Are Thine own compassionate sons;
   Then art Thou, O Blessed Lady,
   Grandam thus of beings all.

8. All th'immaculate perfections
   At all times encircle Thee,
   As the stars surround the crescent,
   O Thou blameless holy one!

9. Those in need of light considering,
   The Tathagatas extol
   Thee, the Single One, as many,
   Multiformed and many-named.

10. As the drops of dew in contact
    With the sun's rays disappear,
    So all theorizings vanish,
    Once we have obtainèd Thee.

11. When as fearful Thou appearest
    Thou engender'st fear in fools;
    When benignly Thou appearest
    Comes assurance to the wise.

12. How will one who no affection
    Has for Thee, though yet Thy Lord,
    Have, O Mother, greed and loathing
    For the many other things?

13. Not from anywhere Thou comest,
    And to nowhere doest Thou go;
    In no dwelling place have sages
    Ever apprehended Thee.

14. Not to see Thee in this manner
    Is to have attained to Thee,
    Gaining thus the final freedom,—
    O how wonderful is this!

15. One indeed is bound who sees Thee;
    One who sees not bound is too.
    One again is freed who sees Thee;
    One who sees not freed is too.

16. Wonderful, profound, illustrious,
    Hard Thou art to recognize.
    Like a mock show Thou art seen, and
    Yet Thou art not seen at all.

17. By all Buddhas, Single Buddhas,
    By Disciples courted, too,
    Thou the one path to salvation,
    There's no other, verily.

18. Saviours of the world, from pity,
    So that men might understand,
    Speak of Thee, observing custom,
    Yet of Thee they do not speak.

19. Who is able here to praise Thee,
    Lacking signs and featureless?
    Thou the range of speech transcending,
    Not supported anywhere.

20. In such words of current language
    Constantly we laud Thee, whom
    None of our acclaim concerneth;
    So we reach beatitude.

21. By my praise of Perfect Wisdom
    All the merit I may rear,
    Let that make the world devoted
    To this wisdom without peer.

    Rāhulabhadra. Prajñāpāramitāstotra.

THE ELUSIVENESS OF PERFECT WISDOM

143.

Subhuti: Is it at all possible, O Lord, to hear the perfection of wisdom, to distinguish and consider her, to make statements and to reflect about her? Can one explain, or learn, that because of certain attributes, tokens or signs this is the perfection of wisdom, or that here this is the perfection of wisdom, or that there that is the perfection of wisdom?

The Lord: No indeed, Subhuti. This perfection of wisdom cannot be expounded, or learnt, or distinguished, or considered, or stated, or reflected upon by means of the skandhas, or by means of the elements, or by means of the sense-fields. This is a consequence of the fact that all Dharmas are isolated, absolutely isolated. Nor can the perfection of wisdom be understood otherwise than by the skandhas, elements or sense-fields. For just the very skandhas, elements and sense-fields are empty, isolated and calmly quiet. It is thus that the perfection of wisdom and the skandhas, elements and sense-fields are not two, nor divided. As a result of their emptiness, isolatedness and quietude they cannot be apprehended. The lack of a basis of apprehension in all Dharmas, that is called 'perfect wisdom'. Where there is no perception, appellation, conception or conventional expression, there one speaks of 'perfect wisdom'.

Ashṭasāhasrikā VII, 177

144.

Subhuti: When one speaks of a 'Bodhisattva', what dharma does the word 'Bodhisattva' denote? I do not, O Lord, see that dharma 'Bodhisattva', nor a dharma called 'perfect wisdom'. Since I neither find, apprehend, nor see a dharma 'Bodhisattva', nor a 'perfect wisdom', what Bodhisattva shall I instruct and admonish in what perfect wisdom? And yet, O Lord, if, when this is pointed out, a Bodhisattva's heart does not become cowed, nor stolid, does not despair nor despond, if he does not turn away, or become dejected, does not tremble, is not frightened or terrified, it is just this Bodhisattva, this great being, who should be instructed in perfect wisdom. It is precisely this that should be recognized as the perfect wisdom of that Bodhisattva, as his instruction in perfect wisdom. When he thus stands firm, that is his instruction and admonition.

Ashṭasāhasrikā I, 5

145.

Manjusri: What are the qualities and what the advantages of a perfection of wisdom which is without qualities? How can one speak of the qualities or advantages of a perfect wisdom which is incapable of doing anything, neither raises up nor destroys anything, neither accepts nor rejects any dharma, is powerless to act and not at all busy, if its own-being cannot be cognized, if its own-being cannot be seen, if it does not bestow any dharma, and does not obstruct any dharma, if it brings about the non-separateness of all dharmas, does not exalt the single oneness of all dharmas, does not effect the separateness of all dharmas, if it is not made, not something to be done, not passed, if it does not destroy anything, if it is not a donor of the dharmas of the common people, of the dharmas of the Arhats, of the dharmas of the Pratyeka-buddhas, of the dharmas of the Bodhisattvas, and not even of the dharmas of a Buddha, and does not take them away, if it does not toil in birth-and-death, nor cease toiling in Nirvana, neither bestows nor destroys the dharmas of a Buddha, if it is unthinkable and inconceivable, not something to be done, not something to be undone, if it neither produces nor stops any dharmas, neither annihilates them nor makes them eternal, if it neither causes to come nor to go, brings about neither detachment nor non-detachment, neither duality nor non-duality, and if, finally, it is non-existent?

The Lord: Well have you, Manjusri, described the qualities of perfect wisdom. But nevertheless a Bodhisattva should train in just this perfection of wisdom, in the manner of no-training, if he wants to train in, and to accomplish, that concentration of a Bodhisattva which allows him to see all the Buddhas, the Lords, if he wants to see their Buddha-fields, and to know their names, and if he wants to perfect the supreme worship of those Buddhas and Lords, and firmly to believe in and to fathom their demonstration of dharma.

Manjusri: For what reason is this the perfection of wisdom?

The Lord: It is called 'perfect wisdom' because it is neither produced nor stopped. And it is so because it is calmly quiet from the very beginning, because there is escape, because there is nothing to be accomplished, and, finally, because of its non-existence. For what is non-existence, that is perfect wisdom. It is for this reason that one should expect Bodhisattvas to develop perfect wisdom. It is the range of the Bodhisattvas, the great beings, ranging in all dharmas.

Saptaśatikā 32b–34a

THE DOCTRINE OF PERFECT WISDOM

146. *The Heart Sutra*

Homage to the Perfection of Wisdom, the lovely, the holy! Avalokita, the holy Lord and Bodhisattva, was moving in the deep course of the wisdom which has gone beyond. He looked down from on high; he beheld but five heaps; and he saw that in their own being they were empty. Here, O Sariputra, form is emptiness and the very emptiness is form; emptiness does not differ from form, nor does form differ from emptiness; whatever is form, that is emptiness, whatever is emptiness, that is form. The same is true of feelings, perceptions, impulses and consciousness. Here, O Sariputra, all dharmas are marked with emptiness, they are neither produced nor stopped, neither defiled nor immaculate, neither deficient nor complete. Therefore, O Sariputra, where there is emptiness there is neither form, nor feeling, nor perception, nor impulse, nor consciousness; no eye, or ear, or nose, or tongue, or body, or mind; no form, nor sound, nor smell, nor taste, nor touchable, nor object of mind; no sight-organ element, and so forth, until we come to: no mind-consciousness element; there is no ignorance, nor extinction of ignorance, and so forth, until we come to, there is no decay and death, no extinction of decay and death; there is no suffering, nor origination, nor stopping, nor path; there is no cognition, no attainment and no non-attainment.

Therefore, O Sariputra, owing to a Bodhisattva's indifference to any kind of personal attainment, and through his having relied on the perfection of wisdom, he dwells without thought-coverings. In the absence of thought-coverings he has not been made to tremble, he has overcome what can upset, in the end sustained by Nirvana. All those who appear as Buddhas in the three periods of time,—fully awake to the utmost, right and perfect enlightenment because they have relied on the perfection of wisdom. Therefore one should know the Prajnaparamita as the great spell, the spell of great knowledge, the utmost spell, the unequalled spell, allayer of all suffering, in truth,—for what could go wrong? By the

Prajnaparamita has this spell been delivered. It runs like this:
Gone, gone, gone beyond, gone altogether beyond, O what an
awakening, all hail!

Prajñāpāramitāhṛdaya.

147.

Subhuti: How is perfect wisdom marked?
 The Lord: It is marked with the non-attachment of space.
It is, however, no mark, nor does it have one.

Subhuti: Would it be possible for all dharmas to be found
by the same mark by which the perfection of wisdom is to be
found?

The Lord: So it is, Subhuti, so it is. The mark by which
perfect wisdom exists, through just that mark all dharmas also
exist. Because all dharmas are isolated in their own-being,
empty in their own-being. In that way all dharmas exist
through the mark by which perfect wisdom exists, i.e. through
the mark of emptiness, through the mark of isolation.

Subhuti: If all dharmas are isolated from all dharmas, if all
dharmas are empty of all dharmas, how can one then conceive
of the defilement and purification of beings? Because what is
isolated, that is neither defiled nor purified. Emptiness also is
neither defiled nor purified. Neither the isolated, nor emptiness,
can fully know the supreme enlightenment. The isolated does
not apprehend any dharma in emptiness. The isolated does
not apprehend in emptiness any being that can know full enlightenment. How shall we understand the meaning of this
teaching, O Lord?

The Lord: What do you think, Subhuti, do beings indulge
for a long time in I-making and mine-making?

Subhuti: They do, O Lord.

The Lord: Are then I-making and mine-making isolated and
empty?

Subhuti: They are, O Lord.

The Lord: Is it because of I-making and mine-making that
beings run and wander about in birth-and-death.

Subhuti: Yes, so it is, O Lord.

The Lord: It is surely in this sense that one conceives
of beings as defiled. Insofar as they indulge in I-making and

mine-making, insofar as they take hold of things, they are defiled. Insofar, however, as they do not take hold of things, insofar they are considered as purified, and do not run about and wander in birth-and-death.

Śatasāhasrikā XLV, f. 119

148.

The Elder Subhuti said to the Buddha, "How does the Bodhisattva Mahasattva, when he is practising the deep perfection of wisdom, come to knowledge of the five skandhas?"

Buddha said to Subhuti, "If a Bodhisattva Mahasattva, when he is practising the deep perfection of wisdom, is able to know in accordance with truth form and the other four skandhas in respect to their marks, their origin-and-extinction, and their Suchness, this is called a Bodhisattva Mahasattva, when he practises the deep perfection of wisdom, being able to come to knowledge of the Five Skandhas.

"Subhuti, what is meant by a Bodhisattva Mahasattva knowing in accordance with truth the marks of form? It means that a Bodhisattva in accordance with truth knows that form is nothing but holes and cracks, and is indeed like a mass of bubbles, with a nature that has no hardness or solidity. This is what is called a Bodhisattva Mahasattva knowing in accordance with truth the marks of form.

"Subhuti, what is meant by a Bodhisattva Mahasattva knowing in accordance with truth the origin and extinction of form? It means that a Bodhisattva Mahasattva knows in accordance with truth that when form originates it comes from nowhere, and when it is extinguished, it goes nowhere, but that though it neither comes nor goes, yet its origin and extinction do jointly exist.[1] This is what is called a Bodhisattva Mahasattva knowing in accordance with truth about the origin and extinction of form.

"Subhuti, what is meant by a Bodhisattva Mahasattva knowing in accordance with truth about the Suchness of form? It means that a Bodhisattva Mahasattva knows in accordance

[1] Are samprayukta.

with truth that the Suchness of form is not subject to origin or extinction, that it neither comes nor goes, is neither foul nor clean, neither increases nor diminishes, is constant to its own nature, is never empty, false or changeful, and is therefore called Suchness. That is what is called a Bodhisattva Mahasattva knowing according to truth the Suchness of form.

"Subhuti, what is meant by a Bodhisattva Mahasattva knowing in accordance with truth about the marks of feeling? It means that a Bodhisattva Mahasattva knows in accordance with truth that feelings are all like a boil or an arrow, swiftly rising and swiftly vanishing, and are indeed like floating foam, empty, false and fleeting, arising only from the coincidence of the three factors.[1] This is what is called a Bodhisattva Mahasattva knowing in accordance with truth about the marks of feeling.

"Subhuti, what is meant by a Bodhisattva Mahasattva knowing in accordance with truth about the origin and extinction of feeling? It means that a Bodhisattva Mahasattva knows in accordance with truth that when feeling originates it comes from nowhere and when it is extinguished it goes nowhere. Yet though it neither comes nor goes, yet its origin and extinction do jointly exist.[2] This is what is called a Bodhisattva Mahasattva knowing in accordance with truth about the origin and extinction of feeling.

"Subhuti, what is meant by a Bodhisattva Mahasattva knowing in accordance with truth about the Suchness of feeling? It means that the Bodhisattva Mahasattva knows in accordance with truth that the Suchness of feeling has no origin or extinction, neither comes nor goes, is neither foul nor clean, neither increases nor diminishes, is constant to its own nature, is never empty, false or changeful, and is therefore called Suchness. That is what is called a Bodhisattva Mahasattva knowing according to truth the Suchness of feeling.

Subhuti, what is meant by a Bodhisattva Mahasattva knowing in accordance with truth about the marks of perception? It means that the Bodhisattva Mahasattva knows in accordance with truth that perception is like a mirage-pool; it cannot be laid hand upon. He knows that when causes leading to thirst and craving mistakenly arise, then thought

[1] Sense-organ, object and consciousness. [2] samprayukta.

impels to unreal utterances. This is what is called a Bodhi-sattva Mahasattva knowing in accordance with truth about the marks of perception.

"Subhuti, what is meant by a Bodhisattva Mahasattva knowing in accordance with truth about the origin and extinction of perception? It means that a Bodhisattva Mahasattva knows in accordance with truth that when perception originates it comes from nowhere and when it is extinguished it goes nowhere. But though it neither comes nor goes, yet its origin and extinction do jointly exist. This is what is called a Bodhisattva Mahasattva knowing in accordance with truth about the origin and extinction of perception.

"Subhuti, what is meant by a Bodhisattva Mahasattva knowing in accordance with truth about the Suchness of perception? It means that a Bodhisattva Mahasattva knows in accordance with truth that the Suchness of perception is not subject to origin or extinction, that it neither comes nor goes, is neither foul nor clean, neither increases nor diminishes, is constant to its own nature, is never empty, false or changeful, and is therefore called Suchness. That is what is called a Bodhisattva Mahasattva knowing in accordance with truth about the Suchness of perception.

"Subhuti, what is meant by a Bodhisattva Mahasattva knowing in accordance with truth about the marks of impulse? It means that a Bodhisattva Mahasattva knows in accordance with truth that impulse is like the banana-tree which, though you strip it leaf-sheath by leaf-sheath, you cannot lay hand on. This is called a Bodhisattva Mahasattva knowing in accordance with truth about the marks of impulse.

"Subhuti, what is meant by a Bodhisattva Mahasattva knowing in accordance with truth about the origin and extinction of impulse? It means that the Bodhisattva Mahasattva knows in accordance with truth that when impulse originates it comes from nowhere and when it is extinguished it goes nowhere. Yet though it neither comes nor goes, its origin and extinction do jointly exist. This is what is called the Bodhisattva Mahasattva knowing in accordance with truth about the origin and extinction of impulse.

"Subhuti, what is meant by the Bodhisattva Mahasattva knowing in accordance with truth about the Suchness of impulse? It means that the Bodhisattva Mahasattva knows in accordance with truth that the Suchness of impulse is not subject to origin or extinction, that it neither comes nor goes, is neither foul nor clean, neither increases nor diminishes, is constant to its own nature, is never empty, false nor changeful, and is therefore called Suchness. That is what is called a Bodhisattva Mahasattva knowing in accordance with truth about the Suchness of impulse.

"Subhuti, what is meant by the Bodhisattva Mahasattva knowing in accordance with truth about the marks of consciousness? It means that a Bodhisattva Mahasattva knows in accordance with truth that consciousness is like things of magic. Conditions are brought together which create the supposition that something exists. But actually there is nothing that can be laid hand upon. It is as when a master of magic or his disciple at a crossroads magically creates the four kinds of army—that is to say, an elephant-army, a cavalry-army, a chariot-army and an army of foot-soldiers, or again magically creates other kinds of form, complete with their various characteristics. Such things seem to exist, but have no reality. Consciousness is also like this, and cannot really be laid hand upon. This is called the Bodhisattva Mahasattva knowing according to truth about the marks of consciousness.

"Subhuti, what is meant by a Bodhisattva Mahasattva knowing in accordance with truth about the origin and extinction of consciousness? It means that the Bodhisattva Mahasattva knows in accordance with truth that when consciousness is born it comes from nowhere, and that when it is extinguished it goes nowhere. But though it neither comes nor goes, yet its origin and extinction do jointly exist. This is what is called the Bodhisattva Mahasattva knowing in accordance with truth about the origin and extinction of consciousness.

"Subhuti, what is meant by a Bodhisattva Mahasattva knowing in accordance with truth about the Suchness of consciousness? It means that the Bodhisattva Mahasattva knows in accordance with truth that the Suchness of consciousness is not subject to origin or extinction, that it neither comes nor goes, is neither foul nor clean, neither increases nor diminishes, is constant to its own nature, is never empty, false or changeful, and is therefore called Suchness. That is what is called a Bodhisattva Mahasattva knowing in accordance with truth about the Suchness of consciousness."[1]

> *Mahāprajñāpāramitā, trsl. Hsüan-tsang, fasc. 532, ch. 29 (1).*

EMPTINESS

PRELIMINARY MEDITATIONS

149. *The Conditioned*

The following stanzas were spoken by the Gods to remind the Buddha that the time had come to leave his home:

95. Impermanent and unstable are all conditioned things,
    Essentially brittle, like an unbaked pot.
    Like some borrowed article, like a town built on sand,
    They last for a short while only.

96 These complexes are doomed to destruction,
    Like plaster washed away by the rainy season,
    Like sand on a river's bank.
    They are subject to conditions, and their own-being is
    hard to get at.

97. Like the flame of a lamp are the complexes.
    Suddenly it arises, soon it is doomed to stop.
    Without any staying power they are, like air, or a mass of
    foam,
    Unsubstantial and weak in themselves.

98. Complexes have no inner might, are void in themselves;
    Rather like the stem of the plantain tree, when one re-
    flects on them,
    Like a mock show which deludes the mind,
    Like an empty fist with which a child is teased.

99. Everything that is a complex event
    Proceeds by way of causes and conditions,
    And the events mutually cause and condition each other.
    This fact is not understood by foolish people.

[1] Translated from the Chinese by Arthur Waley.

100. Out of pieces of Munja-grass a rope is twisted
  By the force of effort;
  Well-buckets are raised by several revolutions of the
    wheel;
  Yet each revolution, by itself, can do nothing.

101. Just so, the turning of all the components of becoming
  Results from their mutual interaction;
  In each of them singly it cannot be apprehended,
  Either at the beginning or at the end.

102. Where there is a seed, there is the sprout;
  But the seed is by its nature not the sprout,
  Nor is it other than that, nor just that.
  Just so the true nature of Dharma is neither annihilated
    nor eternal.

103. Ignorance is the condition of all conditioned things;
  But in real truth these conditioned things are not.
  For conditioned things and ignorance are just empty,
  By their own inner nature without any ability to act.

104. One can see the impression made by a seal,
  But the transmission of the seal one cannot apprehend.
  It is not therein, nor anywhere else.
  Just so are conditioned things not annihilated or eternal.

105. Dependent on eye and sight-object
  An act of eye-consciousness springs up here.
  But the sight-object is not based on the eye,
  Nor has any sight-object been transferred to the eye.

106. Without self and impure are these dharmas;
  Yet one imagines that they are with self and pure.
  The act of eye-consciousness springs up from that
  Which is pervertedly seen, which is discriminated
    although it does not exist.

107. The wise discern of an act of consciousness
  The origin and the stopping, the production and the
    passing away.
  The Yogin sees that it has come from nowhere, gone to
    nowhere,
  That it is empty, and like unto a mock show.

108. Conditioned by the concourse of three factors,—
     The tinderstick, the fuel, the exertion of the hand,—
     Does fire arise; it does its work,
     And then it quickly stops again.

109. Then a wise man searches all around
     Whence it has come and whither it goes.
     Through every region, in every direction he searches.
     He cannot find it as it was before it came or went.

110. Skandhas, sense-fields, elements, craving and ignorance,
     These are the conditions which bring about our deeds.
     Where they are complete one thinks of a being.
     In ultimate truth such a being can never be found.

111. When words are uttered the conditions are
     The throat, the lips, the palate and the rolling of the
       tongue.
     But the words have not come from the throat or the
       palate,
     And in each single of these conditions they cannot be
       found.

112. Speech comes about when all these conditions are com-
       plete,
     With mind and intellect as the driving force.
     Invisible and immaterial are mind and speech;
     Without or within they cannot be found.

113. The wise man discerns the rise and fall,
     Of speech, or song, or noise, or any sound.
     They are but momentary and empty,
     All speech is similar to an echo.

114. From a lute, or other stringed musical instruments,
     Sound comes forth when three conditions are present—
     The strings, the wooden body, and the hand's exertion.
     It is their concourse which brings forth the sound.

115. Then the wise man searches all around
     Whence it has come and whither it goes.
     Through every region, in every direction he searches,
     He cannot find the sound as it was before it came.

116. Thus immersed in causes and conditions
Proceeds all that belongs to this conditioned world.
The Yogin again with his vision of the truly real
Sees the complexes as empty and without inner might.

117. The skandhas, the sense-fields, the elements
They are empty inward, empty outward.
The beings are separated from their self and homeless,
The dharmas marked with the own-being of space.

Lalitavistara XIII, 95–117

150. The Marks of the Conditioned

As stars, a fault of vision, as a lamp,
A mock show, dew drops, or a bubble,
A dream, a lightning flash, or cloud,
So we should view what is conditioned.

Commentary: The marks of the elements of samsaric existence should be considered from nine points of view: 1. As
regards their visibility,—all mental constituents disappear
when right gnosis is realized, just as *stars* disappear when the
sun shines. 2. As regards the sign,—because things are wrongly
perceived, just as the hairs in front of the eyes of a man who
has an *eye disease*. 3. As regards consciousness,—which is like
a *lamp*, because passions are born insofar as things are seen.
4. As regards their support,—the elements composing this
world are essentially unreal like things appearing in *a mock
show*. 5. As regards the body,—which lasts for a short time,
like *drops of dew*. 6. As regards fruition, which is like a *bubble*.
7. As regards the past, because like *dreams* the things of the
past remain only as a memory. 8. As regards the present, because this disappears quickly like *lightning*. 9. As regards the
future, which is like *clouds*, because the store consciousness
contains all the seeds of the elements which are going to
develop.

*Vajracchedikā 32a, Asanga Saptati, v. 76,
and Vasubandhu's Commentary*

151. *Contemplation of Thought* [1]

He searches all around for his thought. But what thought? It is either passionate, or hateful, or confused. What about the past, future or present? What is past that is extinct, what is future that has not yet arrived, and the present has no stability. For thought, Kasyapa, cannot be apprehended, inside, or outside, or in between both. For thought is immaterial, invisible, non-resisting, inconceivable, unsupported and homeless. Thought has never been seen by any of the Buddhas, nor do they see it, nor will they see it. And what the Buddhas never see, how can that be an observable process, except in the sense that dharmas proceed by way of mistaken perception? Thought is like a magical illusion; by an imagination of what is actually unreal it takes hold of a manifold variety of rebirths. A thought is like the stream of a river, without any staying power; as soon as it is produced it breaks up and disappears. A thought is like the flame of a lamp, and it proceeds through causes and conditions. A thought is like lightning, it breaks up in a moment and does not stay on. Thought is like space, and it is defiled by adventitious defilements. Thought is like a bad friend, for it generates all kinds of ill. Thought is like a fish-hook, which looks pleasant although it is not. Thought is like a bluebottle-fly, because it looks for what is lovely in what is not. Thought is like an enemy, because it inflicts much agony. Thought is like a strength-sucking goblin, because it always searches for weak points. Thought is like a thief, because it steals all the roots of good. Thought takes delight in forms like a fly's eye, in sounds like a battle-drum, in smells like a pig in the dirt, in tastes like a servant maid who enjoys the leavings of food, and in touchables like a fly in a dish of oil. Thought, though one searches for it all round, cannot be found. What cannot be found, that cannot be apprehended. What cannot be apprehended, that is not past, future or present. What is not past, future or present, that is beyond the three dimensions of time. What is beyond the three dimensions of time, that neither is nor is not.

[1] This meditation is a development of the mindfulness as to mind, described in no. 32.

Searching for thought all round, he does not see it within or without. He does not see it in the skandhas, or in the elements, or in the sense-fields. Unable to see thought, he seeks to find the trend of thought, and asks himself: Whence is the genesis of thought? And it occurs to him that "where there is an object, there thought arises". Is then the thought one thing, and the object another? No, what is the object, just that is the thought. If the object were one thing, and the thought another, then there would be a double state of thought. So the object itself is just thought. Can then thought review thought? No, thought cannot review thought. As the blade of a sword cannot cut itself, as a finger-tip cannot touch itself, so a thought cannot see itself. Moreover, vexed and pressed hard on all sides, thought proceeds, without any staying power, like a monkey or like the wind. It ranges far, bodiless, easily changing, agitated by the objects of sense, with the six sense-fields for its sphere, connected with one thing after another. The stability of thought, its one-pointedness, its immobility, its undis-traughtness, its one-pointed calm, its non-distraction, that is, on the other hand, called mindfulness as to thought.

Śikshāsamuccaya, 233–34 (Ratnakūṭa and Ratnacūḍa)

DEFINITION AND SYNONYMS OF EMPTINESS

152.

One who is convinced of the emptiness of everything is not captivated by worldly dharmas, because he does not lean on them. When he gains something he does not rejoice, when he does not gain it he is not depressed. Fame does not make him proud, lack of fame does not depress him. Scorn does not cow him, praise does not win him over. Pleasure does not attract, pain does not repel him. One who in such a way is not captivated by the worldly dharmas is said to be one who knows emptiness. So one who is convinced of the emptiness of everything has no likes or dislikes. For he knows that that which he might like is just empty, and he sees it as just empty.

But one does not know emptiness if he likes or dislikes any dharma. Neither does one know it if he quarrels or disputes with anyone. For one would know that that also is just empty, and would see it as just empty.

Śikshāsamuccaya, 264 (*Dharmasangīti Sūtra*)

153.

Manjusri: What is the root of the imagination which constructs something that is not actually there?

Vimalakirti: A perverted perception.

Manjusri: And what is the root of the perverted perception?

Vimalakirti: The fact that it has no support.

Manjusri: And what is the root of that?

Vimalakirti: This fact, that it has no support, it has no root at all. In this way all dharmas are supported on roots that have no support.

Śikshāsamuccaya, 264 (*Vimalakīrtinirdeśa*)

154.

Thus much should be cognized, i.e. the conventional view of the world and the ultimately real. And the Lord has well seen, well known, well realized this from the point of view of emptiness. That is why he is called the 'Omniscient One'. There the Lord has seen the conventional point of view as the observed range of the world. But the ultimately real, that is inexpressible, it cannot be understood, discerned, shown or revealed; it is inactive; it is not gain or no gain, not ease or suffering, not fame or lack of fame, not form or no form, etc. . . . All dharmas are enlightenment. One should understand them as devoid of own-being. Even the five deadly sins are enlightenment. For enlightenment has no essential nature of its own, neither have the five deadly sins. In that sense can one say that the deadly sins are enlightenment. People are therefore ridiculous if they desire to win Nirvana. For if someone has fallen into birth-and-death, then he seeks for Nirvana. . . .

The Leader has preached the delightful meditation on friendliness with beings for its object;

But as He further examined those beings, he clearly knew
the entire world to be without beings.

In this the Best of men is without any obscurity, and his
mind is free from doubts.

Let us therefore worship you, the Sugata, worthy of worship, whose intellect is fully developed.

Although, O Sugata, nowhere in the ten directions do you
see any suffering,

Yet you preach compassion for all beings, O you God above
the Gods!

It is thus that we must, O mighty Jina, understand the
Jina's doctrine as it truly is.

Let us therefore worship you, the chief and best of men,
worthy of our worship.

You, O Sakyamuni, see no beings and no suffering, yet you
take their suffering away.

They are pleased, joyous and content because their distress
has been removed from them.

Thus we should understand the Buddha's method, the unthinkable method, as it really is . . .

You told us to develop calm and insight, as the way to the
appeasing of suffering.

Appeased, O Lord, are these impurities, with their residues,
by which the world is defiled.

But that calm, that insight and those taints, O Sage, they
all are empty . . .

Understand activity and inactivity as I explained them.

Consider that a waggon is a conglomeration (without a will
of its own), and yet the waggon does its work.

I have spoken of karma, but no doer exists anywhere in the
ten regions.

A fire blazes up when the wind blows along a smouldering
tree.

The winds and the tree do not think that they produce the
fire,

Yet there is the fire. So with the doers of karma.

And, as you say, there is no heaping up of merit, and no

accumulation of good practices. Be instructed in that also and hear the truth of the matter. One says that the measure of man's life-span is a hundred years of living, and yet the years are not heaped up together in a lump. Just like that is the accumulation (of merit).

Śikshāsamuccaya, 256, 257, 259–61, 262
(Pitṛputrasamāgama)

155. *Not-self, Emptiness and Reality*

One may object that the heretics believe in a self which is distinct from the skandhas, and speak of its separate character. But how the heretics speak about the separate character of the self, that the Madhyamakavatara (VI 142) explains as follows:

"The self is imagined by the heretics[1] as essentially permanent,
> Not a doer, but an enjoyer, without qualities, without activity.
> And according to which of these characteristics of the self is stressed,
> According to that do the systems of the heretics differ."

One replies: It is true that the heretics speak of a self which is distinct from the skandhas. But they describe its mark without having apprehended the true status of the self. They have not understood that it is a merely metaphorical designation, and from fear they do not progress to the insight that the self is nothing but a mere word. In consequence they fail to see that they deal with what is conventionally true, and, through a wrong thought-construction, deceived by what is a mere semblance of reasoning, in their delusion they falsely imagine a self, and speak of its character.[2] And it is said[3]:

"As by means of a mirror one sees a reflected image of one's own face,

---

[1] I.e. the Samkhya school.
[2] A reference to ch. VIII is here omitted.
[3] Ratnāvalī I, 31–34: JRAS. 1934, 314–15.

Though in actual reality this reflected image is nothing at
  all,
Just so one apprehends the idea of I through the skandhas,
Though in actual reality, like the image of one's own face,
  it is nothing at all.
As without the mirror one cannot see the reflected image
Of one's own face, so also the I without the medium of the
  skandhas.
Because he had heard this kind of truth, the holy Ananda
Won for himself the dharma-eye; and constantly he repeated it to the monks."
v. 4. "When the ideas of I and mine are extinct, both with
  regard to things within and without,
Then grasping is stopped. Its extinction leads to the
  extinction of birth."

It is said in the Sutra that all defilements have the false
theory of individuality for their root, for their origin, for their
cause. But this false theory of individuality is forsaken when
one does not apprehend a self or what belongs to a self. And by
the forsaking of that one also forsakes the fourfold grasping,
i.e. at sense-desire, false views, reliance on mere rule and
ritual, and the theory of self. The extinction of grasping leads
to that of birth, which consists in becoming again and again.
The sequence of events which leads to the cessation of birth
being thus established, Nagarjuna therefore says:

v. 5. "From the extinction of karma and defilement results
  deliverance."

For when grasping is extinct, becoming, which is conditioned
by it, does not take place. When becoming has stopped, how
can birth, old age, death and so forth be possible? It is thus
established that deliverance results from the extinction of
karma and defilements.

It must now be explained by the extinction of what, karma
and the defilements reach complete extinction:

v. 5. "Karma and the defilements derive from discrimination.
They spread as a result of discursive ideas, they are
  stopped by emptiness."

The defilements, passion, and others, arise in the foolish common person who unwisely discriminates form, and so on. For he (Nagarjuna) will say (xxiii 1):

"One says that passion, hate and delusion originate in thought-construction.
And they are possible because one pervertedly mistakes the unlovely for the lovely."

And in the Sutra[1] it is said:

"O sense-desire, I know your root. From thought-construction do you arise.
I shall no longer construct you in my thought. Then I shall no longer have you. . . ."

All worldly ideas are stopped without exception in emptiness, where there is a vision of the emptiness of the own-being of all existents. How does that come about? Because, if one has the apprehension of an object, then the whole net of discursive ideas comes about. If one would not apprehend that, which is really the daughter of a barren woman, as a handsome young woman, then one would not, with her as an object, enter on a trend of discursive ideas; this would not lead to unwise discriminations; the net of thought-constructions, by an inclination to the ideas of I and mine, would not give rise to a host of defilements which are rooted in the false view of individuality; one would not do deeds, wholesome, unwholesome and immovable[2]; and in consequence one would not experience the jungle of Samsara, which is just a network made up of birth, old age, death, sorrow, lamentation, pain, sadness and despair. But the Yogins who abide in the vision of emptiness do not at all apprehend the skandhas, elements and sense-fields as if they were something in themselves; in consequence they do not enter upon discursive ideas with these as objects, make no discriminations, by inclination to the ideas of I and mine do not give rise to a host of defilements which have the false view of individuality for its root, do not perform any actions, and, in consequence, do not experience the transmigration which consists in birth, old age and death. It is thus, when one

[1] Udānavarga II, 1.   [2] Aninñja.

resorts to emptiness, characterized as blissful and as the appeasing of all discursive ideas, that all the discursive ideas, which are a net of thought-construction, disappear. When discursive ideas have disappeared, discrimination comes to rest, and with it all karma and defilement, and all kinds of rebirth. Hence one calls emptiness Nirvana, as it brings to rest (nirvriti) all discursive ideas. As it is said in the Sataka (XII 23):

> "In brief the Tathagatas proclaim the Dharma as Non-violence,
> And emptiness as Nirvana. In their doctrine there are only these two items."

The teaching of the Lord aims at leading us to true reality. Which then are the marks of that true reality?

Answer: We have already said (xviii 6):

> "When the objective sphere of thought disappears, the object which one could designate has also gone."

If that is so, what else could one ask?

Question: Let that be so. But could you conform to the conventional truth, and adjust yourself to worldly ways, and speak of the marks of true reality by way of super-imposition?

Answer:

> v. 9. "Not dependent on anything else, calm, unimpeded by discursive ideas,
> Indiscriminate, undifferentiated, those are the marks of true reality."

Not dependent on anything else, which means that with regard to it one does not depend on anything else, that one cannot come to it through someone else's instruction, but that one must discover it for oneself. Those who suffer from an eye-disease falsely see things which look like hairs, gnats, flies, etc. Even when instructed by those with healthy eyes, they cannot be brought to see that they can discover the true nature of the hairs, as it actually is, by not seeing them, as those without eye-disease do. They can by instruction only progress far enough to understand that what they see is wrong. It is only when an ointment has taken away the

disease from their eyes, and when they have become like
people with healthy eyes, that they can discover the true
nature of those hairs by not seeing them. Similarly the saints
can explain reality by superimposition; but that is not
sufficient to allow the unconverted to discover its own-being.
But when the eyes of their intelligence are anointed with the
ointment of the unperverted vision of emptiness, which dispels
the eye-disease, and when thereby they become people who
can cognize true reality, then they can discover for themselves
that true reality by not seeing (the multiplicity of things). In
this way that true nature of existents, which is not dependent
on anything else, is the true reality.

And this is *calm* in its own-being, which means that it is
devoid of own-being. It is like the hairs which are not seen by
those with healthy eyes.

In consequence it is *unimpeded by discursive ideas*. 'Discursive ideas' are words which develop meanings. This means
'not expressed by words'.

And that is *indiscriminate*. Discrimination is the function of
thought. Because this is suppressed, the true reality is indiscriminate. As it is said in the Sutra: "What is ultimate
truth? Where even cognition no longer functions, how much
less verbal expressions." In that sense is it indiscriminate.

'Differentiated' is that which has differentiations, which is
multiple. *Undifferentiated* is that which has no differentiations,
is not multiple.

> *Candrakīrti, Prasannapadā XVIII, 344, 2-345,
> 12; 349, 8-351, 14; 372, 7-374, 4*

156. *The Synonyms of Emptiness*

*Three authors have contributed to this extract: the stanzas are
by Maitreyanatha, the commentary (placed into " ") by Vasubandhu, and the sub-commentary by Sthiramati.*

One now speaks of the synonyms (of emptiness):

I, 14. Suchness, reality-limit, the signless, the ultimate reality,
The element of dharma,—these, briefly, are the synonyms of emptiness.

Synonyms are different expressions for one single thing. One speaks of a 'synonym', because it defines the meaning of the word of which it is a synonym. These definitions are explained as just emptiness in the Sutras. The five synonyms (of the verse) are, as particularly important, mentioned in the stanza. But there are others, not mentioned here, which should be considered as following from the fundamental doctrine. They are: non-duality, the realm of non-discrimination, the true nature of dharma, the inexpressible, that which has not been stopped, the Unconditioned, Nirvana, etc. "How the meaning of the synonyms can be cognized", that he now shows. And the expressions are not figurative, but should be taken literally.

I, 15. As not being otherwise, as unperverted, because that (i.e. the sign) is stopped, because it is the sphere of the saints

And because it is the root-cause of the dharmas of the saints,—in this way we have the meaning of the synonyms in due order.

"It is Suchness in the sense that it is not otherwise." In the sense that it is without modification, that is the meaning. And in order to show this more clearly, he (Vasubandhu) says: "It is permanent, because of its Suchness." It is permanent because it is at all time unconditioned. It is not affected (by anything), that is the meaning. "It is Reality-limit in the sense of non-perversion." 'Reality' has the meaning of 'true', 'unperverted'; 'limit' is the extremity beyond which there is nothing else that can be cognized. Therefore the 'extremity of reality' is called 'Reality-limit'. And why is Suchness called 'cognizable'? Because it is the sphere of the cognition which consists in the purification from the covering of the cognizable. 'In the sense of non-perversion' means that there is neither affirmation nor negation. He then gives the reason for that: "Because it cannot become the object of perverted thinking." For perversion is discrimination, therefore it is not an object of perverted thinking. "It is signless, because the sign has been stopped." Here signlessness is understood as the stopping of signs. In order to show this more clearly, he says: "Because of the non-existence of all signs." For emptiness is empty of all signs, of the conditioned and the unconditioned, in that way is it called signless. Because of the non-existence of all signs it is signless. Signless means just without signs. "It is ultimate reality as the sphere of the cognition of the saints." For 'ultimate' means the supramundane cognition. The object of that is the ultimate reality. In order to show this more clearly, he says: "Because it is the sphere of the ultimate (or, supreme) cognition." "It is the Element of Dharma as the root cause of the dharmas of the saints." The word 'dharma' here means the saintly dharmas, i.e. those beginning with right views, etc., and ending with the right cognition of deliverance. It is an 'Element' because it is their root cause. Explaining this further, he says: "Because the dharmas of the Saints are brought forth in dependance on it." Since this word 'Element' is also used to denote 'something which has a (certain) form on account of its own marks', he adds: "For 'Element' has here the sense of 'root cause'." As one speaks of gold, copper or silver as 'elements'. (The other synonyms, which are taught in the Sutras, must be defined in their own meaning by the same method.)

Sthiramati, Madhyāntavibhāgaṭīkā, pp. 49–51

NEGATIONS

157. *No Beings*

The Lord: Here, Subhuti, one who has set out on the career of a Bodhisattva should reflect in such a wise: "As many beings as there are in the universe of beings, comprehended under the term 'beings',—egg-born, or born from a womb, or moisture born, or miraculously born, with or without form, with perception, without perception, with neither perception nor non-perception,—as far as any conceivable universe of beings is conceived; all these I should lead to Nirvana, into the realm of Nirvana which leaves nothing behind. But, although innumerable beings have thus been led to Nirvana, no being at all has been led to Nirvana. And why? If in a Bodhisattva the perception of a 'being' should take place he would not be called a 'Bodhi-being'. He is not to be called a

'Bodhi-being', in whom the perception of a being should take place or the perception of a living soul, or the perception of a person.

Vajracchedikā 3

158. *No dharmas*

The Lord: Bodhisattvas, great beings have no notion of a dharma, Subhuti, nor a notion of non-dharma. They have no notion or non-notion at all. For if these Bodhisattvas should have the notion of a dharma, then they would thereby seize on a self, on a being, on a soul, on a person. A Bodhisattva should therefore certainly not take up a dharma, nor a non-dharma. Therefore this saying has been taught by the Tathagata in a hidden sense: "Those who know the discourse on dharma as a raft should forsake dharmas, and how much more so non-dharmas."

Vajracchedikā 6

159. *No Mindings*

The Lord: It is through absolute emptiness that Bodhisattvas, practising perfect wisdom, cleanse the road to the knowledge of all modes. Established in the perfection of giving they do not grasp at anything; established in the perfection of morality they commit no offence; established in the perfection of patience they remain imperturbable; established in the perfection of vigour they are indefatigable in body and mind; established in the perfection of concentration they know no distraction in their thoughts; established in the perfection of wisdom they have expelled all stupid thoughts. In this way Bodhisattvas cleanse through absolute emptiness the road to the knowledge of all modes, practising perfect wisdom, and having stood in the six perfections. One conceives of giving on account of taking, of morality on account of immorality, of patience on account of impatience, of vigour on account of sloth, of concentration on account of the unconcentrated, of wisdom on account of the stupid. A Bodhisattva does not put his mind to such ideas as having crossed or not having crossed, of giver or non-giver, persons of good or bad conduct, patient or angry people, vigorous or slothful people, concentrated or unconcentrated people, wise or stupid people, or to such ideas as 'I am abused', 'I am praised', 'I am treated with respect', 'I am not treated with respect'. For non-production cannot put its mind to such ideas. Perfect wisdom cuts off all mindings.

Pañcaviṃśatisāhasrikā 89–90

Non-duality

160.

The Lord: A Bodhisattva, Sariputra, who practises perfect wisdom produces an even state of mind towards all beings. As a result he acquires insight into the sameness of all dharmas, and learns to establish all beings in this insight.

Pañcaviṃśatisāhasrikā, 90

161.

Subhuti: How should a Bodhisattva be trained so as to understand that 'all dharmas are empty of marks of their own'?

The Lord: Form should be seen as empty of form, feeling as empty of feeling, and so forth.

Subhuti: If everything is empty of itself, how does the Bodhisattva's coursing in perfect wisdom take place?

The Lord: A non-coursing is that coursing in perfect wisdom.

Subhuti: For what reason is it a non-coursing?

The Lord: Because one cannot apprehend perfect wisdom, nor a Bodhisattva, nor a coursing, nor him who has coursed, nor that by which he has coursed, nor that wherein he has coursed. The coursing in perfect wisdom is therefore a non-coursing, in which all these discoursings are not apprehended.

Subhuti: How then should a beginner course in perfect wisdom?

The Lord: From the first thought of enlightenment onwards a Bodhisattva should train himself in the conviction that all dharmas are baseless. While he practises the six perfections he should not take anything as a basis.

Subhuti: What makes for a basis, what for lack of basis?

The Lord: Where there is duality, there is a basis. Where there is non-duality there is lack of basis.

Subhuti: How do duality and non-duality come about?

The Lord: Where there is eye and forms, ear and sounds, etc., to: where there is mind and dharmas, where there is enlightenment and the enlightened, that is duality. Where there is no eye and forms, nor ear and sounds, etc., to: no mind and dharmas, no enlightenment and enlightened, that is non-duality.

Śatasāhasrikā LIII, f. 279–83

CONTRADICTIONS

162.

Sariputra: For what reason should a Bodhisattva be known as not lacking in perfect wisdom?

Subhuti: Form is lacking in the own being of form. And so for all things.

Sariputra: What then is the own being of form, etc.?

Subhuti: Non-positivity is the own being of form, etc. It is in this sense that form is lacking in the own-being of form. And so with the other skandhas. Moreover, form, etc. is lacking in the mark which is characteristic of form, etc. The mark, again, is lacking in the own being of a mark. The own being, again, is lacking in the mark of (being) own being.

Sariputra: A Bodhisattva who trains himself in this method, will he go forth to the knowledge of all modes?

Subhuti: He will. Because all dharmas are unborn and do not go forth.

Sariputra: For what reason are all dharmas unborn, and do not go forth?

Subhuti: Form is empty of the own being of form. And so are all other dharmas. With regard to them no birth or going forth can be apprehended. It is thus that a Bodhisattva who practises perfect wisdom comes near to the knowledge of all modes.

Pañcaviṃśatisāhasrikā, 136–38

163.

Subhuti: The Bodhisattva, the great being who practises perfect wisdom, should come to know of a thought which is even and exalted but he should not put his mind to it. For that thought is non-thought, since thought, in its essential, original, nature is a state of transparent luminosity.

Sariputra: What is the transparent luminosity of thought?

Subhuti: Thought which is neither conjoined with passion, nor disjoined from it; which is neither conjoined with, nor disjoined from, hate, confusion, obsessions, coverings, unwholesome tendencies, fetters or what makes for views, That is the transparent luminosity of thought.

Sariputra: That thought which is non-thought, is that something which is?

Subhuti: Can one find, or apprehend, in this state of absence of thought either a 'there is' or a 'there is not'?

Sariputra: No, not that.

Subhuti: Was it then a suitable question when the Venerable Sariputra asked whether that thought which is non-thought is something which is?

Sariputra: What then is this non-thoughthood?

Subhuti: It is without modification or discrimination, it is the true nature of Dharma.

Sariputra: Are also form, and the other skandhas without modification and discrimination, as non-thoughthood is?

Subhuti: In the same way also form, and all the rest, are without modification and discrimination.

Śatasāhasrikā III, 495–502

164.

The Lord: 'Beings, beings', O Subhuti, as non-beings have they been taught by the Tathagata. Therefore are they called 'beings'. It is because of that that the Tathagata teaches, "Without self are all dharmas, without a living soul, without manhood, without personality."

Vajracchedikā, 17 f

UNREALITY OF THE WORLD

165.

Thereupon the thought came to some of the Gods in that assembly: What the fairies talk and murmur, that we understand though mumbled. What Subhuti has just told us, that we do not understand!

Subhuti read their thoughts and said: There is nothing to understand, there is nothing to understand. For nothing in particular has been indicated, nothing in particular has been explained.

Thereupon the Gods thought: May the holy Subhuti enlarge on this! May the holy Subhuti enlarge on this! What the holy Subhuti here explores, demonstrates and teaches, that is remoter than the remote, subtler than the subtle, deeper than the deep.

Subhuti read their thoughts, and said: No one can attain any of the fruits of the holy life, or keep it,—from the Stream-winner's fruit to full enlightenment—unless he patiently accepts this elusiveness of the Dharma.

Then those Gods thought: What should one wish those to be like who are worthy to listen to the doctrine from the holy Subhuti?

Subhuti read their thoughts, and said: Those who learn the doctrine from me one should wish to be like an illusory magical creation, for they will neither hear my words, nor experience the facts which they express.

The Gods: Beings that are like a magical illusion, are they not just an illusion?

Subhuti: Like a magical illusion are those beings, like a dream. For magical illusion and beings are not two different things, nor are dreams and beings. All objective facts (dharmas) also are like a magical illusion, like a dream. The various classes of Saints,—from Streamwinner to Buddhahood —also are like a magical illusion, like a dream.

The Gods: A fully enlightened Buddha also, you say, is like a magical illusion, is like a dream? Buddhahood also, you say, is like a magical illusion, is like a dream?

Subhuti: Even Nirvana, I say, is like a magical illusion, is
like a dream. How much more so anything else!

The Gods: Even Nirvana, holy Subhuti, you say is like an
illusion, is like a dream?

Subhuti: Even if perchance there could be anything more
distinguished, of that too I would say that it is like an illusion,
like a dream. For illusion and Nirvana are not two different
things, nor are dreams and Nirvana.

Thereupon the Venerable Sariputra, the Venerable Purna,
son of Maitrayani, the Venerable Mahakoshthila, the Venerable Mahakatyayana, the Venerable Mahakashyapa, and the
other great Disciples, together with many thousands of
Bodhisattvas, said: Who Subhuti, will be those who grasp this
perfection of wisdom as here explained?

Thereupon the Venerable Ananda said to those Elders:
Bodhisattvas who cannot fall back will grasp it, or persons who
have reached sound views, or Arhats in whom the outflows
have dried up.

Subhuti: No one will grasp this perfection of wisdom as here
explained, (i.e. explained in such a way that there is really no
explanation at all). For no Dharma at all has been indicated, lit
up, or communicated. So there will be no one who can grasp it.

Ashṭasāhasrikā II, 38–40

166.

The Lord: What do you think Subhuti? Do the five grasping
skandhas, after they have trained themselves in the perfection of wisdom, go forth to the knowledge of all modes?

Subhuti: No, Lord. For the own-being of the five grasping
skandhas is non-existent. The five skandhas are similar to a
dream. The own-being of a dream cannot be apprehended,
because it does not exist. In this way the five skandhas cannot
be apprehended, because of the non-existence of their own-
being.

The Lord: What do you think, Subhuti, the five skandhas
which are similar to an echo, to an apparition, to a magical
creation, to an image of the moon reflected in water,—do they,
after they have trained themselves in perfect wisdom, go forth
to the knowledge of all modes?

Subhuti: No, Lord. For the own-being of an echo is non-existent, and so is that of an apparition, of a magical creation, of a reflected image. And thus the five skandhas cannot be apprehended, because of the non-existence of their own-being.

Pañcaviṃśatisāhasrikā, 153–54

EMPTINESS AND SALVATION

167.

Subhuti: It is wonderful to see the extent to which the Tathagata has demonstrated the true nature of all these dharmas, and yet one cannot properly talk about the true nature of all these dharmas (in the sense of predicating distinctive attributes to separate real entities). As I understand the meaning of the Tathagata's teaching, even all dharmas cannot be talked about in any proper sense?

The Lord: So it is, for one cannot properly express the emptiness of all dharmas in words.

Subhuti: Can something have growth, or diminution, if it is beyond all distinctive words?

The Lord: No, Subhuti.

Subhuti: But if there is no growth or diminution of an entity which is beyond all distinctive words, then there can be no growth or diminution of the six perfections. And how then could a Bodhisattva win full enlightenment through the force of these six perfections, if they do not grow, and how could he come close to full enlightenment, since, without fulfilling the perfections, he cannot come close to full enlightenment?

The Lord: So it is, Subhuti. There is certainly no growth or diminution of a perfection-entity. A Bodhisattva who practises perfect wisdom, who develops perfect wisdom, and who is skilled in means, does obviously not think that "this perfection of giving grows, or diminishes". But he knows that "this perfection of giving is a mere word". When he gives a gift he dedicates to the supreme enlightenment of all beings the mental activities, the productions of thought, the roots of good which are involved in that act of giving. But he dedicates them in such a way that he respects the actual reality of full enlightenment. And he proceeds in the same way when he takes upon himself the moral obligations, when he perfects himself in patience, when he exerts vigour, enters into the trances, practises perfect wisdom, develops perfect wisdom.

Subhuti: What then is this supreme enlightenment?

The Lord: It is Suchness. But Suchness neither grows nor diminishes. A Bodhisattva, who repeatedly and often dwells in mental activities connected with that Suchness, comes near to the supreme enlightenment, and he does not lose those mental activities again. It is certain that there can be no growth or diminution of an entity which is beyond all words, and that therefore neither the perfections, nor all dharmas, can grow or diminish. It is thus that, when he dwells in mental activities of this kind, a Bodhisattva becomes one who is near to perfect enlightenment.

Ashṭasāhasrikā XVIII, 348–51

168. *Emptiness and Friendliness*

For hatred, friendliness is the antidote, and not to see unpleasant people; or by encouraging the pleasure that comes from association in such matters as common meals. Friendliness means to have hopes for the welfare of others, to long for it, to crave for it, to delight in it. It is affection unsullied by motives of sense-desire, passion or hope of a return.

In the holy Akshayamati Sutra friendliness is explained as threefold: In Bodhisattvas who have first raised their hearts to enlightenment it has beings for its object. In Bodhisattvas who progress on the course it has dharmas for its object. In Bodhisattvas who have acquired the patient acceptance of dharmas which fail to be produced it has no object at all.

Śikshāsamuccaya, 212

THE GERM OF BUDDHAHOOD IN ALL BEINGS

169.

All beings are potentially Tathagatas:

27. Because the Buddha-cognition is contained in the mass of beings,
    Because it is immaculate and non-dual by nature,
    Because those who belong to the Buddha's lineage go towards it as their reward,
    Therefore all animate beings have the germ of Buddhahood in them.

28. The Body of the perfect Buddha irradiates everything,
    Its Suchness is undifferentiated,
    And the road to Buddhahood is open to all.
    At all times have all living beings the Germ of Buddhahood in them.

40. If the Element of the Buddha did not exist (in everyone),
    There could be no disgust with suffering,
    Nor could there be a wish for Nirvana,
    Nor striving for it, nor a resolve to win it.

41. The suffering and the faults of becoming,
    The virtues and the happiness of Nirvana,
    Are taken into account because this lineage exists.
    Those who are without the lineage cannot do so.

45. As to its Suchness identical in common people, Saints and perfect Buddhas,
    Thus has the Jina's Germ been shown to be in beings, by those who have seen the true Reality.

46. But the difference lies in that common people are perverted in their views,
    Whereas those who have seen the Truths have undone this perversion;
    The Tathagatas again are unperverted as to what truly is,
    And without intellectual impediments.

47. It is impure in ordinary beings,
    Partly pure and partly impure in the Bodhisattvas,
    And perfectly pure in the Tathagatas.

49. Just as space, essentially indiscriminate, reaches every-
    where,
    Just so the immaculate Element which in its essential
    nature is Thought, is present in all.

50. It pervades, as a general mark, the vicious, the virtuous
    and the perfect;
    Just as ether is in all visible forms, be they base, inter-
    mediate or superior.

It has been said in a Sutra: "Therefore, Sariputra, the world
of beings is not one thing, and the Dharma-body another. The
world of beings is just the Dharma-body, the Dharma-body
is just the world of beings. Objectively they are not two. The
distinction lies in the words only." And the Element of
Tathagatahood, as it is present in all, is immutable, and
cannot be affected by either defilement or purification.

51. In spite of the adventitious faults, and because of the
    virtues essential to its nature,
    The Nature of Dharma remains immutable, the same in
    former and in subsequent states.

96. Like the Buddha in a faded lotus flower, like honey
    covered by a swarm of bees,
    Like the kernel of a fruit in the husk, like gold within
    impurities,
    Like a treasure hidden in the soil, the fruit in a small seed,
    An image of the Jina in tattered garments,

97. The universal monarch in the vile belly of a woman,
    And like a precious statue covered with dust,
    So is this Element established in beings
    Who are covered with the stains of adventitious defile-
    ments.

108. Suppose that gold belonging to a man on his travels
     Had fallen into a place full of stinking dirt.
     As it is indestructible by nature, it would stay there
     For many hundreds of years.

109. A deity, with a pure heavenly eye, would see it there,
And say to people:
"When I have cleansed this gold, the most precious sub-
stance of all,
I will bring it back to its precious state."

110. Just so, the great Sage, when he has seen the virtue in
beings,
Sunk as they are in defilements which are like filth,
In order to cleanse off the mud of these defilements,
Rains down the rain of Dharma on all that lives.

118. Suppose that an image of the Jina, made of precious
material,
Were covered by a garment, evil-smelling and stinking.
A deity travelling by that way would see it in its neglected
state,
Would explain its significance to others so that they
might release it.

119. So the Buddha's unattached eye,
Having perceived even in animals the personality of a
Sugata,
Though concealed by the taints of manifold defilements,
Shows the means which allow its release.

145. The Dharma-body should be known as twofold:
The completely immaculate element of Dharma,
And its outpourings, the demonstration of the principle
(of Dharma),
In its depth and in its variety.

148. Being immutable in its essential nature, lovely, and pure,
To a golden disk has this Suchness been compared.

153. The State of the Self-Existent can, in the ultimate sense,
be approached only by faith.
For those who have no eyes cannot see the blazing disk of
the sun.

154. Nothing should be taken from it, and nothing added on to
it;
The Real must be seen in its reality, and one who sees the
Truth is emancipated.

155. Empty is the Element of the adventitious properties which are distinct from it.

It is not empty of the supreme dharmas, which are properties indistinct from it.

Ratnagotravibhāga I, vv. 27–28, 45–47, 49–51, 96–97, 108–10, 118–20, 145, 148, 153–55

THE BUDDHISM OF FAITH

THE FIVE CARDINAL VIRTUES
AND
THE DEFINITION OF FAITH

170.

The five faculties are Faith, Vigour, Mindfulness, Concentration and Wisdom. Here what is *Faith?* By this faith one has faith in four dharmas. Which four? He accepts the right view which assumes a transmigration in the world of birth-and-death; he puts his trust in the ripening of karma, and knows that he will experience the fruit of any karma that he may have done; even to save his life he does not do any evil deed. He has faith in the mode of life of a Bodhisattva, and, having taken up this discipline, he does not long for any other vehicle. He believes when he hears all the doctrines which are characterized by the true, clear and profound knowledge of conditioned co-production, by such terms as lack of self, absence of a being, absence of a soul, absence of a person, and by emptiness, the signless and the wishless. He follows none of the false doctrines, and believes in all the qualities (dharmas) of a Buddha, his powers, grounds of self-confidence and all the rest; and when in his faith he has left behind all doubts, he brings about in himself those qualities of a Buddha. This is known as the virtue of faith. His *vigour* consists in his bringing about (in himself) the dharmas in which he has faith. His *mindfulness* consists in his preventing the qualities which he brings about by vigour from being destroyed by forgetfulness. His *concentration* consists in his fixing his one-pointed attention on these very same qualities. With the faculty of *wisdom* he contemplates those dharmas on which he has fixed his one-pointed attention, and penetrates to their reality. The cognition of those dharmas which arises in himself and which has no outside condition is called the virtue of wisdom. Thus these

five virtues, together, are sufficient to bring forth all the
qualities of a Buddha.

Śikshāsamuccaya, 316 (Akshayamati Sūtra)

THE ACTS AND REWARDS OF DEVOTION

171.

Endowed with ten wholesome dharmas Bodhisattvas are
born unstained by the impurities of a womb. Which ten?
They are: to manufacture an image of the Tathagata; to re-
build a decayed shrine; to give perfumes and ointments to the
shrines of the Tathagata; to give scented water for the images
of the Tathagata to be bathed; to endow (gifts so that) the
shrines of the Tathagata can be swept and anointed; personal
attendance on parents; personal attendance on teachers and
instructors; personal attendance on companions in the holy
life; and all that with a heart disinterested and free from any
thought of gain; and, finally, the dedication of the merit from
all this with the intense thought, "May, as a result of this
meritorious action all beings be born unstained by the impurities of a womb."

Śikshāsamuccaya, 313 (Ratnamegha)

172.

Verily, for countless aeons he is not reborn blind or lame,
If, after he has decided to win enlightenment, he venerates
a Stupa of the Teacher.
Firm in strength and vigour, a hero, firm in courage,
Speedily he wins fortune after he has circumambulated a
Stupa.
One who in this last age, this dreadful age, reveres a Stupa,
greater is his merit,
Than if for hundreds of thousands of Nayutas of Kotis of aeons
he had honoured a similar number of Buddhas.
For the Buddha is pre-eminent, unequalled, most worthy of
offerings, he who has travelled along the noblest pre-
eminent way.

One who does worship to this Chief of Men, he has the best and
unequalled reward.

Deceased here among men, he goes to the Heavens of the
Thirty-Three,

And there he obtains a brilliant palace made of jewels.

If he here gives a pointed tower, he will there be waited upon
by Apsaras.

If he places a garland on a Stupa, he will be reborn among the
Thirty-Three.

And there he gets a celestial lotus-pond, full of excellent water,

With a floor of golden sand, bestrewn with vaidurya and
crystal.

And when he has enjoyed that celestial delight, and completed
his life-span there,

The wise man, deceased from the Deva-world, becomes a man
of wealth.

In hundreds of thousands of Nayutas of Kotis of births he will
everywhere

Be honoured after he has placed a garland on a shrine.

And he will become a universal monarch, and a Sakra, a world-
ruler,

And a Brahma in the Brahma world, for having placed a
garland on a shrine.

When he has but given a strip of cloth to the Saviour of the
world, to the Protector,

All his aims will prosper, both among Gods and among
men.

He keeps out of the inferior and unlucky modes of life, and is
not reborn in them.

When he has made a bower of garlands over the relics of the
Saviour of the world,

He becomes a powerful king with a loyal retinue.

He is dear and cherished, honoured and praised,

By Gods and Nagas, and the wise men in this world.

Wherever that hero is born, glorious with his merit's glory,

There his family is honoured, his country and his town.

Listen to me telling you of his advantages if he takes a speck
of incense finer than a mustard seed,

And burns it at the shrines of the Lord: Serene in heart he forsakes all obstructions and all taints;

In whichever region he is, there he is full of merit, altogether
full of health, firm in his intelligence, and alert;
He averts sorrow, and he goes his way dear and pleasant to
many people.
If he should gain a kingdom, he honours the supreme Jina, a
wise universal monarch of great might,
Golden his colour, adorned with marks, his body emits a
pleasant odour in all worlds.
At birth already he receives the best of clothes, silken gar-
ments, heavenly, superb, well made.
He is blessed with a beautiful body when he has clothed the
Saviour's shrines with robes.
It is because he has done worship with robes at the shrines of
the unequalled Saviours,
That here in this world his body becomes unequalled, and
armoured with the thirty-two marks.

Śikshāsamuccaya, 299–301 (Avalokana Sūtra)

173.

As it is said in the holy Gandavyuha:
    " It is difficult, even in the course of hundreds of kotis of
aeons, to hear a Buddha preach;
How much more to see him, his sight being the supreme
remover of all hesitations.
Good is the sight of the light of the world, who has fully
understood all dharmas,
Who is the ford to merit for the triple world, and who
purifies all beings;
A great field of merit, a gladdening circle of cognition,
He illuminates the infinite world, and increases the mass of
merit.
He tears up the net of suffering, purifies the mass of cognition.
Those have no fear of the states of woe, who here have
pleased the Jina.
Wide becomes the thought of those who see the Best of Men.
In them arises a force of wisdom which is immeasurable and
translucent."

Again, in the same place it is said:

"For the weal of all beings arise the Tathagatas,
  Great in compassion, mighty heroes, who turn the wheel of
    Dharma.
  How can all that lives, even in hundreds of kotis of aeons,
  Repay the Buddhas who have been devoted to the welfare of
    beings?
  Better is it to roast for Kotis of aeons in the three states of
    woe, terrible though they are,
  Than not to see the Teacher, who turns away from all
    created things.
  However many the states of woe which spread through this
    world,
  Better it is to dwell in them for long than not to hear the
    Buddhas.
  For what reason is even a long abode in the states of woe
    to be preferred?
  Because the sight of the Jina, the Chief, causes cognition to
    grow.
  Annulled are all the sufferings when one has seen the Jina,
    the Lord of the world,
  And it becomes possible to enter on gnosis, the sphere of the
    supreme Buddhas.
  One extinguishes all coverings when one has seen the Buddha,
    best of men,
  One heaps up infinite merit which helps to win enlighten-
    ment."

This is the opportunity for increasing merit by meeting with
the Buddhas. Even now to see an image of the Tathagatas
brings an immeasurable reward, how much so when they are
seen in their own form?

For it is said in the holy Sraddha-bala-adhana-avatara-
mudra Sutra: "If, Manjusri, a son or daughter of good family
should give to Pratyekabuddhas, as numerous as the particles
of dust in all the world systems, day by day most excellent
food and superb raiment, and should go on doing so for aeons
countless like the sands of the Ganges; and if another son or
daughter of good family should see a Buddha, whether on a
painting or on an illuminated manuscript; then the latter will

beget an infinitely greater merit. What do I say of him who reverently holds out his hands (to the image), or who gives it a flower, or incense, or perfume, or a lamp? Such a one will beget a still greater merit."

Śikshāsamuccaya, 310–11

THE OBJECTS OF DEVOTION

174. *The Buddha*

1. All the faults can never in any way be in him;
   All the virtues are in every way in him established.

2. To go to him for refuge, to praise and to honour him,
   To abide in his religion, that is fit for those with sense.

3. The only Protector, he is without faults or their residues;
   The All-knowing, he has all the virtues, and that without fail.

4. For even the spiteful cannot find with any justice
   Any fault in the Lord,—in his thought, words or deeds.

8. Homage to the Self-Existent! Wonderful his many works,
   Virtues potent and abundant, which refuse to be defined.

9. There is no end to their number, for their nature words must fail,
   But to speak of them brings merit, and so we have much to say.

27. In the world you have gone to pre-eminence, without feeling envy for the élite,
    Without despising the low, without competing with your equals.

28. On the causes of virtues did you set your heart, and not on their rewards.
    It is thus that your right progress led you to the culmination of the virtues.

29. So much merit have you gathered by your good actions
    That even the dust of your feet has become a field of merit.

30. Your faults diminished and uprooted, your virtues grown and purified,
    This wise procedure brought you the supreme success.

31. You smote your faults with all your might, and even
    No residues of them remain within the series of your continuity.

32. Step by step you have deposited virtues in yourself,
    And now no likeness of them can be seen elsewhere.

33. Any worldly thing one might compare can be damaged or obstructed,
    Time and place set limits to it, to surpass it is not hard.

34. How can there be a likeness to your virtues, untouched by foe or obstacle,
    Everlasting, unlimited, and which cannot be surpassed?

40. There is only one thing which resembles you, O kindly one,
    The jewel of the Dharma, by gaining which you won pre-eminence.

52. This form of yours, calm yet lovely, brilliant without dazzling,
    Soft but mighty,—whom would it not entrance?

53. Whether one has seen it a hundred times, or beholds it for the first time,
    Your form gives the same pleasure to the eye.

54. Each time one sees it your body gives new joy,
    For its sight cannot ever satiate, its aspect is so pleasing.

56. Where else would these virtues of a Tathagata be well housed
    Except in this form of yours, blazing with signs and marks?

58. Without distinction all this world was bound to the defilements,
    That you might free it you were long in bondage to compassion.

59. Which shall I praise first, you or the great compassion, by which
   For so long you were held in Samsara, although you well knew its faults?

60. It was your compassion, given free course, which made you pass your time
   Among the crowds, when the happiness of seclusion suited you so much better.

92. To hear you gives satisfaction, to see you makes serene,
   Your speech gives gladness, your religion brings release.

93. Your birth gives joy to people, and your growth delights them;
   While you are there they benefit, on your departure they feel lost.

94. To praise you takes all guilt away, to recollect you lifts up the heart,
   To seek you brings understanding, to comprehend you purity.

95. To approach you brings good fortune, to tend you the highest wisdom,
   To resort to you takes away fear, to honour you is propitious.

96. A great lake of merit you are, pure through the achievement of moral conduct,
   Calmly serene through that of meditation, imperturbable through that of wisdom.

98. An island you are to those swept along by the flood, a shelter to the stricken,
   A refuge to those terrified by becoming, the resource of those who desire release.

99. To all that breathes you are a good vessel because of your pure conduct,
   A good field because of your perfect fruits, a good friend because of the benefits you confer.

113. Fatigue, loss of the bliss of quietude, the meeting with
men of little worth,
Contentions, and the press of the crowd, these evils you
bear as if they were benefits.

114. With a mind unattached you struggle for the weal of the
world,—
How splendid is this Blessed Buddha-nature of the
Buddhas!

115. You ate even bad food, and sometimes you agreed to
remain hungry,
You trod uneven paths, and slept on mud trampled by
cattle.

117. You are a master, O Saviour, and yet you never make use
of that fact for yourself;
All can use you as a servant for their own advantage.

118. No matter by whom or where or how provoked,
Never do you transgress your own fair path of conduct.

119. Other men do not as much study the welfare of those who
mean them well,
As you study that of those who seek you harm.

120. To an enemy intent on ill you are a good friend intent on
good.
To one who constantly seeks for faults you respond by
seeking for virtues.

122. Revilers you conquered by patience, plotters by blessing,
Slanderers by the truth, the malicious by friendliness.

123. You vanquished the manifold natures of men, depraved
since beginningless time,
And instantly you reversed their rebirth in the states of
woe.

124. It was through your skill in means that the harsh became
gentle,
That the niggard became bountiful, and the cruel tender-
hearted.

138. You have declared how the defilements are slain, you have broken through Mara's illusions,
     You have explained the evil of Samsara, you have shown the region where there is no fear.

139. Those who wish to benefit beings, and who are compassionate,
     What can they do wherein you have not led the way?

142. Out of pity for the world you have promoted the good Dharma for a long time,
     Many worthy disciples able to help the triple world have you raised,

143. You have trained many personal converts, with Subhadra as the last,—
     What yet remains of your debt to living creatures?

147. What steadfastness! What conduct! What form! What virtues!
     In a Buddha's dharmas there is nothing that is not wonderful.

> *Mātrçeţa, Śatapañcāśatkastotra I, 1–4,*
> *8–9; III, 27–34, 40; V, 52–54, 56; VI,*
> *58–60; IX, 92–96, 98–99; XI, 113–15,*
> *117–20, 122–23; XII, 124; XIII, 138–*
> *139, 142–43, 147*

175. *Devotion to Avalokiteśvara*

17. Strong in fine knowledge, Avalokitesvara surveys
    Beings afflicted by countless ills,
    And by many ills oppressed.
    He thus becomes the Saviour of the world with its Gods.

18. He has reached perfection in wonderworking power,
    He is trained in abundant cognition and skill in means.
    Everywhere in all the ten directions in the world,
    In all the Buddha-fields he can be seen.

19. And the terrors of the untoward and bad rebirths,
    In hells, in brute creation, and in Yama's kingdom,
    And the oppressions from birth, old age and sickness,
    Will slowly come to an end for living beings.

Thereupon the Bodhisattva Akshayamati, joyous and contented in his heart, spoke these verses:

20. O you, whose eyes are clear, whose eyes are friendly,
    Whose eyes betray distinguished wisdom-knowledge;
    Whose eyes are pitiful, whose eyes are pure,
    O you, so lovable, with beautiful face, with beautiful eyes!

21. Your lustre is spotless and immaculate,
    Your knowledge without darkness, your splendour like the
        sun,
    Radiant like the blaze of a fire not disturbed by the wind,
    Warming the world you shine splendidly.

22. Eminent in your pity, friendly in your words,
    One great mass of fine virtues and friendly thoughts,
    You appease the fire of the defilements which burn
        beings,
    And you rain down the rain of the deathless Dharma.

23. In quarrrels, disputes and in strife,
    In the battles of men, and in any great danger,
    To recollect the name of Avalokitesvara
    Will appease the troops of evil foes.

24. His voice[1] is like that of a cloud or drum;
    Like a rain-cloud he thunders, sweet in voice like Brahma.
    His voice is the most perfect that can be.
    So one should recall Avalokitesvara.

25. Think of him, think of him, without hesitation,
    Of Avalokitesvara, that pure being.
    In death, disaster and calamity
    He is the saviour, refuge and recourse.

26. As he who has reached perfection in all virtues,
    Who looks on all beings with pity and friendliness,
    Who is virtue itself, a great ocean of virtues,
    As such Avalokitesvara is worthy of adoration.

[1] voice=svara, a play on Avalokite-śvara.

27. He who is now so compassionate to the world,
    He will a Buddha be in future ages.
    Humbly I bow to Avalokitesvara
    Who destroys all sorrow, fear and suffering.

                      Saddharmapuṇḍarīka XXIV, vv. 17–27

176. Devotion to Tārā

The 108 Names of the Holy Tara.

Om. Homage to the Holy Tara!

1. The beautiful and delightful Potalaka is resplendent with
   various minerals,
   Covered with manifold trees and creepers, resounding with
   the sound of many birds,

2. And with murmur of waterfalls, thronged with wild beasts
   of many kinds;
   Many species of flowers grow everywhere,

3. And it is furnished with many savoury fruits; one hears
   there the humming of the bees,
   And the sweet songs of the Kinnaras; throngs of elephants

4. Frequent it by hosts of accomplished Holders of the
   magical lore,
   Gandharvas and sages free from passion,

5. A profusion of hosts of Bodhisattvas, and other masters
   of the ten stages,
   Thousands of goddesses and queens of the sacred lore,
   Taras and others,

6. Hosts of wrathful deities defend it, Hayagriva and many
   like him.
   There the wonderful Lord Avalokita, who labours for the
   weal of all beings,

7. Dwelt, seated in the lotus seat,
   A great ascetic, full of friendliness and compassion.

8. He taught Dharma in this great assembly of deities.
Vajrapani, greatly powerful, came to him who was seated there,

9. And, impelled with supreme pity, he questioned Avalokita:
"Beset by thieves, snakes, lions, fire, elephants and tigers,

10. "These beings, O Sage, are drowned in the ocean of birth-and-death;
They are bound by the snares of this world, placed there by passion, hate and confusion;

11. "Tell me, O great sage, whereby they can be freed from birth-and-death."
Avalokita, Saviour of the World, then addressed

12. These sweet words to Vajrapani, who is always vigilant:
"Listen, O Chief of the Guhyaka clan, to Amitabha, the Protector![1]

13. "The mothers of the world, born of the power of my vow and understanding,
Endowed with great compassion, created for the world's saving,

14. "Like the risen sun to behold, shining like the full moon,
The Taras illuminate the trees with their Gods, Asuras and men,

15. "They shake the triple world, and terrify the Yakshas and Rakshasas.
The Goddess who holds the blue lotus in her hands, says: 'Have no fear, have no fear!

16. 'It is for the protection of the world that I have been produced by the Jinas.
In places of terror, which bristle with swords, and where dangers abound,

17. 'When only my names are recollected, I always protect all beings,
I, O Saviour, will ferry them across[2] the great flood of their manifold fears.

[1] It is he who speaks through Avalokita.   [2] tārayishyāmi.

18. "Therefore the great Seers sing of me in the world under
the name of Tara,
Having reverently stretched forth their hands, full of
respect and awe.' "

19. Vajrapani, he who blazes through the sky, then said:
"Tell the 108 names which in the past were proclaimed by
the Jinas,

20. "By the saviours who are masters of the ten stages, by the
Bodhisattvas great in psychic power,
Names which remove all evil, bring merit and happiness,
and increase one's glory,

21. "Make for wealth and riches, increase one's health and
prosperity,
—Out of your friendliness for beings, recite them, O great
Sage!"

22. When this had been said, the Lord Avalokita, smiling all
over,
Surveyed[1] all the ten regions with eyes that radiated
friendliness,

23. Raised his right hand, making a propitious sign, and,
Great in wisdom, said to him: "Well said, well said, you
great ascetic!

24. "Listen, O you who are greatly endowed and beloved by
all beings, to the names:
People who correctly repeat them become men of princely
wealth,

25. "Free from all kinds of disease, endowed with all the virtues
of sovereignty.
They avoid an untimely death, and, when deceased, go to
the Happy Land.[2]

[1] vyavalokya.
[2] Sukhāvatī, the paradise of Amitābha (see no. 177).

26. "These I will now enumerate. Deities, assembled here, listen to me,
Rejoice at the true Dharma, and may you find peace through it!

27. "Om. You who are bright, of the beautiful eyes, Tara, joy of starlight,[1] full of pity for all beings,
Saviour of all beings, thousand-armed, thousand-eyed,

28. "Om. Homage to the Blessed Lady! Look down, look down on me,
On all beings, and also me, phaṭ svāhā! Oṃ tāre tuttāre ture svāhā!

29. "Om, pure, quite pure, cleanser, purifier,
Daughter of the Sugatas, heart of friendliness, immaculate, green, green in appearance,

30. "Of great wisdom, excellent, beautifully adorned, invincible,
Greatly formidable, able to take on all forms, great in power,

31. "Fierce like the heat of the fire at the end of an aeon, nurse of the world, most famous,
Sarasvati, with large eyes, who increases wisdom, beauty and intelligence.

32. "Om, giver of fortitude, giver of prosperity, svaha! You are Om, who can take on any shape you will,
Who labour for the weal of all beings! Saviour and victor in battle,

33. "Goddess of the perfection of wisdom, holy Tara who delights the heart,
Friend of the drum, perfect Queen of sacred lore who speaks kindly,

34. "With a face like the moon, shining brilliantly, unconquered, with a yellow garment,
The great Maya,[2] quite white, most strong and heroic,

---

[1] tārotsave. [2] The illusion which creates the world.

35. "Greatly formidable, capable of fierce anger, slayer of evil
beings,
Quite calm, calm to behold, victorious, blazing with
splendour,

36. "Girt with lightnings, standard-bearer, armed with a
sword, a wheel, and a bow,
Devourer, supporter, Kali, the night of destruction at the
world's end, who walketh about at night,

37. "Protector, deluder, calm, dear and well-loved, lovely,
Brahmani and mother of the Vedas, hidden and a dweller
in hidden places,

38. "Propitious, auspicious, gentle, knowing all created beings,
swift as thought,
Adorned with skulls, of great energy, the twilight, truly
invincible,

39. "Leader of the caravans, of the pitiful looks, who showeth
the way to those who have lost it,
Granter of boons, instructor, teacher, of unbounded valour
with a woman's form,

40. "Variegated in colour, practitioner of Yoga, accomplished
magician, a Pariah, and yet deathless and everlasting,
Wealthy, full of merit, of great parts, of good parts,
pleasant to behold,

41. "Who terrifies Death even, fearsome, terrible, fierce in
your great austerities,
Labouring only for the weal of the world, a worthy refuge,
affectionate to your devotees,

42. "Mistress of language, fortunate, exquisite, constant, the
mother of all projects,
The assistant in all projects, a gracious defender, a nurse, a
conqueror of wealth,

43. "Fearless, a Gautami, the worthy daughter of the holy
Lokesvara.
Tara, infinite by the virtues of her names, she fulfills all
hopes.

44. "These 108 names have been proclaimed for your welfare;
They are mysterious, wonderful, secret, hard to get even
by the Gods,

45. "They bring luck and good fortune, destroy all sin,
Heal all sickness, and bring ease to all beings.

46. "When one recites them three times, intelligently, clean
from having taken a bath, and with concentration,—
Then before long one attains to the splendours of royalty;

47. "Those in pain will permanently be at ease, the poor will
become rich,
The stupid wise and intelligent,—that admits of no doubt;

48. "Those bound will be freed from their bonds, in lawsuits
they will be victorious,
Foes will become friends, so will horned and tusked beasts.

49. "In battles, straits and difficulties, crowded with many
dangers,
The mere recollection of these names takes all evils away.

50. "He knows no untimely death, he gains abundant
prosperity,
And rebirth as a human being is fruitful to him who is thus
great-souled.

51. "A man who, risen early in the morning, will recite them,
He will win prosperity for a long time.

52. "Gods, Nagas, and also Yakshas, Gandharvas, Kataputana
demons,
Pisacas, Rakshasas, Ghosts and the Mothers of the
Terrible Glow,

53. "Those who bring death and epilepsy, the demons who
torment people in hell,
The Dakshinis, the Tarakas, the Pretas, Skandas, Maras,
and great ghosts,

54. "Cannot even jump on his shadow, and how much less can
they take hold of him;
Evil beings cannot oppress, diseases cannot approach him.

55. "Of great psychic powers, he experiences even the battles
between Gods and Asuras,
He has all the virtues of sovereignty, and he waxes great
through his children and children's children.

56. "He remembers his former births, is intelligent, well born,
pleasant to behold,
Affectionate, most eloquent, and well versed in all the
Sastras.

57. "He will tend his spiritual teacher, will be adorned with the
thought of enlightenment,
And wherever he may be reborn, he will never be deprived
of the Buddhas."

Āryatārābhaṭṭārikānāmāshṭottaraśatakastotra

THE PURE LAND

177.

15. This world Sukhavati, Ananda, which is the world
system of the Lord Amitabha, is rich and prosperous, com-
fortable, fertile, delightful and crowded with many Gods and
men. And in this world system, Ananda, there are no hells, no
animals, no ghosts, no Asuras and none of the inauspicious
places of rebirth. And in this our world no jewels make their
appearance like those which exist in the world system
Sukhavati.

16. And that world system Sukhavati, Ananda, emits many
fragrant odours, it is rich in a great variety of flowers and
fruits, adorned with jewel trees, which are frequented by
flocks of various birds with sweet voices, which the Tathagata's miraculous power has conjured up. And these jewel
trees, Ananda, have various colours, many colours, many
hundreds of thousands of colours. They are variously composed of the seven precious things, in varying combinations,[1]
i.e. of gold, silver, beryl, crystal, coral, red pearls or emerald.
Such jewel trees, and clusters of banana trees and rows of

[1] This phrase abbreviates two and a half pages of the text.

palm trees, all made of precious things, grow everywhere in this Buddha-field. On all sides it is surrounded with golden nets, and all round covered with lotus flowers made of all the precious things. Some of the lotus flowers are half a mile in circumference, others up to ten miles. And from each jewel lotus issue thirty-six hundred thousand kotis of rays. And at the end of each ray there issue thirty-six hundred thousand kotis of Buddhas, with golden-coloured bodies, who bear the thirty-two marks of the superman, and who, in all the ten directions, go into countless world systems, and there demonstrate Dharma.

17. And further, Ananda, in this Buddha-field there are nowhere any mountains,—black mountains, jewel mountains, Sumerus, kings of mountains, circular mountains and great circular mountains. But the Buddha-field is everywhere even, delightful like the palm of the hand, and in all its parts the ground contains a great variety of jewels and gems. . . .

18. And many kinds of rivers flow along in this world system Sukhavati. There are great rivers there, one mile broad, and up to fifty miles broad and twelve miles deep. And all these rivers flow along calmly, their water is fragrant with manifold agreeable odours, in them there are bunches of flowers to which various jewels adhere, and they resound with various sweet sounds. And the sound which issues from these great rivers is as pleasant as that of a musical instrument, which consists of hundreds of thousands of kotis of parts, and which, skilfully played, emits a heavenly music. It is deep, commanding, distinct, clear, pleasant to the ear, touching the heart, delightful, sweet, pleasant, and one never tires of hearing it, it always agrees with one and one likes to hear it, like the words 'Impermanent, peaceful, calm, and not-self'. Such is the sound that reaches the ears of those beings.

And, Ananda, both the banks of those great rivers are lined with variously scented jewel trees, and from them bunches of flowers, leaves and branches of all kinds hang down. And if those beings wish to indulge in sports full of heavenly delights on those river-banks, then, after they have stepped into the water, the water in each case rises as high as they wish it to, —up to the ankles, or the knees, or the hips, or their sides, or their ears. And heavenly delights arise. Again, if beings wish

the water to be cold, for them it becomes cold; if they wish it
to be hot, for them it becomes hot; if they wish it to be hot and
cold, for them it becomes hot and cold, to suit their pleasure.
And those rivers flow along, full of water scented with the
finest odours, and covered with beautiful flowers, resounding
with the sounds of many birds,[1] easy to ford, free from mud,
and with golden sand at the bottom. And all the wishes those
beings may think of, they all will be fulfilled, as long as they
are rightful.

And as to the pleasant sound which issues from the water
(of these rivers), that reaches all the parts of this Buddha-field.
And everyone hears the pleasant sound he wishes to hear, i.e.
he hears of the Buddha, the Dharma, the Samgha, of the (six)
perfections, the (ten) stages, the powers, the grounds of self-
confidence, of the special dharmas of a Buddha, of the
analytical knowledges, of emptiness, the signless, and the
wishless, of the uneffected, the unborn, of non-production,
non-existence, non-cessation, of calm, quietude and peace, of
the great friendliness, the great compassion, the great sympathetic joy, the great evenmindedness, of the patient acceptance
of things which fail to be produced, and of the acquisition of
the stage where one is consecrated (as a Tathagata). And,
hearing this, one gains the exalted zest and joyfulness, which
is associated with detachment, dispassion, calm, cessation,
Dharma, and brings about the state of mind which leads to
the accomplishment of enlightenment. And nowhere in this
world-system Sukhavati does one hear of anything unwholesome, nowhere of the hindrances, nowhere of the states of
punishment, the states of woe and the bad destinies, nowhere
of suffering. Even of feelings which are neither pleasant nor
unpleasant one does not hear here, how much less of suffering!
And that, Ananda, is the reason why this world-system is
called the 'Happy Land' (Sukhavati). But all this describes
it only in brief, not in detail. One aeon might well reach its end
while one proclaims the reasons for happiness in the world-
system Sukhavati, and still one could not come to the end of
(the enumeration of) the reasons for happiness.

19. Moreover, Ananda, all the beings who have been reborn
in this world-system Sukhavati, who are reborn in it, or who

[1] Here the descriptions have been abbreviated.

will be reborn in it, they will be exactly like the Paranirmita-vasavartin Gods: of the same colour, strength, vigour, height and breadth, dominion, store of merit and keenness of super-knowledges; they enjoy the same dresses, ornaments, parks, palaces and pointed towers, the same kind of forms, sounds, smells, tastes and touchables, just the same kinds of enjoy-ments. And the beings in the world-system Sukhavati do not eat gross food, like soup or raw sugar; but whatever food they may wish for, that they perceive as eaten, and they become gratified in body and mind, without there being any further need to throw the food into the body. And if, after their bodies are gratified, they wish for certain perfumes, then the whole of that Buddha-field becomes scented with just that kind of heavenly perfumes. But if someone does not wish to smell that perfume, then the perception of it does not reach him.[1] In the same way, whatever they may wish for, comes to them, be it musical instruments, banners, flags, etc.; or cloaks of different colours, or ornaments of various kinds. If they wish for a palace of a certain colour, distinguishing marks, construction, height and width, made of various precious things, adorned with hundreds of thousands of pinnacles, while inside it various heavenly woven materials are spread out, and it is full of couches strewn with beautiful cushions,—then just such a palace appears before them. In those delightful palaces, surrounded and honoured by seven times seven thousand Apsaras, they dwell, play, enjoy and disport themselves.

21. . . . And the beings who are touched by the winds, which are pervaded with various perfumes, are filled with a happiness as great as that of a monk who has achieved the cessation of suffering.

22. And in this Buddha-field one has no conception at all of fire, sun, moon, planets, constellations, stars or blinding dark-ness, and no conception even of day and night, except (where they are mentioned) in the sayings of the Tathagata. There is nowhere a notion of monks possessing private parks for retreats.

24. And all the beings who have been born, who are born, who will be born in this Buddha-field, they all are fixed on the right method of salvation, until they have won Nirvana. And

[1] In the following passage some enumerations have been abbreviated.

why? Because there is here no place for and no conception of
the two other groups, i.e. of those who are not fixed at all,
and those who are fixed on wrong ways. For this reason also
that world-system is called the 'Happy Land'. . . .

26. And further again, Ananda, in the ten directions, in each
single direction, in Buddha-fields countless like the sands of
the river Ganges, Buddhas and Lords countless like the sands
of the river Ganges, glorify the name of the Lord Amitabha,
the Tathagata, praise him, proclaim his fame, extol his virtue.
And why? Because all beings are irreversible from the supreme
enlightenment if they hear the name of the Lord Amitabha,
and, on hearing it, with one single thought only raise their
hearts to him with a resolve connected with serene faith.

27. And if any beings, Ananda, again and again reverently
attend to this Tathagata, if they will plant a large and immeasurable root of good, having raised their hearts to enlightenment, and if they vow to be reborn in that world
system, then, when the hour of their death approaches, that
Tathagata Amitabha, the Arhat, the fully Enlightened One,
will stand before them, surrounded by hosts of monks. Then,
having seen that Lord, and having died with hearts serene,
they will be reborn in just that world-system Sukhavati. And
if there are sons or daughters of good family, who may desire
to see that Tathagata Amitabha in this very life, they should
raise their hearts to the supreme enlightenment, they should
direct their thought with extreme resoluteness and per-
severance unto this Buddha-field and they should dedicate
their store of merit to being reborn therein.

Sukhāvativyūha ch. 15–17, 18, 19, 21 (in
part), 22, 24 (in part), 26, 27

YOGACARINS

MIND-ONLY

178. *Mind-only and Suffering*

Further, Mahamati, afraid of the sufferings arising from the discrimination of birth-and-death, they seek for Nirvana. They do not know that there is no difference between birth-and-death and Nirvana. They distinguish Nirvana as the absence of the discrimination of all existents, and as the termination of future objects for the sense-organs, but they do not understand that it is the store-consciousness which is realised inwardly, after a revulsion has taken place. In consequence these deluded people teach a trinity of vehicles, but not a state of mind-only, in which nothing makes its appearance. Therefore, Mahamati, they are ignorant of the range of what is seen by the own mind of the past, future and present Tathagatas, settle down in a range which is outside that which is seen of the mind, and go on rolling themselves along the wheel of birth-and-death.

Lankavatāra Sūtra, 61–62

179. *Mind-only and Nirvana*

Finally, Mahamati, there are others who, roaring the lion's roar of all-knowledge, explain Nirvana as follows: It is where one understands that everything is merely that which is seen in (of) one's own mind only; where there is no inclination to believe in outside existents or non-existents; where one is free from the four logical possibilities[1]; where one has a vision of the truly real situation; where one does not fall into the dualism of discriminating between 'is' and 'is not' in that which is seen of one's own mind; where one does not apprehend

[1] I.e. it is, it is not, it both is and is not, it neither is nor is not.

either subject or object; where all the means of logical proof are not seized upon, because one has seen that they do not assert themselves; where there is no seizing on the real truth, but a disregard for it, as being a likely cause of infatuation; where there is a full attainment of the holy Dharma in the inside of one's being; where the two forms of egolessness[1] are understood; where the two forms of defilement [2] are kept away, and where one is purified of the twofold covering[3]; where there are the successive stages, up to the stage of a Tathagata, all the concentrations, beginning with the one (which sees everything as) 'illusion', and where there is a revulsion from thought, mind and mind-consciousness.

Lankavatāra Sūtra 184-85

180. *Mind-only, Permanence and Impermanence*

I, however, Mahamati, am neither for permanence nor for impermanence. And why? For these reasons: External existents are not admitted; the triple world has been explained as mind-only; a variety of marks (which would distinguish objects) is not accepted; the combination and separation of the great elements does not take place and does not disappear, and there are no primary and secondary elements; a duality of what is discriminated takes place in spite of the fact that object and subject cannot be defined; one comprehends duality as a result of false discrimination; one has moved away from false views about external existents or non-existents, and one has understood that they are merely one's own mind. Discrimination takes place because one effects the karma-producing activity of discriminating, and fails to desist from such activity. If someone did desist, he would leave behind the discrimination between existence and non-existence which is the work of his own mind. He would understand that, as they are merely what is seen of his own mind, all dharmas, from the worldly to the highest supramundane, have neither permanence nor impermanence. With their continuity (per-

---

[1] See no. 182.

[2] (*a*) Evil inclination, (*b*) the realistic error.

[3] The covering over of the truth which comes from evil inclination, and the one which is due to the realistic error.

sonality) fallen into the false view of two extremes,[1] all the heretics, who, because they have not understood their own discriminations, are people without spiritual success, have constructed talk about impermanence. The triple mark[2] of all dharmas, from the worldly to the highest supramundane, has issued from verbal discriminations. But the foolish common people do not understand that. As it is said:

121. Mind-only is all this; dual does the mind proceed;
    In the absence of subject and object, a self and what belongs to it cannot exist.

122. Up to the realm of Brahma, all is mind-only, I say.
    Outside mind-only, Brahma and so forth cannot be apprehended.

Lankavatāra Sūtra, 208–09

181. *Mind-only and Salvation*

26. "As long as consciousness does not abide in representation-only,
    So long does one not turn away from the tendency towards the twofold grasping."

Commentary: As long as consciousness does not abide in the true nature of thought, which is also called 'representation-only', so long it proceeds with the object and the subject as a basis. 'The twofold grasping' means the grasping of the object and the grasping of the subject. 'The tendency towards it' is the germ of the future genesis of the twofold grasping, which they have placed in the store-consciousness. Until the time when the thought of the Yogin is supported on representation-only, which is marked by non-duality, so long he 'does not turn away from', does not forsake the tendency towards the twofold grasping. And here the non-forsaking of the external basis implies also the non-forsaking of the internal basis. And he thinks to himself, "I grasp at sight-objects, etc., with my eyes, etc."

Next one explains, why to take as a basis thought-only

---

[1] It is, it is not.   [2] Impermanence, ill, not-self.

which is devoid of an object, is not sufficient for the abiding in the true nature of thought:

27. As long as he places something before him, taking it as a basis, saying:
    'This is just representation-only', so long he does not abide in that alone."

This refers to someone who, conceited and acting on hearsay alone, thinks, "I am established in the pure representation-only." "This is mere representation-only, it is devoid of an object, there is here no external object," thus he grasps at a basis and esteems himself. 'Before him' means 'face to face with him'. 'He places', as he has heard it said, with his mind. . . . 'He does not abide in That alone', because he has not forsaken the apprehension of (his own) consciousness.

Then he (Vasubandhu) says with regard to the forsaking of the grasping at consciousness, and how thereby one becomes one who is supported by thought-only:

28. "But when cognition no longer apprehends an object, then It stands firmly in consciousness-only, because, where there is nothing to grasp there is no more grasping."

At the time when outside thought 'he does not apprehend', not see, not grasp, not take as real, any object whatsoever, be it the demonstration (of Dharma) and instruction (in it), or an ordinary object, like form, sound, etc.—and that because he sees that which really is, and not because he is as one born blind—at that time there is a forsaking of the grasping at consciousness, and he is established in the true nature of his own thought. The reason for this is that 'where there is nothing to grasp, there is no more grasping'. Where there is an object there is a subject, but not where there is no object. The absence of an object results in the absence also of a subject, and not merely in that of grasping. It is thus that there arises the cognition which is homogeneous, without object, indiscriminate and supramundane. The tendencies to treat object and subject as distinct and real entities are forsaken, and thought is established in just the true nature of one's own thought.

When thought thus abides in representation-only, then how can one describe it? He says:

29. "It is without thought, without basis, and is the supramundane cognition.
The revulsion from the substratum results from the loss of
the twofold corruption.

30. "This is the element without outflows, inconceivable,
wholesome and stable,
The blissful body of emancipation, the Dharma-body of the
great Sage."

Vasubandhu, Trimśikā, 26–30

TWOFOLD EGOLESSNESS AND EMPTINESS

182.

A Bodhisattva, a great being, should become one who is
skilful in investigating the mark of the twofold egolessness.
1. There is first the lack of self in *persons*. (*a*) Persons are a
conglomeration of skandhas, elements and sense-fields, devoid
of a self or anything belonging to a self. (*b*) Consciousness arises
from ignorance, karma and craving, and it keeps going by
settling down in the grasping at form, etc., by means of the
eye, etc. (*c*) Through all the sense-organs a world of objects and
bodies is manifested owing to the discrimination that takes
place in the world which is of mind itself, that is, in the store-
consciousness. (*a*)[1] Like a river, a seed, a lamp, wind, a cloud
beings are broken up from moment to moment. (*b*) Always
restless like a monkey, like a fly which is ever in search of unclean things and defiled places, like a fire never satisfied,
(consciousness persists) by reason of the habit-energy stored up
by false imagination since beginningless time. (*c*) (The world)
proceeds like a water-drawing wheel or machine, rolling the
wheel of Samsara, carrying along various bodies and forms,
resuscitating the dead like the demon Vetala, moving beings
about as a magician moves puppets. The skill in the cognition

---

[1] *a–c* illustrate the triple mark, i.e. impermanence, ill, not-self.

of these marks, that is called the cognition of the absence of self in persons.

2. What, then, is the cognition of the absence of self in *dharmas*? It is the recognition that own-being and marks of the skandhas, elements and sense-fields are imagined. Since the skandhas, elements and sense-fields are devoid of a self,—a mere agglomeration of heaps, closely tied to the string of their root cause (i.e. ignorance), karma and craving, proceeding by mutual conditioning, (and therefore) inactive,—therefore the skandhas are also devoid of the special and general marks. The variety of their marks is the result of unreal imagination, and they are distinguished from one another by the fools, but not by the saints.

Lankavatāra Sūtra, 68–69

THE IRREALITY OF THE WORLD

183.

This passage illustrates the irreality of the world by twelve comparisons, of which only six are given here.

Mahamati, foolish common people do not understand that what is seen is merely their own mind. Being convinced that there exists outside a variety of objects and,—as a result of the habit-energy, acquired in past lives,—being addicted to discriminate between existence and non-existence, oneness and otherness, bothness and non-bothness, permanence and impermanence, as true to the own-being of things, they produce false imaginings.

1. It is as with animals who imagine in a mirage the existence of water. Scorched by the summer heat, desirous of drinking it, they run towards it. They do not understand that it is an erroneous vision in their own minds, and they do not comprehend that there is no water there. Just so the foolish common people, accustomed as they are since beginningless time to all kinds of discursive ideas and discriminations, their minds burning with the fires of passion, hatred and confusion, coveting a variety of forms and objects, bent on viewing things

as produced, breaking up and subsisting, unskilled in understanding the true meaning of within and without, of existence and non-existence, fall into the grasping at oneness and otherness, existence and non-existence.

3. It is as if some man, asleep, dreams of a country, full of women and men, elephants, horses, cars, pedestrians, villages, cities and market towns, cows, buffaloes, woods, parks, and adorned with various mountains, rivers and lakes. In his dream he enters the women's apartments of the king's palace, and then he wakes up. Awake, his memory runs back over the country and the women's apartments. It would not be an intelligent thing to do for this man, to go in his memory through the various unreal experiences which he had in his dream, or would it, Mahamati? In the same way, the foolish common people, bitten by false views and under the influence of the heretics, do not realize that what is seen by their own mind is like a dream, and they rely on notions of oneness and otherness, of being and non-being.

5. It is like people with an eye-disease, who see a hair-net before their eyes, and who exclaim to one another, saying: "This is wonderful, this is wonderful! Look, sirs, just look!" But that hair-net has never been produced. It is not an existent, and not a non-existent, because it is seen, and not seen. Just so those who believe in the discriminations and false views to which the heretics are addicted,—who are convinced that there are the alternatives of 'is' and 'is not', of oneness and otherness, bothness and non-bothness—will oppose the good Dharma, and will destroy themselves and others.

6. It is like a wheel made by a firebrand. Fools imagine that it is a real wheel, but not so intelligent people. Just so, those who have fallen into the false views to which the heretics are addicted will, with regard to the genesis of all existents, imagine oneness and otherness, bothness and non-bothness.

10. Just as an echo is heard, when it occurs caused by the connection between a man, a river and the wind. But it is not an existent, nor a non-existent, because it is heard as a voice and yet not as a voice. Just so, existence and non-existence, oneness and otherness, bothness and non-bothness, are visions falsely constructed by the habit-energy in one's own mind.

149. The skandhas, with consciousness as the fifth, are similar
   to reflections of trees in water;
   They should be seen as a mock show, and a dream. Do not
   discriminate them by representation!

150. The triple world resembles a hair-net, or water whirling
   about in a mirage;
   It is like a dream or a mock show. When that is distinctly
   perceived, one is emancipated.

151. Like a mirage in summer, so palpitates the deluded mind;
   The animals seize on something to drink, but there is no
   reality to it.

152. Just so the seed of consciousness palpitates in the range
   of false views;
   The fools seize on something that is born, like dim-eyed
   people in the dark.

153. In his wanderings throughout beginningless time the fool
   is wrapped up in his grasping at existence.
   As a wedge is driven out by another wedge, so he is
   gradually led into abandoning it.

154. See the world always as a mock show, a corpse animated
   by a ghost, a machine, a dream, lightning or a cloud,
   Then the triple continuity is severed, and one is set free.

155. And do not employ any representation, but regard it like
   a mirage in the air;
   When thus one discerns dharmas, there is nothing that
   one recognizes as real.

156. All this is but words and thought-construction. Its
   distinguishing marks have no existence.
   The skandhas are like a hair-net, to which one falsely
   attributes a distinct existence.

157. The variety of things is like a hair-net, a mock show, a
   dream, a fairy city,
   A firebrand or mirage. It is not, it is just a way of talking
   among men.

158. Permanence and impermanence, and so oneness, and likewise both and not-both;
The fools think them out, deluded as they are and bound
up with faults since beginningless time.

159. In a mirror, in water, in an eye, in a vessel, and in gems,
Images can be seen. But the images in turn do not come
from anywhere real.

160. A mere appearance of existence is thus the variety of
things, like a mirage in the air.
It is seen in a variety of forms, like a barren woman's
child in a dream.

Lankavatāra Sūtra, 90–96

184.[1]

*In order to remove unjustified hesitation, the Sutra gives these
comparisons:*

1. One may ask, "How can the non-existent become a sense-
object?" In order to remove this doubt, the Sutra compares
things to a *magical illusion.*

2. One may ask, "How can thought and mental acts arise
without an object?" To remove this doubt, there is the comparison to a *mirage.*—Here thought and mental acts correspond
to the mirage, and the object to the water. When a mirage
makes its appearance, no real water is there, and yet the notion
of real water arises.

3. One may ask, "How, in the absence of an object, can one
experience desirable and undesirable impressions?" To remove
this doubt, things are compared to a *dream.*—In a dream also
there is no real object, and yet pleasant and unpleasant impressions are felt.

4. One may ask, "How, in the absence of an object, can
wholesome and unwholesome actions produce desirable or
undesirable fruits?" In answer, things are compared to an
image.—The image is not the real object. It is relative to a
model that one produces the notion of an image. Yet, as

---

[1] See introduction, p. 12.

distinct from the model, it has no reality. Likewise a desirable or undesirable fruit, though unreal, can be perceived.

5. One may ask, "How, in the absence of objects, can different acts of consciousness arise?" In answer, things are compared to a *reflection*.—In a shadow play one sees all sorts of things reflected. Although these reflections are seen, they are not really what they seem to be. In the same way, acts of consciousness are not different things, although they appear to be so.

6. One may ask, "How, in the absence of objects, can different verbal expressions arise?" In answer things are compared to an *echo*.—An echo is not a real sound, and yet it is heard. Similarly verbal expressions are not real things, and yet they are understood.

7. One may ask, "How, in the absence of an object, can the images apperceived in trance arise?" In answer, things are compared to the *moon reflected in water*.—The moon reflected in water is not really in the water, and yet, because the water is wet and limpid, the moon is seen in it. So with concentrated thought. The objects which form its range are not real things, and yet they are perceived, the state of trance playing the part of the water.

8. One may ask, "How, in the absence of an object, can Bodhisattvas, whose thought is unperverted, be born at will for the service of beings?" In answer, things are compared to a *magical creation*.—A magical creation is not a real thing, and yet a conjurer has the power to conjure up all sorts of objects, which can be perceived. The same holds good here. The personality which a Bodhisattva assumes is not real, and yet it is perceived when he works for the benefit of beings.

*Asanga Mahāyānasamgraha II, 27, with
some of Vasubandhu's comments*

THE BUDDHA AS THE BASIS OF ALL

185.

Tathagatahood consists in the manifestation of the three bodies of a Buddha. The element of the Tathagata is therefore the cause of their attainment. 'Element' has here the meaning of cause. As it is said: "In each being there exists in embryonic form the element of the Tathagata, but people do not look through to that." Moreover it is said (Abhidharma-mahāyānasūtra):

"The Element is without beginning in time,
It is the common foundation of all dharmas.
Because it exists there also exist
All places of rebirth and the full attainment of Nirvana."

Ratnagotravibhāga, pp. 72–73

Third Part

THE TANTRAS

by
David Snellgrove

THE TANTRAS

THE CLEANSING OF THOUGHT

186.

Those who do not perceive the truth think in terms of Samsara and Nirvana, but those who perceive the truth think neither of Samsara nor of Nirvana. Discriminating thought is then the great demon that produces the ocean of the Samsara. But being free of this discriminating thought, the great ones are freed from the bonds of existence. Ordinary folk are afflicted with the poison of fear as though with poison itself, but he who has identified himself with compassion should uproot it completely and go his way. Just as crystal, which is clear, becomes coloured from the colour of another object, so likewise the jewel of the mind becomes coloured with the colour of mental conceits. Like a jewel the mind is naturally free from the colour of these mental conceits; it is pure from the beginning, unproduced, immaculate and without any self-nature. So one has to do with all one's might those very things that fools condemn, remaining in union with one's chosen divinity and with purity of mind as one's motive.

Just as water that has entered the ear may be removed by water and just as a thorn may be removed by a thorn, so those who know how, remove passion by means of passion itself. Just as a washerman removes the grime from a garment by means of grime, so the wise man renders himself free of impurity by means of impurity itself.

Cittaviśuddhiprakaraṇa, vv. 24–94, 37–38

SUPREME ENLIGHTENMENT

187.

Then the Lord who is ruler of the Body, Speech and Mind of all the Tathagatas, expounded this chapter on supreme enlightenment, the mantra-practice of the great sacramental truth.

"By the enjoyment of all desires, to which one devotes oneself just as one pleases, it is by such practice as this that one may speedily gain Buddhahood.

"With the enjoyment of all desires, to which one devotes oneself just as one pleases, in union with one's chosen divinity, one worships oneself, the Supreme One.

"One does not succeed by devoting oneself to harsh discipline and austerities, but by devoting oneself to the enjoyment of all desires one rapidly gains success.

"Don't move your lips for the eating of food you've begged, nor should you be attached to these offerings. It is by moving one's lips in the recitation of mantras that the body becomes whole and confirmed in the enjoyment of all desires.

"One gains enlightenment, when one has first attained to a condition of well-being of Body, Speech and Mind. Otherwise untimely death will certainly bear its fruit in hell.

"Buddhas and Bodhisattvas, followers of the Mantra-practice supreme, have attained to the supreme place of the Dharma by devoting themselves to all desires.

"Those who aspire to the five kinds of knowledge[1] should always devote themselves to the five kinds of desirable things. They should gratify the Bodhisattvas, and gladden them with the sun of enlightenment.

"Knowing Form to be threefold, one should worship it, identifying oneself with the worship, for this is that knowing Lord, the Great Buddha Vairocana.

"Knowing Sound to be threefold, one should entrust it to the divinities, for this is that Lord, the Great Buddha Ratnasambhava.

"Knowing Smell to be threefold, one should entrust it to the Buddhas, Bodhisattvas and the rest, for this is that Lord, the Great Buddha Amitabha.

"Knowing Taste to be threefold, one should entrust it to the divinities, for this is that Lord, the Great Buddha Amogha-siddhi.

---

[1] The five kinds of knowledge typify perfect enlightenment. They are (1) the pure knowledge of the dharma-sphere, (2) mirror-like knowledge, (3) knowledge of sameness, (4) perceptual knowledge and (5) knowledge of needful activity. They will be found again below in 'The Fivefold Manifestation' associated with the Five Tathagatas.

"Knowing Touch to be threefold, one should entrust it to one's own Buddha-family, for this is that adamantine Lord, endowed with the form of Akshobhya.

"Form and Sound and the other three, one should always endow with Thought, for of all those Five Buddhas Thought is the secret essence."

Now how is that mental concentration that recollects Body as its object?—That Body of all the Buddhas, which is filled with the five skandhas, O that I might be endowed with such a one, with the self-nature of that Buddha-body!

And how is that mental concentration that recollects Speech as its object?—The Word of the Vajra-Dharma, the sure word of perfection, O may such Speech be mine as for all possessors of the Dharma!

And how is that mental concentration that recollects Mind as its object?—That mind of Samantabhadra, the wise one, the hidden Lord, O may such Mind be mine as for all holders of the Vajra!

And how is that mental concentration that recollects Being as its object?—That mind of all beings, which is characterized by Body, Speech and Mind, O may such Mind be mine, of the nature of the sameness of space!

And how is that mental concentration which recollects Body, Speech and Mind, the embodiment of all mantras, as its object?—That Body of adamantine mantras, that bodily manifestation of Speech, O may this ever be mine as for all possessors of mantras.

And how is that mental concentration which recollects the sacrament as its object?—He who desires the fruit (i.e. effective results) should drink the sacrificial drop in accordance with the rite, and thus he should honour the whole array of the Tathagatas and quite certainly gain perfection.

And how is that mental concentration that recollects the Perfection of Wisdom as its object?—It is naturally translucent, completely unproduced and without any basis, for there is no enlightenment and no understanding, no end and no beginning.

And how is that mental concentration that has non-production as its object?—It is naturally translucent, completely signless and unchanging; it is neither duality nor the absence of duality, calm and immaculate like space.

And how is that mental concentration which has as its object the worship of the Family of Wrath (i.e. the Buddha-family of Akshobhya)?—Having found a maiden of twelve years, whose mind is firm, one should worship her in accordance with the family-practice. One will gain thereby in this very life the Body of a Tathagata, the Mind of a Vajra-holder and the Speech of a supreme Dharma-knower.

Even those who are considered poor wretches succeed by means of this recitation of mantras, by this concentration where there is no discriminating of the triple-vajra, in this complete perfection of Body, Speech and Mind.

Guhyasamājatantra, ch. 7

SARAHA'S TREASURY OF SONGS

188.[1]

1. The Brahmins who do not know the truth,
   Vainly recite the Vedas four.

2. With earth and water and kusha-grass they make
   preparations,
   And seated at home they kindle fire,
   And from the senseless offerings that they make,
   They burn their eyes with the pungent smoke.

3. In lordly garb with one staff or three,
   They think themselves wise with their brahmanical lore.
   Vainly is the world enslaved by their vanity.
   They do not know that dharma's the same as non-dharma.

[1] See introduction, pp. 13–14.

4. With ashes these masters smear their bodies,
   And on their heads they wear matted hair.
   Seated within the house they kindle lamps.
   Seated in a corner they tinkle bells.

5. They adopt a posture and fix their eyes,
   Whispering in ears and deceiving folk,
   Teaching widows and bald-headed nuns and such like,
   Initiating them as they take their fee.

6. The Jain monks mock the Way with their appearance,
   With their long nails and their filthy clothes,
   Or else naked and with dishevelled hair,
   Enslaving themselves with their doctrine of release.

7. If by nakedness one is released,
   Then dogs and jackals must be so.
   If from absence of hair there comes perfection,
   Then the hips of maidens must be so.

8. If from having a tail there comes release,
   Then for the peacock and yak it must be so.
   If wisdom consists in eating just what one finds,
   Then for elephant and horse it must be so.

9. For these Jain monks there is no release, Saraha says.
   Deprived of the truth of happiness, they do but afflict
   their own bodies.

10. Then there are the novices and bhikshus with the teaching
    of the Old School,
    Who renounce the world to be monks.
    Some are seen sitting and reading the scriptures,
    Some wither away in their concentration on thought.

11. Others have recourse to the Great Vehicle.
    This is the doctrine which expounds the original texts,
    (they say).
    Others just meditate on mandala-circles.
    Others strive to define the fourth stage of bliss.[1]

---

[1] In some Tantric schools the progress towards enlightenment is
envisaged as four stages of bliss: mere bliss, extreme bliss, the bliss of
cessation and the bliss of the Innate. To define the fourth stage, which
is enlightenment itself, is conceived as an impossible task.

12. With such investigating they fall from the Way;
    Some would envisage it as space,
    Others endow it with the nature of voidness,
    And thus they are generally in disagreement.

13. Whoever deprived of the Innate, seeks nirvana,
    Can in no wise acquire the absolute truth.

14. Whoever is intent on anything else, how may he gain
    release?
    Will one gain release, abiding in meditation?
    What's the use of lamps? What's the use of offerings?
    What's to be done by reliance on mantras?

15. What is the use of austerities?
    What is the use of going on pilgrimage?
    Is release achieved by bathing in water?

16. Abandon such false attachments and renounce such
    illusion!
    Than knowledge of This there is nothing else.
    Other than This no one can know.

17. It is This that's read and This that's meditated,
    It's This that's discussed in treatises and old legends.
    There is no school of thought that does not have This as
    its aim,
    But one sees it only at the feet of one's master.

18. If the word of one's master but enter the heart,
    It seems like a treasure in the palm of one's hand.
    The world is enslaved by falsehood, says Saraha,
    And the fool does not perceive his true nature.

19. Without meditating, without renouncing the world,
    One may stay at home in the company of one's wife.
    Can that be called perfect knowledge, Saraha says,
    If one is not released while enjoying the pleasures of
    sense?

20. If it's already manifest, what's the use of meditation?
    And if it is hidden, one is just measuring darkness.

Saraha cries: The nature of the Innate is neither existent
nor non-existent.

21. By means of that same essence by which one is born and
lives and dies,
By means of that one gains the highest bliss.
But although Saraha speaks these profound and
mysterious words,
This stupid world seems not to understand.

22. If it exists apart from meditation, how may one meditate
upon it?
If it is ineffable, how may it be discussed?
The whole world is enslaved by the appearance of
things,
And no one apprehends his true nature.

23. Mantras and tantras, meditation and concentration,
They are all a cause of self-deception.
Do not defile in contemplation thought that is pure in its
own nature,
But abide in the bliss of yourself and cease those
torments.

24. Eat and drink, indulge the senses,
Fill the mandala (with offerings) again and again,
By things like these you'll gain the world beyond.
Tread upon the head of the foolish worldling and pro-
ceed!

25. Where vital breath and mind no longer roam about,
Where Sun and Moon do not appear,[1]
There, O man, put thy thought to rest,
This is the precept taught by Saraha.

---

[1] Sun and Moon are synonyms for the two veins, *lalanā* and *rasanā*,
conceived as passing to the left and right of the yogin's body, and up and
down which pass the two streams of vital breath in the psycho-physical
process. These two streams (or waves, see verse 45 below) are conceived
as uniting in the central vein where they are consumed and are now
known as *Caṇḍālī* (see p. 254 below). For a fuller account of this process
see Evans-Wentz, *Tibetan Yoga and Secret Doctrines*, pp. 171–207.

26. Do not discriminate, but see things as one,
    Making no distinction of families.[1]
    Let the whole of the threefold world become one in the
        state of Great Passion.[2]

27. Here there is no beginning, no middle, no end,
    Neither samsara nor nirvana.
    In this state of highest bliss
    There is neither self nor other.

28. Whatever you see, that is it,
    In front, behind, in all the ten directions.
    Even today let your master make an end of delusion!
    There is no need to ask of anyone else.

29. The faculties of sense subside,
    And the notion of self is destroyed.
    O friend, such is the Body Innate.
    Ask for it clearly of your master.

30. Where thought is held and breath passes hence,
    That is the highest bliss.
    Elsewhere one goes nowhere.

31. Now it is a matter of self-experience,
    So do not err with regard to it.
    To call it existence or non-existence or even stage of bliss
        would impose a limitation.

32. Know your own thought completely, O yogin!
    Like water meeting with water.

[1] All beings are conceived as belonging to one or other of five Buddha-families, the Vajra-family, the Tathagata-family, the Lotus-family, the Gem-family and the Karma-family. Of these five families the Five Tathagatas as they appear below in 'The Fivefold Manifestation' are the family-heads.

[2] This refers directly to the ritual of union. See p. 221 above: "those who know how, remove passion by means of passion itself." This is a constantly recurring idea. "Those things by which men of evil conduct are bound, others turn into means and gain thereby release from the bonds of existence. By passion the world is bound and by passion it may be released." (Hevajratantra, Part II, Chapter 2.)

33. How by meditation should one fondly gain release?
And why accept such falsehood?
Have confidence in the word of your good master.
This is the advice that I Saraha give.

34. The nature of the sky is originally clear,
But by gazing and gazing the sight becomes obscured.
Then when the sky appears deformed in this way,
The fool does not know that the fault's in his own mind.

35. Through fault of pride he does not see truth,
And therefore like a demon he maligns all ways.
The whole world is confused by schools of thought,
And no one perceives his true nature.

36. They do not perceive the true basis of mind,
For upon the Innate they impose a threefold falsification.[1]
Where thought arises and where it dissolves,
There you should abide, O my son.

37. For one who thus ponders the truth without its true basis,
A master's instruction would make everything clear.
Saraha says, O fool, surely know,
The diversity of existence is but a form of thought.

38. One's own true nature cannot be explained by another,
But it is revealed by one's master's instruction.
There exists in it not an atom of evil,
Both dharma and non-dharma are cleansed and consumed.

39. When one's own mind is cleansed,
Then one's master's good qualities may enter the heart.
It is in knowledge of this that Saraha sings,
Paying no regard to tantra or mantra.

40. Men are bound by karma and by release from karma the
mind is released.
And by this release of the mind they gain for a certainty
this highest Nirvana.

[1] The threefold falsification is that of perceiver, thing perceived and
act of perceiving.

41. Mind is the universal seed.
    Both Samsara and Nirvana spring forth from it.
    Pay honour to this that like a wish-granting gem
    Gives all desirable things.

42. Thought bound brings bondage, and released brings
    release,
    Of that there is no doubt.
    By that with which fools are bound, the wise are quickly
    released.

43. When so bound it dashes in all directions,
    But released, it stays still.
    Just consider the camel, my friend.
    I see there a similar paradox.

44. Don't concentrate on yourself, restricting your breath.
    Fie, yogin, don't squint at the end of your nose.
    O fool, hold fast to the Innate,
    And abandon the clinging bonds of existence.

45. Bring together in thought the restless waves of breath.
    Then know the true nature of the Innate,
    And this becomes still of itself.

46. When the mind goes to rest
    And the bonds of the body are destroyed,
    Then the one flavour of the Innate pours forth
    And there is neither outcast nor brahmin.

47. Here is the sacred Jumna and here the River Ganges,
    Here are Prayaga and Benares, here are Sun and Moon.

48. I have visited in my wanderings shrines and other places
    of pilgrimage,
    But I have not seen another shrine blissful like my own
    body.

49. Lotuses in clusters with leaves and blossoms and
    fragrance and petals and tendrils,
    Abandon this discrimination, O Fool, do not torment
    yourself and cling to such fondness.

50. As objects of desire mantras and treatises go to destruction.
Ask, O thou of no family,[1]
For Brahma and Vishnu and all the three worlds return here to their source.

51. Know the taste of this flavour which consists in absence of knowledge.
Those who recite commentaries do not know how to cleanse the world.

52. Listen, my son; this taste cannot be told by its various parts.
For it is free from conceits, a state of perfect bliss, in which existence has its origin.

53. It is the very last segment that remains of the creation of illusion,[2]
Where intellect is destroyed, where mind dies and self-centredness is lost.
Why encumber yourself there with meditation?

54. A thing appears in the world and then goes to destruction.
If it has no true existence, how may it appear again?
If it is free from both manifestation and destruction, what then arises?
Stay! Your master has spoken.

55. Look and listen, touch and eat,
Smell, wander, sit and stand,
Renounce the vanity of discussion,
Abandon thought and be not moved from singleness.

56. Those who do not readily drink the ambrosia of their master's instruction,
Die of thirst in the desert of multitudinous treatises.

57. Abandon thought and thinking and be just as a child.
Be devoted to your master's teaching, and the Innate will become manifest.

[1] See v. 26 above.
[2] The idea of the last segment of phenomenal existence comes from analogy with the moon, which likewise grows to its developed form only to wane once more.

58. It is devoid of names and other qualities;
    I have said it cannot be known by discussion.
    So how may the Supreme Lord be described?
    It is like a maiden's experiencing of bliss.

59. Completely devoid of the notions of being and non-being,
    It is there that the whole world is absorbed.
    For when the mind abides motionless,
    One is released from the toils of existence.

60. So long as you do not recognize the Supreme One in
        yourself,
    How should you gain this incomparable form?
    I have taught that when error ceases,
    You know yourself for what you are.

61. One should not think of molecules or atoms;
    It is this supreme bliss that pours forth unceasingly as
        existence.
    Error such as that is madness, says Saraha.
    Know but the pure and perfect state!

62. He is at home, but she goes outside and looks.
    She sees her husband, but still asks the neighbours.
    Saraha says, O fool, know yourself.
    It is not a matter of meditation, or concentration or the
        reciting of mantras.

63. "If one's master just speaks, would one know every-
        thing?
    And without knowing everything would one gain
        release?"
    So they wander about gaining experience,
    But they know not the Innate. They just amass evil.

64. Enjoying the world of sense, one is undefiled by the world
        of sense.
    One plucks the lotus without touching the water.
    So the yogin who has gone to the root of things,
    Is not enslaved by the senses although he enjoys them.

65. One may worship a divinity, and (in trance) even his
    form may be seen.
    But one is still oneself subject to death, for what can he
    do?
    All this does not destroy the Samsara,
    "Without perseverance", they say, "there is no escape."

66. "One fixes the eyes, obstructs the thought, restrains the
    breath.
    This is the teaching of our lord and master."
    But when the flow of his breath is quite motionless
    And the yogin is dead, what then?

67. So long as one is in the sphere of the senses,
    Desire[1] pours forth of itself.
    Who can deal with this awkward problem?
    In so far as one is within something, one cannot see it
    (from without).

68. All these pandits expound the treatises,
    But the Buddha who resides within the body is not
    known.
    Comings and goings are not destroyed in that way.
    But they shamelessly say: "We are pandits."

69. He who among living men never grew old,
    Such a one would be free from old age and death.
    (This is their impossible aim.)
    But at one's master's word the mind is cleared.
    What treasure is there other than this?

70. He who does not enjoy the senses purified,
    And practises only the Void,
    Is like a bird that flies up from a ship
    And then wheels round and lands back there again.[2]

[1] The translation of this word is doubtful, as the reading is uncertain.
The Tibetan versions translate it as 'inaction' (Sanskrit: akarman).

[2] He who practises only the Void, that is to say, he who pursues
Wisdom alone, and neglects Compassion, may well experience flights
of ecstasy, but he makes no more real progress than a bird who flies
up only to return from where it started. See the last verses on p. 239.

71. But do not be caught by attachment to the senses,
    Saraha says.
    Consider the fish, the butterfly, the elephant, the bee and
    the deer.[1]

72. Whatever pours forth from the mind,
    Possesses the nature of the owner.
    Are waves different from the water?
    Their nature like that of space is one and the same.

73. Who speaks, who listens, and what is confided?
    Like the dust in a dusty tunnel,
    That which arises in the heart goes to rest in the heart.

74. Even as water entering water
    Has an identical savour,
    So faults and virtues are accounted the same
    As there's no opposition between them.

75. Do not cling to the notion of voidness,
    But consider all things alike.
    Indeed even the husk of a sesame-seed
    Causes pain like that of an arrow.

76. One thing is so, another is not so.
    The action is like that of a wish-granting gem.
    Strange how these pandits go to grief through their own
    errors,
    For in self-experience consists this great bliss.

77. In it all forms are endowed with the sameness of space,
    And the mind is held steady with the nature of this same
    sameness.
    When the mind ceases thus to be mind,
    The true nature of the Innate shines forth.

78. In this house and that the matter is discussed,
    But the basis of the great bliss is unknown.
    The world is enslaved by thought, Saraha says,
    And no one has known this non-thought.

[1] The commentary explains that each of these creatures is caught
because of its particular attachment to one of the senses: the fish by
taste, the butterfly by colour, the elephant by touch, the bee by smell
and the deer by sound.

79. There is one Lord revealed in many scriptures,
    Who becomes clearly manifest at your wish.

80. Oneself is the Lord, and another is the enemy.[1]
    This is the notion they have in their houses.
    In eating the one, he consumes all the other,
    But she goes outside and looks for her master.

81. He is not seen to come,
    Nor known to stay or go;
    As signless and motionless the supreme Lord is known.

82. If you do not abandon coming and going,
    How may you gain this rare one, this splendour?

83. Thought is pure when consigned to the forehead.[2]
    Do not then conceive differences in yourself.
    When there is no distinction between Body, Speech and
        Mind,
    Then the true nature of the Innate shines forth.

84. There how should another arise,
    Where the wife without hesitation consumes the house-
        holder?
    This yogini's action is peerless.

85. She consumes the house-holder and the Innate shines
        forth.
    There is neither passion nor absence of passion.
    Seated beside her own, her mind destroyed, thus I have
        seen the yogini.

    [1] There is but one Lord universally manifest, but fools, conscious of
their own ego think: "I am the Lord", that is to say, "I am right in
my views and the others who oppose me are wrong." But in consuming
the notion of one's own lordship, that is to say, one's own selfhood, all
notions of otherness are consumed at the same time. The last line of the
verse refers back to verse 62.
    [2] This is again a reference to the psycho-physical process. Thought
(*citta*) in its pure state is the Thought of Enlightenment (*bodhicitta*),
which is conceived as ascending the central vein (see p. 227, note), to
the head. Its arrival here corresponds with the fourth stage of bliss
(see p. 225, note).

86. One eats and drinks and thinks what occurs to the
    thought.
    It is beyond the mind and inconceivable, this wonder of
    the yogini.

87. Here Sun and Moon lose their distinction,
    In her the triple world is formed.
    O know this yogini, perfecter of thought and unity of the
    Innate.

88. The whole world is tormented by words
    And there is no one who does without words.
    But in so far as one is free from words
    Does one really understand words.

89. The same without as within,
    Firmly established at the 14th stage,[1]
    The bodiless form is concealed in the body.
    He who knows this is therein released.

90. I used to recite (the text-book, which begins with the
    words), "Let there be success".
    But I drank the elixir and forgot it.
    There is but one word that I know now,
    And of that, my friend, I know not the name.

91. At the moment of the embrace does he then win the
    great bliss,
    Who does not comprehend that everything is of his own
    nature?
    He is like a thirsty deer that runs for water which is but
    a mirage.
    It dies of thirst, and how should he obtain the divine
    waters?

---

[1] There was a constant tendency to add to the traditional number of
stages to be traversed by the bodhisattva, for one might indicate
thereby the superiority of Vajrayana over Mahayana. The number
grows from ten to twelve, then a thirteenth is added and finally a
fourteenth.

92. The five skandhas, the five material elements, the twelve
sense-fields, the six faculties of sense and their spheres,
these with their various modifications are the water.
In these doha-verses which are altogether new nothing
is anywhere concealed.

93. So pandits, please have patience with me,
For here there is no hesitating.
That which I have heard by the word of my master,
Why should I speak of it secretly?

94. That blissful delight that consists between lotus and
vajra,
Who does not rejoice there?
In the triple world whose hopes does it fail to fulfil?

95. This moment may be the bliss of Means or of both[1]
(Wisdom and Means),
And by the favour of their master and by merit it is
known by a few.

96. It is profound, it is vast.
It is neither self nor other.
O know this self-experience
Of the Innate in the Fourth Moment!

97. Even as the moon makes light in black darkness,
So in one moment the supreme bliss removes all
defilement.

98. When the sun of suffering has set,
Then arises this bliss, this lord of the stars.
It creates with continuous creativity,
And of this comes the mandala-circle.[2]

99. See thought as thought, O fool, and leave all false views,
Gain purification in bliss supreme,
For here lies final perfection.

[1] Enlightenment may be realized by the yogin alone, who represents
Means, or by means of the ritual involving both yogin and yogini, who
are Means and Wisdom in symbol.
[2] The mandala here represents the whole of phenomenal existence.

100. Question not with hesitation.
   Release this elephant which is your mind,
   That he may drink the river-waters
   And stay on the bank at his pleasure.

101. Held in the trunk of the elephant that now represents the
      senses,
   One may appear as lifeless,
   But the yogin like a nimble rider slips away and goes.

102. As is Nirvana, so is Samsara.
   Do not think there is any distinction.
   Yet it possesses no single nature,
   For I know it as quite pure.

103. Do not sit at home, do not go to the forest,
   But recognize mind wherever you are.
   When one abides in complete and perfect enlightenment,
   Where is Samsara and where is Nirvana?

104. O know this truth,
   That neither at home nor in the forest does enlightenment
      dwell.
   Be free from prevarication
   In the self-nature of immaculate thought!

105. "This is myself and this is another."
   Be free of this bond which encompasses you about,
   And your own self is thereby released.

106. Do not err in this matter of self and other.
   Everything is Buddha without exception.
   Here is that immaculate and final stage,
   Where thought is pure in its true nature.

107. The fair tree of thought that knows no duality,
   Spreads through the triple world.
   It bears the flower and fruit of compassion,
   And its name is service of others.

108. The fair tree of the Void abounds with flowers,
    Acts of compassion of many kinds,
    And fruit for others appearing spontaneously,
    For this joy has no actual thought of another.

109. So the fair tree of the Void also lacks compasssion,
    Without shoots or flowers or foliage,
    And whoever imagines them there, falls down,
    For branches there are none.

110. The two trees spring from one seed,
    And for that reason there is but one fruit.
    He who thinks of them thus indistinguishable,
    Is released from Nirvana and Samsara.

111. If a man in need approaches and goes away hopes unful-
        filled,
    It is better he should abandon that house
    Than take the bowl that has been thrown from the door.

112. Not to be helpful to others,
    Not to give to those in need,
    This is the fruit of Samsara.
    Better than this is to renounce the idea of a self.

> He who clings to the Void[1]
> And neglects Compassion,
> Does not reach the highest stage.
> But he who practises only Compassion,
> Does not gain release from toils of existence.
> He, however, who is strong in practice of both,
> Remains neither in Samsara nor in Nirvana.
>
> *Saraha, Dohākosha*

[1] These are verses 16 and 17 of Shahidullah's version, but in that
position they interrupt the context.

THE ATTAINMENT OF THE REALIZATION OF WISDOM AND MEANS

by

Anangavajra

189.

SALUTATION TO VAJRASATTVA!

Having made salutation again and again to him who consists of Wisdom and Means, of him I now speak, in whom there arises the threefold body of Buddhahood: the matchless Dharma-Body, pure in essence and untrammelled by the whole veil of unreal phenomena, the Sambhoga-Body which is the basis for the spreading of the Good Law, the Nirmana-Body which is effected in diverse forms. Of him I Anangavajra shall now briefly speak for the benefit of all beings who are ignorant of his true nature.

The wise explain phenomenal existence, that deluder of simple minds, as the result of a false construction, the essence of which is the notion of existence. Thence there arises continually and under varying forms a whole mass of defilements, so hard to bear, and a vast accumulation of karma. For those whose minds thus cling to falsehood these two produce perpetual suffering of diverse kinds, of which the chief are death and birth. So long as the notion of existence remains the fixation of men who tarry in the prison of phenomenal life, what good can they do themselves or others in such deprivation of wisdom? And so the wise who desire to bring joy to the triple world and remove their own mental confusion must abandon altogether the fixation of this notion of existence. But having abandoned the fixation of existence, the wise man should not conceive a state of non-existence, for if indeed he should discriminate between these two, his conceits are not destroyed. Far preferable is a conception of existence, but never the conceit of non-existence; a burning lamp may be extinguished, but if it is already extinguished, then what course should one pursue? So long as one conceives of existence, one remains aware of existence (and there is always the possibility of realizing its true nature), but there can be no realization of the end of space which has here no beginning, and nothing can be realized as mere non-existence, for it would be deprived of all means. It would be useless to oneself and others, for it would be as non-existent as flowers that grow in the sky. Thus those who desire the fruit of Buddhahood should renounce the notion of existence because it is deluding like a magical display, but they should also renounce the notion of non-existence, for it is non-existent. O Wise Ones, do ye now hearken, for in so far as one renounces both extremes, the state in which one abides is neither Samsara nor Nirvana, for one has renounced these two.

The non-substantiality of things which is realized by reflection and by discriminating between the act of knowing and what is known, is called the essence of Wisdom.

Because one is passionately devoted to all beings who have failed to extricate themselves from a whole flood of suffering, this passionate devotion of which their suffering is the cause is known as Compassion. In that one thereby brings a man to the desired end by a combination of appropriate measures; it is also called the Means.

The mingling of both, which is like that of water and milk, is known as Wisdom-Means in a union free of duality. It is the essence of Dharma, to which nothing may be added and from which nothing may be withdrawn. It is free from the two notions of subject and object, free from being and non-being, from characterizing and characteristics; it is pure and immaculate in its own nature. Neither duality nor non-duality, calm and tranquil it consists in all things, motionless and unflurried; such is Wisdom-Means which may be known intuitively. It is this that is called the supreme and wondrous abode of all Buddhas, the Dharma-sphere, the divine cause of the perfection of bliss. It is Nirvana Indeterminate (apratiṣṭhitanirvāṇa) and is frequented by the Buddhas of the Past, Present and Future; it is the blissful stage of self-consecration (svādhiṣṭhāna), the beatitute of the Perfection of Wisdom. The three Buddha-bodies, the three Buddhist vehicles, mantras in their innumerable thousands, mudras and mandala-circles, phenomenal existence and that which transcends it, all

arise from the same source; gods and asuras and men, dis-
embodied spirits and whatever else exists, all spring from here
and return here to their cessation. It abides always in all
things like a wish-granting gem; it is the final stage of Enjoyment and Release. It is here that the Blessed Ones met in
times past and so became Buddhas, and it is here that those
intent on the good of the world become Buddhas now and will
always do so in future. It is called the Great Bliss, for it consists of bliss unending; it is the Supreme One, the Universal
Good, the producer of Perfect Enlightenment. The great sages
define this truth, which is the supreme bliss of self and others,
as the union of limitless Compassion which is intent alone on
the destruction of all the world's suffering, and of perfect
Wisdom which is free from all attachment and is an accumulation of knowledge which may not be reckoned, so great is its
diversity.

II

And now in order that the jewel of this truth may be
obtained, I Anangavajra, my mind penetrated with compassion, will discourse a little concerning the Means, but
briefly, for it is just as has been taught by the Buddhas of old.
It should benefit all those who are bewildered by the delusion
of phenomenal existence which is so hard to destroy. But even
Buddhas may not speak on this matter, saying that this is thus,
for since it must be realized intuitively, it cannot be contained
in words. And so it has been revealed as a process by means of
the practices of many sutras and mantras by those Buddhas
of the Past, Present and Future who have brought joy to the
world. But this process itself can in no wise express the actual
knowledge of tradition and so on, and since there is no
connection between the sound and the true meaning, it merely
shows the characteristics of a particular treatise. So a wise
man must resort to a good master, for without him the truth
cannot be found even in millions of ages. And if truth is not
found, the final goal can never be reached, just as without a
seed a plant will not grow even in the best and clearest of
fields. So when in the course of life one comes upon masters
with this truth, those who are teachers of Wisdom-Means,
firm in line of succession, wondrous as a wish-granting gem

and established in the path that is free from querulous thought, one should honour them to the best of one's ability if final perfection of the self is really one's aim. It is by means of their splendour that the bliss of infinite enlightenment is gained which is the highest goal possible for all beings in this triple world of moving and motionless things. So good men who desire their own perfection always pay with their whole being full honour to their master, who is the bestower of infinite rewards. They abandon envy and malignancy, and pride and self-conceit, their determination set on enlightenment and the concept of weariness renounced, and thus they always honour their guru, master of the world, who bestows success in all things. They are zealous in conduct and unwavering in mind and without thought for their own affairs they bow with head to his feet three times with great devotion. Thereby they gain by the grace of their guru and without any obstruction that truth supreme which is taught by all the Buddhas. It is eternal, resplendent and pure, the abode of the conquerors, the divine substance in all things and the source of all things. Just as a sun-stone shines brightly from the proximity of the sun-light which dispels the enclosing darkness, even so does the jewel of a pupil's mind, freed from the murkiness of impurity, light up from the proximity of a world-teacher who is bright with the fire of the practice of truth. As soon as he becomes thus enlightened, ablaze with the jewel of truth, this happy pupil is quickly approached by the Buddhas of the ten directions whose thoughts are pervaded with compassion, and by them he is firmly consecrated as a perfect Buddha. From the consecration of these Buddhas he becomes himself the equal of all Buddhas.

Thus those who abandon the cloak of pride and envy and deceit, and firm in their resolve serve with unequalled faith their master who embodies the traditional succession, they certainly shall gain the jewel of truth, which is the abode of all Buddha-qualities, for they have won supreme enlightenment which is the possession of all the Blessed Ones.

III

Now the rite of consecration, the basis of the triple world, shall be expounded for the benefit of all practisers who aim to

reach the stage of Vajrasattva. When a wise man is consecrated in the tradition of the way of mantras, all Buddhas
become manifest to him in the mandala which is their abode.
So the thoughtful man who fears the loss of this sacramental
experience does not let go of the Lord of the realms of endless
worlds, when once he has attained the process of self-
consecration. By perfected Buddhas it is taught that in the
mantra-way there exists in its absolute aspect that sacramental experience of Vajrasattva and the other divine beings
which is so hard to withstand. And so a son of the Conquerors
for the sake of this consecration strives with all his might, and
with the observation of all due ceremony approaches his vajra-
guru, that ocean of all good qualities. Having found a yogini
with wondrous eyes and endowed with youth and beauty, he
should deck her with fair raiment, and garlands and the scent
of sandal-wood, and commit her to his master, and together
with her he should honour and praise him with all his might,
using scents and garlands and milk and other kinds of offerings. Then placing in all faith his knee upon the ground, he
should beseech his master with this hymn of praise, stretching
forth his hands in supplication:

"Hail to thee, womb of the Void, who art free of all conceits,
omniscient one, thou mass of knowledge, knowledge per-
sonified, all hail to thee!

"Thou, teacher of the pure essence of truth which makes an
end of worldly knowledge, O Vajrasattva, born of the non-
substantiality of all things, hail to thee!

"From you, O Lord, there ever rise into existence Buddhas
and Bodhisattvas, who possess as their good qualities the
great perfections, O Thought of Enlightenment, hail to thee!

"From you, O Lord of the world, come the Three Jewels and
the Great Way and the whole triple world with its moving and
motionless things. All hail to thee!

"Thou art wondrous as a wish-granting gem for producing
the welfare of the world; O Buddha-Son, most blessed, who
dost command all the blessed ones, all hail to thee!

"It is by your grace, O ocean of good qualities, that I have
known the truth, and now, O Omniscient One, may thou
favour me with the vajra-consecration.

"Do thou favour me with the secret of all Buddhas, even as

it has been taught by the Supreme Vajra of Thought, embodiment of the Vajra of the Dharma.

"If once I leave your lotus-feet, I have no other way to go.
Therefore do thou, Lord, conqueror of the foe which is samsara,
have compassion."

Then the worthy vajra-guru, filled with sympathy and
intent on good, makes manifest his compassion and calls the
pupil into the mandala. It is strewn with the five kinds of
delectable things resplendent with a canopy spread above;
it resounds with bells and cymbals, and is pleasant with
flowers and incense and garlands and heavenly perfumes; it
is the most wondrous resort of Vajrasattva and other divine
beings and is prepared for union with the yogini. Then joining
with the yogini the most worthy master places the Thought of
Enlightenment in the lotus-vessel, which is the abode of the
Buddhas. Next he consecrates the pupil, now joined with the
yogini, with chowries and umbrellas held high and with
propitious songs and verses. Having thus bestowed upon him
the consecration, that excellent gem, he should give him the
fivefold sacrament, delightful, divine, essentially pure. It
consists of the precious jewel, with camphor, red sandal-wood
and vajra-water, and as fifth component the empowering
mantra. "This is your sacrament, Beloved, prescribed by
former Buddhas. Do thou protect it always, and hearken now
to the vow you must keep. Never must you take life, and
never abandon the Three Jewels, and never abandon your
master. This is the vow you transgress at your peril."

Then he should give leave of departure to that pupil, who
having been thus consecrated with the Thought of Enlightenment, has become freed from his evil ways and is now the
foremost son of the Buddhas. "O best of beings, until you
enter final enlightenment, cause the excellent wheel of the
Law to revolve everywhere throughout all the quarters. He
who is the essence of Wisdom-Means is said to be like a
wish-granting gem, for he is free of suffering and free of
attachment, so serve now the cause of living beings!"

Having thus received the consecration and his leave to
depart, joyful and content, he should pronounce pleasant
words, which cause joy to the world. "Today my birth has
proved fruitful, and fruitful is now my life. Today I am born

in the Buddha-family, and I am now a son of the Buddhas. Thou, O Lord, hast rescued me from the ocean of ages, vast in its terror, and disturbed with the waves which are our births, from the mud of molestations, which is so hard to cross. I know that it is by your grace that I have emerged; I know that I am free from desire, and that all past influences are cast away." Then falling with devotion at his master's feet, his eyes wide-open with joy, he adds: "And may thou please inform me whatever thing thou desirest most." Then spontaneously his compassionate master should accept the offer, for it will tend to the destruction of the pupil's acquisitiveness and will be for his good. Thus the pupil, having gained the prize he sought, should present his gift with praise and worship, and once again should supplicate his master: "Now upon me has descended your favour, O foremost of Buddhas, and by this favour of yours I achieve the highest enlightenment, such as is your possession. And having gained highest Buddhahood, that stage which is praised by all pre-eminent ones, there I shall establish all beings who wander in the triple world."

Having understood in one's heart a pupil's aspiration, one should grant him consecration in conformity with the methods prescribed, and then in one's own devotion to a discipline so vast and profound, one should give him, also verbally, the jewel of consecration. And he, now a true yogin, who has received the great consecration of the Thought of Enlightenment, which is the matchless enjoyment of perfection of the Bearer of the Vajra, the acquisition of Lakshmi, having received his leave of departure and with his mind set on gaining victory over that evil foe which is the triple world, should raise his thought to enlightenment and pursue the great and immaculate way.

Prajñopāyaviniścayasiddhi, ch. 1–3

Note on The Mandala

The Mandala is a circle of symbolic forms, which is either just mentally produced for special purposes of meditation, or actually marked out on the ground for the purpose of special ritual. Its function is always the same, namely as a means towards the reintegration of the practitioner.

There is a vast variety of different sets of symbolic forms, but they

*The Five Buddhas and the Four Goddesses
and some of the Elements of the Universe they symbolize*

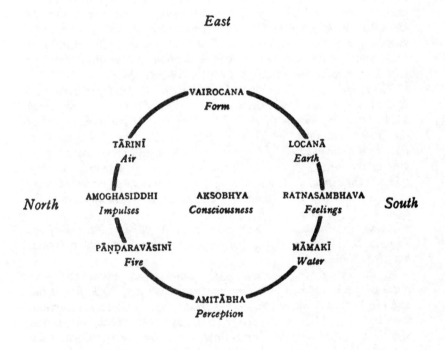

East

VAIROCANA
Form

TĀRINĪ   LOCANĀ
Air   *Earth*

North   AMOGHASIDDHI   AKSOBHYA   RATNASAMBHAVA   South
        Impulses   *Consciousness*   *Feelings*

PĀṆḌARAVĀSINĪ   MĀMAKĪ
Fire   *Water*

AMITĀBHA
Perception

West

all follow the same fundamental pattern: that is to say, one symbol at the centre, which represents absolute truth itself, and other symbols arranged at the various points of the compass, which represent manifested aspects of this same truth. The simplest set of such symbolic forms consists of the group of the Five Buddhas or Tathagatas, who in the extract that now follows are conceived of as emanating from their respective seed-syllables (for they are each associated with a particular sound, the correct intoning of which will conjure them forth), and taking up their positions to the centre, east, south, north and west. It will also be seen that they are each associated with one of the five skandhas, with one of the five fundamental evils (wrath, passion, envy, malignity and delusion), with one of the five Wisdoms, with a particular taste, with a particular season, with a particular time of the day and with a particular substance used for sacramental purposes.

They serve therefore as symbols not only of the final perfection that is the goal of the aspirant, but also as symbols of those very evils which bind him to existence and also of his own fivefold personality and of the fivefold sacrament employed in the rite. The set of five symbolizes then both the condition of nirvana and the condition of samsara, as well as the means towards the realization of their essential identity, which is the aim of all this endeavour. The condition of perfect identity is represented by a sixth Buddha, Vajrasattva, who here appears in the head-dress of Akshobhya, the central Buddha.

These six Buddhas are associated with the various watches of the day and the different seasons, for they comprehend not only all space, but also all time.

At the intermediate points of the compass are manifested four goddesses, who represent the four material elements, earth, fire, water and air, the basic constituents of material things. This set is completed with a fifth goddess at the centre, who represents space, but is also identical in essence with Vajrasattva, for at the centre, which is the absolute, the Perfection of Wisdom itself, no distinctions can be made whatsoever.

It will be noted that she is identified with the Sanskrit vowel-series, while the Buddhas between them make up the whole Sanskrit consonantal series. The mandala therefore symbolizes all sound in addition to all the things already mentioned above, for the right employment of intoned sound has now become a very important part of Buddhist practice at this stage.

This short note should serve as a sufficient guide to the extract that follows. The whole matter is discussed at length in the introduction to the Hevajratantra, shortly to appear.

THE FIVEFOLD MANIFESTATION

190.

Having made obeisance to Vajrasattva, unevolved and supreme, I shall expound in brief for the welfare of my pupils the fivefold manifestation.

With the mantra: OM ĀḤ HŪM one ensures protection for the site, for oneself and for the performance. Then upon this site which has been prepared with perfumes and so on one should worship the Five Buddhas and the Five Yoginis in the centre of the four-sided mandala.

There in the centre one envisages the syllable PAM of many colours. This turns into a fair eight-petalled lotus of many colours with the red syllable RAM at its centre. This becomes a solar disk, upon which is a dark-blue HŪM whence arises Akshobhya with one face and two arms, in the crossed-legged-posture and making the 'earth-touching' gesture. His body exhibits the 32 major and the 80 minor marks of perfection, for it is the repository of the whole host of excellent qualities, the ten powers, fearlessness and the rest. It is without apertures, flesh or bone, for it is neither true nor false like pure light reflected in a mirror. He is black in colour because he is permeated with great compassion and his symbol is a black vajra which embodies the five constituents of the pure absolute. He has no hair on head or body and he is clad in religious garb. His head is marked with Vajrasattva, for he is himself the essence of Vajrasattva, where there is no distinction between Void and Compassion. He also embodies cause and effect, of which the characteristic is the Void in that it comprehends all possible forms. He is the Dharma-Body because he is the embodiment of the Buddhas who are unconditioned; he is the Sambhoga-Body because he is a pure reflection; he is the Nirmana-Body because he represents the true nature of constructive consciousness; he is the Self-Existing Body (svābhāvika) because this is the single flavour of those three bodies. So it is said:

"Dharma is mind unconditioned; Sambhoga is characterized by reciprocal enjoyment;

Nirmana is that which is variously created;
Svabhavika is that which is innate in everything."

As he is undefiled by discriminating thought and so on, he is
of the Vajra-family, and the Vajra-family is undefiled by
worldlings. His external and internal bases of symbolization
are: wrath, vajra-water, midday, pungency, revealed knowledge, space, sound, the CA-series of consonants. His mantra
is: OM ĀH VAJRADHRK HŪM.

Vajrasattva, born of the syllable HŪM, is pure white with
two arms and one face; he holds a vajra and a bell. He is the
true nature of mind. He represents astringency, Autumn, the
consonantal series YA RA LA VA and the second half of the
night up to dawn. He is another name of the absolute.

Then on the eastern petal on a lunar disk appears Vairocana,
born of the syllable OM; he is white in colour with a white
disk as his symbol and makes the gesture indicating enlightenment. He embodies the skandha of form and the nature of
delusion; he is symbolized by dung; he is of the Tathagata-
family; he consists in the Mirror-like Knowledge, he represents
Winter, sweetness, the KA-series of consonants and the
morning watch. His mantra is: OM ĀH JINAJIK HŪM.

Then on the southern petal on a solar disk appears Ratnasambhava, born of the syllable TRĀM, yellow in colour with a
gem as his symbol and making the gesture of giving. He
embodies the skandha of feeling and the nature of malignity
(paiśunya); he is symbolized by blood; he is of the Gem-family;
he consists in the Knowledge of Sameness; he represents
Spring, saltiness, the TA-series of consonants and the third
watch. His mantra is: OM ĀH RATNADHRK HŪM.

Then on the western petal on a solar disk appears Amitabha,
born of the syllable HRĪH, red in colour with a lotus as his
symbol and in the pose of contemplation. He embodies the
skandha of perception and the nature of passion; he is symbolized by seed; he is of the Lotus-family; he consists in
Perceptual Knowledge; he represents Summer, bitterness, the
TA-series of consonants and the evening watch. His mantra
is: OM ĀH ĀROLIK HŪM.

Then on the northern petal on a solar disk appears Amogha-
siddhi, born of the syllable KHAM, dark-green in colour with

a crossed vajra as his symbol and making the gesture of protection. He embodies the skandha of impulses and the nature of envy (īrṣyā); he is symbolized by flesh; he is of the Karma-family; he consists in the Knowledge of Needful Activity; he represents the season of the rains, the hot taste, the PA-series of consonants and the first watch of the night. His mantra is: OM ĀḤ PRAJÑĀDHṚK HŪM. These are all seated in the cross-legged posture with two arms and one face, wearing the Ushuisha but with no hair on head or body; they are clad in religious garb and exhibit the 32 major and 80 minor marks of physical perfection, for they are repositories of the whole host of excellent qualities, the ten powers, fearlessness and the rest. Theirs are Sambhoga-Bodies, free of apertures, flesh and bones, pure light and naught else, like reflections in a mirror and free from such concepts as truth and falsehood. But these four, Vairocana, Ratnasambhava, Amitabha and Amoghasiddhi, who embody the constituents of Form, Feeling, Perception and Impulses, possess indistinguishably the Dharma-Body which is the unconditioned essence of Buddhas, and the Body of Constructive Consciousness, for they all comprise the Self-Existing Body which is the single flavour of the other three bodies. Thus in order to show that they are all mere consciousness they are signed on the head with the sign of Akshobhya, and in order to show that consciousness, which is non-substantial, is the essence of Void and Compassion, Akshobhya is signed with Vajrasattva.[1] Thereby it is asserted that the world consists of cause and effect, which is just the single flavour of Samsara and Nirvana. So it is said:

"When thought is realized as Void and Compassion indistinguishable, that indeed is the teaching of the Buddha, of the Law, of the Assembly. As sweetness is the nature of sugar and heat of fire, so voidness is the nature of all elements." And so it is said: "Thorough knowledge of Samsara is Nirvana."

On the south-eastern petal on a lunar disk appears Locana, born of a white syllable LOM, white in colour and with a disk as her symbol. She represents the element earth, belongs to the Tathagata-family and is affected by delusion. Her mantra is: OM ĀḤ LOM HŪM SVĀHĀ.

---

[1] Iconographically Vajrasattva appears as a small figure in the head-dress of Akṣobhya.

To the south-west on a lunar disk appears Mamaki, born of a black syllable MĀM, black in colour and with a black vajra as her symbol. She represents the element water, belongs to the Vajra-family and is affected by wrath. Her mantra is: OM ĀH MĀM HŪM SVĀHĀ.

To the north-west on a lunar disk appears Panduravasini, born of the syllable PĀM, red in colour and with a lotus as her symbol. She represents the element fire, belongs to the Lotus-family and is affected by passion. Her mantra is: OM ĀH PĀM HŪM SVĀHĀ.

To the north-east on a lunar disk appears Tarini, born of the syllable TĀM which is gold and dark-green in colour, herself dark-green and with a dark-coloured lotus as her symbol. She represents the element air, belongs to the Karma-family and is affected by Envy.

These four are sixteen years old, endowed with uncommon loveliness and youth as though they were beauty herself. Like the Buddhas they are possessed of the essence of the four Buddha-bodies; they are ravishing to the mind, the repository of the qualities of all the Buddhas and of the very nature of the Five Tathagatas.

In their midst is Nāyikā, the essence of ĀLI (the vowel series); she possesses the true nature of Vajrasattva and is Queen of the Vajra-realm. She is known as the Lady, as Such-ness, as Void, as Perfection of Wisdom, as limit of Reality, as Absence of Self.

Advāyavajrasaṃgraha, pp. 40–43

AN EVOCATION OF PRAJÑĀPĀRAMITĀ

191.

One should envisage in one's own heart the syllable DHĪH set upon a lunar disk, and with the rays that emerge from it one should arouse all gurus and Buddhas and Bodhisattvas and drawing them in before oneself, one should envisage them as sitting there in their various positions. Then one should mentally confess one's sins and rejoice at such merit as has accrued, take the threefold refuge, rouse the thought of enlightenment, dedicate merit and beg for pardon. Next one should develop friendliness, compassion, sympathetic joy and even-mindedness. Then with these words one should meditate the Void: "I possess in my essence the adamantine nature which is knowledge of the Void." Next one should envisage that syllable DHĪḤ which is set on the lunar disk, as transformed into the Lady Prajñāpāramitā. She bears a head-dress of twisted hair; she has four arms and one face. With two of her hands she makes the gesture of expounding the dharma and she is adorned with various jewelled ornaments. She blazes like the colour of gold and in her (second) left hand she holds a blue lotus with a Prajñāpāramitā-book upon it. She wears various garments both below and above and with her (second) right hand she makes the gesture of fearlessness. She is seated cross-legged on the lunar disk and on a red lotus. Envisaging her thus, one should perform the act of identification: "Such as is the Lady Prajñāpāramitā, even so am I. Such as am I, even so is the Lady Prajñāpāramitā." Next one should set out the mantras: at the throat OṂ DHĪḤ, on the tongue OṂ GĪḤ and on the ears OṂ JRĪḤ.

Then in one's own heart one should imagine a red eight-petalled lotus, which arises from the syllable ĀḤ and is complete with pericarp and filament, and upon the pericarp and petals of this lotus one should mentally inscribe in yellow these words:

on the eastern petal:	HOMAGE
on the south-eastern petal:	TO THE LADY
on the southern petal:	PRAJÑĀPĀRAMITĀ
on the south-western petal:	WHOSE VIRTUE IS IMMORTALITY
on the western petal:	WHO RESPONDS TO LOVING DEVOTION
on the north-western petal:	WHO IS REPLETE WITH THE KNOWLEDGE OF ALL THE TATHAGATAS
on the northern petal:	WHO IS LOVING TOWARDS ALL
on the north-eastern petal:	OṂ DHĪḤ

Then

on the eastern side of the pericarp:	ŚRU
on the south-eastern side:	TI

on the southern side:	SMṚ
on the south-western side:	TI
on the western side:	VI
on the north-western side:	JA
on the northern side:	YE
on the north-eastern side:	SVĀHĀ

Having thus set out these mantra-words, one should recite them and meditate upon them—for a day, or for a week, for six months or a year. Thereby one becomes possessed of wisdom.

Sādhanamālā

THE MANDALA CONCEIVED WITHIN

192.

Caṇḍālī[1] blazes at the navel,
She burns the Five Tathagatas,
She burns Locana and the others,
AHAM is burned and the Moon is melted.

Caṇḍa is explained as Wisdom, that is to say the left vein,[2] Ālī is explained as Means, that is to say the right vein, Caṇḍālī means these two united in accordance with one's master's word.

The word 'navel' indicates the centre and the centre here is Avadhūtī, and here Caṇḍālī burns. She burns with the great fire of passion the five skandhas of the person, and earth and the other four elements of the material world. And when AHAM (=I) is burned, which means when such notions as I and mine are consumed, then there flows and arises the knowledge of great bliss.

[1] The Tibetan for Caṇḍālī is gTum-mo, translatable as 'mystic heat'. It may be remembered that the Tibetans employed the 'mystic heat' technique in order to keep the body physically warm. See Alexandra David-Neel, *With Mystics and Magicians in Tibet*, Chapter 6.

[2] See p. 227, note.

By no one may the Innate be explained,
In no place may it be found,
It is known of itself by merit,
And by due attendance on one's master.

Hevajratantra, from ch. 1

THE STORY OF TANTI

193.

In the country of Sondhonagara there was a weaver who had many sons. By doing weaving in that country their father became extremely rich. He married his sons to wives of good family and his own family increased greatly in that country. Then his wife died and the weaver himself, now eighty-nine years old, was aged, decrepit and weakened in body, and used to go to his daughters-in-law for sustenance one at a time. But they all used to chide him and laugh at him for the habits brought on by his age. Then all his daughters-in-law took counsel together, saying: "It upsets people to see this old father-in-law of ours and we are ourselves accumulating evil karma by our treatment of him, so let us build him a thatched hut in the garden, and having settled him there, we will take it in turns to carry him food." They all agreed and arranged things in this manner.

Now the Master Jalandhara chanced to arrive in that country, and he went to the house of the eldest son of that weaver and asked for food. He was asked to be seated, and when the wife had finished the various preparations inside, she said: "Now ask him in," and this was done. The Master Jalandhara entered and when he had finished eating, he made as if to go elsewhere. Then the wife of that weaver besought him, saying: "Master, do not go elsewhere; I beg you to sleep here." "I never sleep amongst other people," he replied. "Then please sleep in our garden," she said. So they conducted him into the garden, and the weaver brought lamps and so on, and he settled there.

The old weaver heard the sound of someone else, and asked himself who it might be. "Who is that making a noise?" he called. "I am a guest and a religious man," the Master replied, "but who are you?" "I am the father of all these weavers," he replied; "when I was young I was the true owner of this property and all this wealth, but now my sons and daughters-in-law all chide me, and being anxious lest anyone else should see me, they have hidden me away here in the garden. Even so are the things of the world without substance." Then Jalandhara said to the weaver:

> "All conditioned things are impermanent,
> All phenomenal existence is suffering,
> All dharmas lack self-existence,
> But nirvana is tranquillity and bliss.

Do you not want those things that serve as provisions for death?" "I do want them," he replied. Then Jalandhara initiated the weaver in the tantra of Hevajra, gave him instruction and started him off on the practice. After this he departed for another place.

And the other committed to mind the instruction of his master, and without saying anything to his daughters-in-law and the rest about how things had been, he carried out the instruction, and after practising for twelve years he gained many powers and no one observed them. But on one occasion, the eldest son, having woven a superb cloth of heavy silk, was diverting himself with celebrations and forgot to send food to his father. At night, however, his wife remembered, and unobserved by her husband and the other menfolk, she went to take him food. There in the hut was a great brilliance of light, and he was surrounded by fifteen maidens[1] with vast quantities of different kinds of food and with garments and adornments heaped up in great numbers and such as did not belong to the world of men. Seeing all this, she hastened back and cried to

[1] The number is fifteen because Hevajra's mandala comprises two concentric circles of four and eight female divinities respectively, one at the zenith, one more at the nadir and one as his consort at the centre. Such a mandala presents a more complex pattern than the simple form shown above consisting of just the Five Tathagatas and Four Goddesses.

her husband: "O go and see your old father." Her husband, thinking his father was dead, began to weep, but the other men came and ran into the garden to look, and they saw things just as she had seen them and were seized with amazement. Then returning indoors they talked about what had occurred, and his sons and all his other relatives said: "Things such as this are not human. It is a devil."

In the morning everyone heard about it and all the people of Sondhonagara came to look and pay him honour. And he came forth and transformed his body and became as a sixteen-year-old youth, and from his body brilliant rays of light shot forth and their eyes could not bear to look at him, for his body was like a polished mirror in which everything reflected as light. He was known everywhere as Tanti-pa and he did infinite good for the world, and finally, accompanied by a great host of the people of Sondhonagara, he entered heaven with that same body.

So by being inclined to faith and devotion and by accepting his master's instruction, this old man was able to gain in this life the perfection of the Great Symbol.

From the Stories of the 84 Perfect Ones

MILA REPA AND THE NOVICES

194.

In order to fulfil the command of his master, that chief lord of yogins, the holy Mila Repa, moved from Kyang-pen to Yolmo-Kang and settled in the tiger's cave of Singa-dzong in the forest of Singa-ling. From the very first the local deity of Yolmo was tranquil and displayed a beauteous form. She surrendered herself to his service and paid him the highest honours, so that his meditation prospered greatly.

At that time five novices from the Mon-country came to seek instruction and said to him: "By its very fearfulness there is an advantage in this place, for it is one that greatly prospers meditation. Has it so appeared to you, O Master?" In reply he sang this song, extolling the place and telling how meditation comes about:

I bow at the feet of my holy master.
It was by accumulated merit that I met with him.
And to this place, indicated by my master, I have come.
This joyous site of fields and hills within the land of Mon.
A land of grassy slopes with flowers of many hues,
With glades where fair trees dance
And monkeys ply their sports,
Where resound the many songs of birds
And bees hover in their flight,
Where day-in day-out a rainbow quivers,
Where Summer and Winter a sweet rain falls
And Spring and Autumn a thick mist clings.
It is in such a lonely place as this,
That I, the yogin Mila Repa,
Am joyous in the Clear Light of realization of the Void,
Joyous exceedingly at its many ways of appearance,
Joyous at its greatness of variety,
Joyous with a body free of harmful karma,
Joyous in confusion of diversity,
Joyous midst fearful appearances,
Joyous in my freedom from that state where distractions
    rise and pass away.
Joyous exceedingly where hardship is great,
Joyous in freedom from sickness,
Joyous that suffering has turned to be joy,
Joyous exceedingly in the mandala of spiritual power,
Joyous in the dance of bringing offerings,
Joyous in the treasure of triumphant songs now uttered,
Joyous exceedingly at the sounds and signs of multi-
    tudinous syllables,
Joyous at their turning into groups of words,
Joyous in that sphere where mind is confident and firm,
Joyous exceedingly in its spontaneous arising,
Joyous at its manifestation in diversity.

"Let a present be given to mark this meeting of you faithful pupils with so happy and contented a yogin."

So saying he initiated them and set them practising, and when the right kind of perception arose in them, he was so pleased that he sang this song, expressing the essence of good counsel:

O Master, Buddha, Body of the Law,
Unfailing teacher of the way across,
Joy of living-beings with your works of compassion,
Never parted from me, may you be my inspiration![1]

Now you practisers and learners of the doctrine who are
    seated here,
Though there be many ways of carrying out the holy law,
The practice of this profound way is the best.

When seeking to gain Buddhahood in one life-time,
Do not make much of your likes and dislikes in this life.
If much be made of them, you'll practise good and evil of all
    kinds,
And if you practise thus, you'll fall into an evil state.

When you are rendering service to your master,
Do not boastfully make much of what you've done,
If you do, then master and pupil will come to disagreement,
And if this comes to pass, you'll not gain the aim of your
    intention.

When you are keeping vows and obligations,
Do not sleep amongst the village folk,
If you sleep with them, you'll develop false ideas,
And if these arise your vows and obligations will be lost.

When you are studying the scriptures,
Let there be no intellectual conceits.
If these exist, the ashes of the five poisons[2] will start to life,
And if these arise, your virtuous disposition will become
    confused.

And when you are practising in the company of a friend,
Let not your doings and affairs be many,
If they be many, you'll distract your deep and virtuous
    intent,
And if this be distracted, the blessings of holy law will cease.

[1] Literally: "May you ever remain as my crest-jewel."

[2] The five poisons are delusion, wrath, passion, envy and malignity.
They have been referred to above in association with the Five
Tathagatas.

When practising the rites that you've received as means,
Do not use this power to vanquish demons,
For if you do, your own self will rise up as a demon,
And if this occurs, the religious practice of the townsfolk
    will prevail.[1]

And when spiritual knowledge has arisen,
Do not tell about your special powers;
If these be talked about, the language of secret signs will
    slip away,
And if this is lost, the signs that mark the way will lose
    their value.

Abandon that which you know is wrong,
Evil conduct and lying speech,
Pocketing fees at funeral rites
And giving advice that is sure to please.
Do none of this.
Less indolence and exert yourselves!

Then they asked him in what way they should exert themselves, and in reply he sang this song:

I beseech my gracious lord that he may grant us joy in our
    instruction.
Now you new and youthful pupils,
Do not squander your inheritance midst the townsfolk,
With their deceitful actions sometimes good and sometimes
    evil,
But pay attention, O my sons, to holy law.
Go not astray, but keep with me.
Gathering merit more and more, perform the practice.
There arises spiritual knowledge, the mist of grace.
But this arising is not enough, so now pray exert yourselves.

This instruction in self-exertion is given from love for you,
    so listen with attention.
When keeping a retreat midst lonely mountains,
Do not think about the entertainments of the town.

[1] Presumably this means that one would thereby debase one's
religious practice to the level of simple folk, who are chiefly interested
in the performance of exorcizing rites and so on.

If you think of them, your mind will be distracted by the
   evil one,
So summon your thoughts within and exert yourselves.

When you relax from making effort in the practice,
Think upon the uncertainty of the time of death
And be mindful of the evils of rebirth.
Thus giving no thought to pleasurable things in this life,
Be hardened, and exert yourselves.

And when you seek instruction in this profound practice,
Let there be little of the thirst for knowledge of the scholar;
If there be much of it, the ways of the lay-folk will prevail,
And if these prevail, a human life will go to waste,
So less indolence and exert yourselves.

And when spiritual knowledge manifests itself,
Do not make much of yourselves by a willingness to talk,
If you talk, the goddesses and *ḍākinīs* will be disturbed,
So practise without distraction and exert yourselves.

And when you're in the company of your master,
Do not look for faults and virtues, good and bad.
If you do, you'll see him as a mass of faults.
Just practise clarity of mind and exert yourselves.

And when you're gathered with your fellows for initiation,
Be not desirous of first place and decorations.
If you so desire, you'll disturb your vows by attachment and
   by anger,
So remain in harmony and exert yourselves.

And when you're collecting alms amidst the townsfolk,
Do not deceive these folk with falsehoods.
If they're so deceived, you'll fall yourself into an evil state,
So make your actions honest and exert yourselves.

Thus at all times and in all things,
Let not your self-esteem or own preferences prevail.
If they do, the dharma will be lost in false appearances.
Renounce all lying and deceit and exert yourselves.

To men who exert themselves I now give these precepts,
Which in themselves are beneficent,
That they may benefit both self and others.
At the centre of your heart keep generosity.

When he had sung this, they set about exerting themselves
in the practice of contemplation and in cultivating indifference
to the things of this life, and with complete faith they placed
before the master a mandala in gold and asked for instruction
in the essentials of right views, contemplation and practice in
an abbreviated form. The master replied that they should let
the gold do for their supplies, and sang this song giving the
main points of right views, contemplation and practice:

May the Lord and Master ensure by his power
That the way of right views, contemplation and practice
May be established in completed self-perfection.

For right views, realization, for practice and the fruit they
    all bear,
For each of these four there are three points to drive home.

Now if of right views these three points are explained,
One consists in uniting all appearance as thought,
One consists in the clear nature of thought itself,
One consists in the absence herein of any notion of self.

Now if of realization the three points are explained,
One consists in the transfer of mundane thought to the
    absolute,
One consists in the state of the pure bliss of knowledge,
One consists in unaffected composure.

Now if for the practice three points are explained,
One arises in the power of practising the ten virtues,
One consists in purity while abiding amidst the ten evils,
One is the pure void unaffected by adversity.

Now if for the fruit three points are explained,
Nirvana is not gained as something distinct,
Samsara is not avoided as something distinct,
One's own thought is confirmed in the Buddha-state.

Of all these three points there's one point we drive home,
And that is the point of absolute voidness.
It is done by a master who is skilled at the task.
If you speculate greatly it's not driven in,
But if you comprehend all at once, the point's driven home.

This crest-jewel of all who practise the Dharma,
The yogin has won it when it shines in his mind.
So you my pupils, let your heart rejoice!

When he had sung this, the pupils asked: "Is there then
nothing more in it than to pray earnestly to a chosen master
who is skilled in the way of instruction and never fails?"

The Master was pleased. "As for chosen masters who know
the way, they appear under these headings," he said, and sang
this song:

Master, pupil, instruction, these three,
Effort, fortitude, faith, these three,
Wisdom, Compassion, Absolute, these three,
All these are constant knowers of the way.

A holy and perfected lama is the knower of the way who
    clears the darkness;
Faith that never tires is the knower of the way that leads
    to happy states;
Realization of the five special powers is the knower of the
    way that is released from friendship and from separation.
The instruction of one's master, rightly established in
    succession, is the knower of the way that makes manifest
    the three Buddha-bodies.
The Three Jewels in which we seek protection, these are
    knowers of the way that never fail.

Led by these knowers of the way, the yogin reaches the
    Land of Great Bliss.
He abides in a condition free of perturbation, free of specu-
    lation,
His own joyous realm of self-knowledge and self-release,
His own firm foundation of sure knowledge, true knowledge.

In this desolate valley, this place where no men dwell,
The yogin's joyful song resounds as thunder,
On all sides falls sweet-sounding rain,
And the flower of Compassion spreads out its petals.
The fruit of Pure Thought has ripened to the full,
And the action of Enlightenment now pervades all things.

When he had sung this, they thought that as he was content wherever he was staying, they should invite him to their country. So they besought him, saying: "O holy master, as your calm of spirit is inviolate and there is no need for you to perform deliberate practice, please come to our country, and accepting the meritorious offerings of the generous lay-folk, benefit all beings by turning the wheel of the doctrine."

But he replied: "It is this practice of mine in the mountains that benefits all beings, and although his practice may be inviolate, the strength of a hermit consists in his remaining in the mountains," and so he sang this song:

By responding to the grace of my master we have met together,
May he bless us with a ripening of our natures and complete release.

Now, you worthy practisers of the doctrine who are seated here,
I shall sing you a song of instruction of profound import,
So be not inattentive, but surrender here your power of hearing.

The white leopard of the snowy heights,
The leopard lording it amidst the white and snowy wastes,
From others he has nought to fear,
The leopard lording it amidst the snow,
Herein his strength consists.

The eagle, royal bird of the russet crags,
Stretching his wings through the expanse of the heavens,
Of a fall down the precipice he has no fear,
The eagle's flight to the summit of the heavens,
Herein his strength consists.

Below in the waters of the ocean,
Nimbly moves the darting fish,
Of drowning he has nought to fear,
'Tis in his darting that his strength consists.

In the branches of the mountain trees of Mon
Nimbly move the monkeys, great and small,
Of tumbling down they have no fear,
It is their nature, this playfulness of every kind.

Beneath the bowers of the forest glades,
The striped Indian tiger moves with agility,
He has nought to fear of fearful things,
It is his very nature, such pride in his adroitness.

In the forest of Singala
Mila Repa practises the Void;
Of slipping from this state he has no fear,
'Tis in its long retaining that his strength consists.

Unwavering assimilation of the mandala
That purifies the elemental sphere,
Has of error nought to fear,
'Tis in adhering to the inmost essence that its strength
consists.

In assimilation of the inner practice with veins and breath
and bindu,[1]
The obstructions and the hesitations that manifest them-
selves,
Do not mean the teaching's faulty;
They are the protest of hastily departing notions.

In experiencing the power of this practice of the Innate
The many various forms appearing
Are not the false perception of a mundane mind,
But the arising in dependence of the various notions.

[1] The bindu is the point of final reabsorption, the last segment of
the moon (see p. 231, note 2), the realization of enlightenment itself. It
is called 'point' partly with reference to the mandala, of which it is
the centre, from which all emanates and to which all must return.

In the ripening of potentiality, of the act with its cause and
    effect,
To see the separate forms of good and evil,
Does not mean that one's practice is in error,
For they are clear concepts of discriminating knowledge.

As for hermits who are able to remain firm in their practice,
Their small yearnings towards the world,
Do not mean they're seeking news of it;
They're just an inner sign of the turning back of momentary
    desires.

That I, a yogin, who practises this profound way of the
    doctrine,
Should keep to mountain crags,
Does not imply hypocrisy and foolishness,
But an innate desire to practise one-pointedly.

These many songs of Mila Repa
Are not just foolishness intended for distraction,
But profound admonition for the benefit of you pupils who
    are gathered here.

When he had sung this, they said: "That is all very well, but
although you indeed dwell in the mountains, you must surely
have built up a citadel of meditation and suchlike aids against
hopes and fears."

The master replied: "The citadel of meditation and other
similar aids of mine are like this," and so sang this song:

I bow at the feet of my father, the wish-granting gem,
May he bless you, my children, with an abundance of aids.
I beg him to bring you to firm knowledge
In the divine fortress of your own body.

Frightened by fears, I built up a castle.
The voidness of absolute being, this was that castle,
And of its destruction I now have no fear.

Fearful of cold, I made up a garment,
The producing of warmth within, this was that garment,
And from cold I now have no fear.

Fearful of poverty, I sought for some wealth,
The seven glorious and inexhaustible jewels, these were that
wealth,
And from poverty I now have no fear.

Fearful of hunger, I sought for some food,
Absorption in the absolute, this was that food,
And from hunger I now have no fear.

Fearful of thirst, I sought for a drink,
The nectar of mindfulness, this was that drink,
And from thirst I now have no fear.

Fearful of melancholy, I sought for a friend,
The blissful void, this is my lasting friend,
And from melancholy I now have no fear.

Fearful of straying, I sought for a way,
The practice of two-in-one, this was that way,
And of straying I now have no fear.

So I, a yogin, complete with all desirable wealth,
Am happy wherever I stay.

At Yolmo in the tiger-cave of Singa-dzong
One trembles with fear at the roar of the tigress
And this sends one involuntarily to strict seclusion.
There arises compassion at the play of her cubs,
And this produces involuntarily the thought of enlighten-
ment.

The cries of the monkeys cling to one's mind,
And this causes involuntarily a feeling of sadness,
But at the chattering of their young one just wants to laugh,
And this produces involuntarily an elevation of spirit.

Sweet to the ear is the sad song of the cuckoo with its
tremulous note,
And one is caused to hearken involuntarily,
And the varied cries of the raven are cheering to his
neighbour the yogin.

Happy is the state of one who lives in such a spot as this,
Without the presence of a single companion, and even in
  this one is happy.
And now by the song of this rejoicing yogin
May the sufferings of all beings be removed.

And then those novices, experiencing aversion to the world
and a strong realization of the truth, did not descend from the
mountain, but took their vows, and by dint of practice reached
the very limits of perfection.

Then Mila Repa was instructed by his guardian divinity
that he should now return to Tibet and promote the welfare of
all beings by practising in a lonely mountain place, as this
would be of benefit to the doctrine and to men and animals
and all other beings, so he directed his mind towards Tibet.

Milarepa. mGur-ḥBum.

Fourth Part

TEXTS
from
CHINA AND JAPAN

by
Arthur Waley

Introduction

I feel that the following extracts from Chinese translations of Indian texts and Buddhist works written in Chinese need a few words of introduction. They make, of course, no pretension of representing in a complete or balanced way the vast field that they cover. My choice was dictated by the following considerations: first (in the case of Indian texts) it was essential that they should not exist in Sanskrit or Pali; otherwise they would naturally go into Dr. Conze's or Miss Horner's sections. I have, however, included two or three pieces which exist in Tibetan, the Chinese translations being many hundred years earlier than the Tibetan and therefore probably representing an earlier condition of the text. Then, like the other contributors to the book, I had to avoid texts that needed an undue amount of explanation or were too technical in character.

The total number of Buddhist works preserved in Sanskrit does not, I think, exceed a few hundred. Pali literature is much larger, but cannot compare in bulk to the Buddhist literature preserved in Chinese. To read all through the eighty-five volumes of the Takakusu Tripitaka for the special purpose of making these extracts was, of course, impossible; I doubt indeed whether anyone has ever read through all those very large and thick volumes. My choice was therefore confined to passages I happened to know. Mr. Snellgrove, whose Tibetan scriptures are almost as numerous as the Chinese, would, I am sure, make the same confession. Two or three passages that I knew and might have used have gone into a recently published book of mine, *The Real Tripitaka*, and were therefore not available. The main Mahayana scriptures can, with few exceptions, be read in Sanskrit. One of these exceptions is the *Vimalakirti Nirdesa* which, apart from a few fragments, exists only in Chinese and Tibetan. The scenario of this scripture sounds very promising. Vimalakirti, a lay follower of Buddha, is so holy that he can frequent without damage to his sanctity wine-shops, gambling-dens and brothels. He is also so formidable a dialectician that no one any longer dares to argue with him. He falls ill, and one after another the Bodhisattvas are told by Buddha that it would be civil if one of them went and condoled with him on his illness. Each in turn refuses, for each has on some occasion been routed in argument by Vimalakirti and is still feeling a little sore and apprehensive. Finally the Bodhisattva Manjusri consents to run the gauntlet of Vimalakirti's dialectic shafts, and it is his bedside dialogue with Vimalakirti that forms the main part of the sutra.

The fault in this plot is that it makes us expect too much from Vimalakirti's argumentative power. Modern novelists often make a similar mistake: they announce that their hero is brilliantly clever; which the reader is willing enough to believe, until the hero begins to talk. So it is with Vimalakirti: the actual quality of his discourse is not good enough. We are left wondering why all the Saints stood in such awe of him. The author of the sutra tries to make up for this defect by a series of flighty miraculous episodes, which serve only to enhance the general effect of triviality. I had counted upon including a number of extracts from this celebrated work, but could not in the end find a single passage which satisfied me. The truth is, I think, that it was the legend of Vimalakirti, with all its popular oral expansions, rather than the text of the sutra itself that fascinated the Far East.

Except in one instance I have confined myself to passages which particularly appeal to me. The exception is Seng-Ts'an's *On Trusting in the Heart*. Here I was influenced by Dr. Conze's admiration for this work as a statement of doctrine and his desire that it should be included, as also by its extreme celebrity in China and Japan. It would be possible, of course, to furnish it with an enormous commentary; but I feel that it gains, for the ordinary reader, by remaining slightly mysterious.

The enigmatic *Kung-an* (topics for meditation) of the Dhyana School, as they existed from the end of the 9th century in China, are the most conspicuous Far Eastern contributions to Buddhist literature. But these have been conveyed in such generous measure to the European reader by Dr. Suzuki, many of whose works have recently been reprinted, that there seemed to be little point in including them here. Whether, being in most cases devoid of rational content, they are worth presenting as reading-matter or should only be used in connection with the actual study and practice of Zen, is a matter upon which opinions differ. To see how intelligible sayings, with a full explanatory content, got whittled down during the 9th century till in the 10th they became irrational fragments is, historically speaking, of great interest. But such a study, to which Dr. Suzuki's friend Dr. Ui has pointed the way in his two volumes on the Zen sect, does not belong to the present book. Accordingly about half of the Dhyana excerpts that I give are, or at any rate are alleged to be, of Indian origin.

In one case (*A Hinayana Sect in China*) I have ventured to depart from the general scheme of this book by giving what is a short article rather than simply a translated extract. By using this form I have avoided an unwieldy apparatus of footnotes and explanations. The rather haphazard collection that I offer has at least two merits: the extracts do for the most part, I think, make easy and agreeable reading, and they also have the advantage of novelty, for almost all of them are now translated for the first time. The only item which I have published before is *Buddha's Pity*. This appeared in *The Temple*, which has long been out of print.

A. W.

TEXTS ORIGINATING IN INDIA

195. *The Parable of Me and Mine*

Some children were playing beside a river. They made castles of sand, and each child defended his castle and said, "This one is mine." They kept their castles separate and would not allow any mistakes about which was whose. When the castles were all finished, one child kicked over someone else's castle and completely destroyed it. The owner of the castle flew into a rage, pulled the other child's hair, struck him with his fist and bawled out, "He has spoilt my castle! Come along all of you and help me to punish him as he deserves." The others all came to his help. They beat the child with a stick and then stamped on him as he lay on the ground. . . . Then they went on playing in their sand-castles, each saying, "This is mine; no one else may have it. Keep away! Don't touch my castle!" But evening came; it was getting dark and they all thought they ought to be going home. No one now cared what became of his castle. One child stamped on his, another pushed his over with both his hands. Then they turned away and went back, each to his home.

> *Yogācāra Bhūmi Sūtra, Ch. IV. Trsl. in*
> *284 A.D. Takakusu XV, 211.*

196. *On the curing of illness contracted during Dhyāna practice*

(*The following passage describes the method of curing a Dhyana practitioner who has gone mad owing to being suddenly roused from trance by a loud noise.*)

The practitioner must first be given milk, honey and the fruit of the myrobalan-tree (harītaka). Then he must concentrate his thoughts upon the mental image of a crystal-coloured mirror, and reflected in the mirror he must see himself doing all sorts of mad things. Next the teacher must say to him: "You see yourself in the mirror doing foolish and crazy things. Your father and mother and other kinsmen all see you doing these disastrous things. Now I will tell you how to get rid of your mad folly. You must call to mind what I taught you before about the way to get rid of noise. You will remember it was as follows: Raise your tongue towards the roof of your mouth and think that there is a pearl in each of your ears. From the pointed tip of each pearl drips a balm; it is like milk dripping. This balm saturates your ears and prevents any sound from getting in. However great the noise, it is as though you had lard in your ears. Nothing can now disturb you."

When this has been accomplished he is next to imagine that a diamond canopy in nine tiers comes out of the pearls and closes in above his head. Beneath it is a diamond lotus, upon which he then sits. All around him are diamond mountains hedging him in so completely that no sound from outside can reach him. On each mountain sit seven Buddhas, who proceed to expound to him the Four Topics of Meditation[1] (Smrtyu-pasthāna), and he is so engrossed in following what they say that it would be absolutely impossible for him to hear any sound from outside.

Chih Ch'an Ping Ching. Takakusu XV, 333.
Trsl. in 455 A.D.

197. *Meditation upon the Element Water*

The teacher must say, "Now meditate upon your body and tell me in what part of it you feel that there is water." If the pupil says, "My whole body consists of water", the teacher must tell him to meditate again. If he says, "I see water appearing in my eyes", that is good. If not, the teacher must say, "Meditate upon your body only from the head upwards. Is water coming out from any part of your head?" If he says, "I see water coming out of my eyes; but it does not fall to the ground. My eyes themselves are like foaming water, and my head is also full of water", the teacher must say to

[1] On the body, the feelings, on thought, on the dharma.

him, "What is this water like? Of what kind is it?" If he replies that the water in his head is neither hot nor cold, that is very good. But if he says it is hot, that is a sign that the vision is not genuine. In that case he must be told to meditate again and see to it that the water is neither hot nor cold; for that is the true sign.

Next he must be told to meditate on his body from the throat and chest downward as far as his belly and make this part of him full of water. But he must not let the water get into his arms or legs. It should be of the colour of glass; and this time if it feels warm, that is correct, while if it feels otherwise, it is wrong.

Next he meditates upon his whole body, including his arms and legs, and if he says he feels like a leather water-bottle and also sees water filling the room and spreading to the couch on which he is sitting, and that the water is cold, that is the true vision, and any other is wrong. If he sees nothing but water anywhere, that is very good.

Next he should meditate upon the diminution of the Water Element. If, when asked at what point it is diminishing, he says, "It has entirely drained away from my body, which is now only an empty hide or like a bundle of straw that has caught fire and burnt right out", that means that he has completely eliminated the concept of Self.

> *Wu-mên Ch'an-ching . . . , by Buddhamitra.*
> *Trsl. c. 430 A.D. Takakusu XV, 328.*

198. *Judging the Character of a Dhyāna Pupil*

When a monk comes to the Dhyana-teacher for his first lesson the teacher should say to him, "Have you always observed the Monastic Rules? Have you ever committed any serious crime?" If the pupil says he has observed the Monastic Rules and has never committed a serious crime, the teacher may proceed at once to give him instruction. But if he says he has broken the Rules, the teacher must question him again, saying, "Which Rule did you break?" If it turns out to be one of the important Rules, the teacher must say, "For you to study Dhyana would be like a man whose ears or nose have been cut off insisting upon looking at himself in a mirror. You must go away and apply yourself diligently to the study of the Sutras and learn from them how to acquire Merit. In that way you may be able to plant seeds of karma that will lead you to Dhyana-instruction in some future incarnation; but in your present incarnation you must give up the idea altogether. A dead tree, however much pains one may take to lead the water to it, will never grow leaves or come into flower; still less, produce any fruit."

If it is only a minor Rule that has been broken, the teacher must show him how to perform the proper rites of expiation. As soon as the pupil is purified, if the teacher has the Heavenly Eye and has the gift of being able to look into other people's hearts, he can at once use the method of instruction suitable to the pupil's failings. If he does not possess this gift, he must either ask further questions or else go by outward signs. He may, for example, say to him, "Which of the Three Poisons lies heaviest upon you? Are you prone to lust, or to anger or to folly?" If on the other hand he goes by outward signs, he must know that the lustful man is very talkative and very credulous, his expression is happy and bland, he is expert in all the arts and is fond of acquiring information, he is passionately fond of poetry . . . he likes looking at paintings, he is mean about his own possessions, but reckless about other people's. He likes always to collect his friends round him and is never happy when alone. . . . His skin is very wrinkled and his hair tends to go white . . . it also tends to grow very thin. He takes very little sleep.

Such a man must practise the Meditation upon impurity. He must meditate upon himself as one mass of impurity from the soles of his feet to the top of his head. . . .[1]

*Tso-ch'an San-mei Ching, by Sangharaksha,
2nd cent. A.D.? Trsl. in 402 A.D.
Takakusu XV, 270 c.*

[1] There follows a long list of bodily parts. Similar signs by which to know the 'angry man' and 'the fool' are given. The 'angry man' is to meditate upon compassion, 'the fool' upon the origin of stupidity (avidya), and so on.

199. *The Bracelets*

There was a king of Benares. One summer when the weather was very hot he lay down in an upper room on a couch adorned with gold, silver and many precious stones, and made a servant massage him with ointment of sandal-wood from the Bull's Head Mountain. The servant was wearing a great many bracelets on her arms, and they jangled together while she massaged the king. The sound irritated him and he asked her to take one of the bracelets off. She did so, and there was a little less noise. She took off another, and there was less noise still. He made her go on taking them off till there was only one left, and then there was no jangling at all. When the noise stopped the king had a sudden awakening. "That is just what I ought to do with my kingdom, my ministers, subjects, concubines and attendants," he said to himself. "In fact, with all business and bother." From that moment onward he had no further worldly desires, but spent his time meditating in complete seclusion, and became a Solitary (Pratyeka) Buddha.[1]

Tso-ch'an San-mei Ching. Takakusu XV, 281.

200. *All Words are True*

"Manjusri," said the god Brahma, "is what you have been telling me the Absolute Truth?" "All words are true," said Manjusri. "Are lies then also true?" asked Brahma. "They are," said Manjusri. "And why? Good sir, all words are empty, vain and belong to no point in space. To be empty and vain and to belong to no point in space is the characteristic of Absolute Truth. So in that sense all words are true. Between the words of Devadatta[2] and the words of the Tathagata there is no difference or distinction at all. How is this? All possible words are words of the Tathagata; there is

[1] A Buddha who has had no teacher and himself does not teach others, except in so far as they are turned towards faith by admiration for his magic powers.

[2] Buddha's chief opponent.

no getting outside him or outside what is So. Whatever can be
said in words is able to say something only by dint of saying
nothing at all."

Viśesha-cinta Brahma-paripṛcchā. Takakusu
XV, 50 and 82.

201. *Buddha's Doctrine*

"World-honoured One," said Brahma to Buddha, "if in
the Tathagata's doctrine there is nothing that can be
apprehended, what profit can be got from it, that men should
speak of him as having achieved Enlightenment (Bodhi), and
should call him Buddha? " "Brahma," said Buddha, "what is
your opinion? Is the doctrine that I preach, whether concerning the sphere of action or of non-action, real or a fiction? "
"It is a fiction," said Brahma. "It is not the Truth." "What
is your opinion? " said Buddha. "Is a doctrine that is a fiction
something that exists or something that does not exist? " "If
a doctrine is only a fiction," said Brahma, "one cannot say
that it exists or that it does not exist." "Now in your opinion,"
said Buddha, "can a doctrine that neither exists nor does not
exist, possibly be apprehended? " "No, it cannot," said
Brahma. "Brahma," replied Buddha, "what the Tathagata
did apprehend when he was sitting in the Place of Enlightenment was that all the passions to which vain misconception
and error give rise are utterly void. His apprehension was that
there was nothing to be apprehended; his knowledge was that
there was nothing to be known. And how is this? The doctrine
I apprehended cannot be seen, heard, felt or known. It cannot
be taken or touched, it cannot be preached or controverted.
It transcends all concrete categories. It cannot be put into
words or into writing. . . . Brahma, from a doctrine that is
void as space itself how can you suppose that any *profit* can be
derived? " "No, World-honoured One," said Brahma. . . .
"But this teaching is one that all the world finds hard to
accept. And why? The world longs to get at Truth; but this
teaching is neither false nor true. The world longs for a doctrine; but this teaching gives neither doctrine nor absence of
doctrine. The world longs for Nirvana; but in this teaching

there is neither Birth-and-Death nor Nirvana. The world longs for a good doctrine; but here there is no good or not-good. The world longs for pleasure; but here there is neither pain nor pleasure. The world longs for the advent of a Buddha; but here no Buddha either appears or passes into Extinction. . . . To believe that within the Passions is to be found Enlightenment and that within Enlightenment are to be found the Passions is as hard as to think that fire can come out of water or water out of fire. Yet the Tathagata, by apprehending that this was the true nature of Delusion and Passion, at the same time apprehended the whole of his Doctrine."

Viśesha-cinta Brahma-paripṛcchā. Takakusu
XV, 39 and 70.

202. *The Negation of Dhyana*

"There is no thought, no action which is not substanceless," said Buddha. "In essence (t'i) both are quiescent, giving rise to nothing. . . . But if you allow the idea of quietness or extinction to arise, or again allow the idea of 'giving rise to nothing' to arise, then your Dhyana (meditation) exercise turns into one that does give rise to something; it is no longer an exercise on the plane of 'giving rise to nothing'. Bodhisattva! He who has reduced to quietness and extinction all idea of the Three Feelings,[1] the Three Activities[2] and the Three Vows,[3] for him no conception of 'giving rise' can arise. His mind is in a state of perpetual quietness and extinction; there is no achievement, no manifestation. He does not evince any outward sign of quietness or extinction; nor does he linger[4] upon the absence of such signs. . . . For him there are no Feelings, Activities or Vows. All is quietness, extinction, purity, freedom from any lingering. He does not enter samadhi (concentration), he does not linger upon the practice of Dhyana, he gives rise to nothing, he has no activity."

[1] Pain, Joy and Indifference.
[2] Bodily, verbal and mental.
[3] Monastic, lay, and those common to both.
[4] Or 'abide'. Sanskrit, pratisthā-.

"But surely," replied the Mind-king Bodhisattva, "Dhyana suppresses movement, allays all delusions, quells the disturbances of mind. Why this negation of Dhyana?"

"Bodhisattva," replied Buddha, "Dhyana is movement. 'No movement, no Dhyana' is the true Dhyana that gives rise to nothing. The real nature of Dhyana is to give rise to nothing; it lacks the outward forms of the Dhyana that does give rise. The nature of the true Dhyana is to linger nowhere, it lacks the movement that marks the lingering Dhyana. Know only that in the real nature of Dhyana there is neither stillness nor movement, and you will attain to the perfect Dhyana that gives rise to nothing at all."

Vajrasamādhi Sūtra. Takakusu IX, 368.
Said to have been translated about 400 A.D.,
but probably a Chinese composition.

203. On Reading the Dhyana Sutra
Poem by Po Chü-i

What I must learn is that all substances lack true substance;
To linger on the No-Residue[1] is to make fresh Residue.
Forget the Word even while it is spoken, and there will be nothing you do not understand;
To tell your dream while still dreaming is to pile vanity on vanity.
How expect the flower-in-the-air[2] also to produce fruit?
In mirage waters how suppose you will find real fish?
The suppression of movement is Dhyana; Dhyana itself is movement;
'No Dhyana, no movement'—that is the Truly So.[3]

Written about 835.

[1] Niravaśesha, total extinction that leaves 'no residue'.
[2] White flakes seen by people with eye disease. Common Buddhist symbol of the purely imaginary.
[3] Tathatā.

204. Nationality

Question: How can he (the practitioner of Dhyana) rid himself of attention to nationality?

Answer: If the practitioner has in mind that his country is
fertile and happy, peaceful, and the abode of many good men,
he will (during his Dhyana exercises) be continually tugged at
by the rope of attention to nationality. In order to get rid of
this fault he must turn his attention to the following points:
A man possessed of wisdom ought not to fix his thoughts upon
such a subject. And why? Because his country is consumed
time and again by the fire of many kinds of transgression.
Because there are people in it who are starving and in the last
stage of exhaustion. Let him again reflect that in no country
do things remain quiet for ever; and again, that there is no
country where the bitterness of old age, sickness and death
does not prevail. Flight from the bodily afflictions of one place
leads only to the bodily afflictions of another place. Even if
he could stop living in any kingdom at all, wherever he
escaped to he would still find misery.

In short, even if a country is fertile, happy and peaceful, so
long as the passions are still at work there, the mind will
produce misery and pain. Such a country cannot really be
called good. Only a country that can get rid of these sundry
evils, pare away the bonds of passion and so free the mind
from distress—only such a country can be called a good
country.

All living creatures are subject to two kinds of pain—pain
of the body and pain of the mind—and these two afflict them
perpetually. There can be no country without these two kinds
of affliction. Moreover every country has certain defects. In
one it is too cold, in another too hot; there is not enough to eat,
or there is a lot of illness or many robbers; or again some
countries are misruled by their king. To these countries, with
their various kinds of evil, the practitioner's heart should not
be attached.

Such is the true view which enables him to rid himself
(during Dhyana practice) of attention to nationality.

Tso-ch'an San-mei Ching. Takakusu XV,
274.

205. *The Intermediate State*

When a human being dies and is going to be reincarnated as a human being ... when the time of his death is approaching he sees these signs: he sees a great rocky mountain lowering above him like a shadow. He thinks to himself, "The mountain might fall down on top of me", and he makes a gesture with his hand as though to ward off this mountain. His brothers and kinsmen and neighbours see him do this; but to them it seems that he is simply pushing out his hand into space. Presently the mountain seems to be made of white cloth and he clambers up this cloth. Then it seems to be made of red cloth. Finally, as the time of his death approaches he sees a bright light, and being unaccustomed to it at the time of his death he is perplexed and confused. He sees all sorts of things such as are seen in dreams, because his mind is confused. He sees his (future) father and mother making love, and seeing them a thought crosses his mind, a perversity (viparyāsa) arises in him. If he is going to be reborn as a man he sees himself making love with his mother and being hindered by his father; or if he is going to be reborn as a woman, he sees himself making love with his father and being hindered by his mother. It is at that moment that the Intermediate Existence is destroyed and life and consciousness arise and causality begins once more to work. It is like the imprint made by a die; the die is then destroyed but the pattern has been imprinted.

> *Compare the Abhidharma Kośa IX, De la Vallée Poussin's translation III, 15, p. 50. The above extract is from Ch. XXXIV of the Saddharma-smṛtyupasthāna Sūtra, translated into Chinese c. 542 A.D. Takakusu XVII, 200 c.*

206. *Devas re-people the Earth*

You must know, monks, that after the floods[1] receded and the earth came back into being, there was upon the face of the earth a film more sweet-smelling than ambrosia. Do

---

[1] That put out the great fire at the end of the last cosmic cycle.

you want to know what was the taste of that film? It was like the taste of grape-wine in the mouth. And at this time the gods of the Abhasvara Heaven said to one another, "Let us go and see what it looks like in Jambudvipa now that there is earth again." So the young gods of that Heaven came down into the world and saw that over the earth was spread this film. They put their fingers into the earth and sucked them. Some put their fingers into the earth many times and ate a great deal of the film, and these at once lost all their majesty and brightness. Their bodies grew heavy and their substance became flesh and bone. They lost their magic, and could no longer fly. But there were others who ate only a little, and these did not feel themselves become heavy or lose their magic, and they could still fly about in the air. And those that had lost their magic cried out to one another in dismay, "Now we are in very sad case. We have lost our magic. There is nothing for it but to stay here on earth; for we cannot possibly get back to Heaven." So they stayed and fed upon the film that covered the earth, and gazed at one another's beauty. Then those among them that were most passionate became women, and these gods and goddesses fulfilled their desires and pleasure in one another. And this was how it was, monks, that when the world began love-making first spread throughout the world; it is an old and constant thing. And that woman should appear in the world, this too is an old thing, and not only a matter of today.

And the gods who had returned to Heaven looked down and saw the young gods that had fallen, and they came down and reproached them, saying, "Why are you behaving in this unclean way?" Then the gods on earth thought to themselves, "We must find some way to be together without being seen by others." So they made houses that would cover and hide them. Monks, that was how houses first began.[1]

(Now the people) seeing that this thing of husbands and wives had begun, hated and despised such couples and seized them with the left hand, pushed them with the right hand and drove them away. But always after two months or maybe three they would come back again. Then the people hit them

---

[1] Ekottara-āgama XXXIV (Takakusu II, 737). There is no corresponding passage in the Anguttara-nikāya. What follows is from the Ch'i-shih Ching (Takakusu I, 362).

or pelted them with sticks, clods of earth, tiles or stones. "Go and hide yourselves! Go and hide yourselves properly!" That is why today when a girl is married she is pelted with flowers or gold or silver or pieces of clothing or rajas,[1] and the people as they pelt her say, "May peace and happiness, new bride, be yours!" Monks, in former times ill was meant by these things that were done; but nowadays good is meant.

The Ekottara . . . was translated in 384–385;
the Ch'i Shih Ching in 590.

207. *Buddha's Pity*

My children,
The Enlightened One, because He saw Mankind drowning in the Great Sea of Birth, Death and Sorrow, and longed to save them,
For this was moved to pity.
Because He saw the men of the world straying in false paths, and none to guide them,
For this He was moved to pity.
Because He saw that they lay wallowing in the mire of the Five Lusts, in dissolute abandonment,
For this He was moved to pity.
Because He saw them still fettered to their wealth, their wives and their children, knowing not how to cast them aside,
For this He was moved to pity.
Because He saw them doing evil with hand, heart and tongue, and many times receiving the bitter fruits of sin, yet ever yielding to their desires,
For this He was moved to pity.
Because He saw that they slaked the thirst of the Five Lusts as it were with brackish water,
For this He was moved to pity.
Because He saw that though they longed for happiness, they made for themselves no karma of happiness: and though they hated pain, yet willingly made for themselves a karma of pain: and though they coveted the joys of Heaven, would not follow His commandments on earth,
For this He was moved to pity.

[1] Artificial flowers made of boiled rice or grain (?).

Because He saw them afraid of birth, old-age and death, yet
still pursuing the works that lead to birth, old-age and
death,
For this He was moved to pity.
Because He saw them consumed by the fires of pain and
sorrow, yet knowing not where to seek the still waters of
Samadhi,
For this He was moved to pity.
Because He saw them living in an evil time, subjected
to tyrannous kings and suffering many ills, yet heedlessly
following after pleasure,
For this He was moved to pity.
Because He saw them living in a time of wars, killing and
wounding one another: and knew that for the riotous hatred
that had flourished in their hearts they were doomed to pay
an endless retribution,
For this He was moved to pity.
Because many born at the time of His incarnation had heard
Him preach the Holy Law, yet could not receive it,
For this He was moved to pity.
Because some had great riches that they could not bear to
give away,
For this He was moved to pity.
Because He saw the men of the world ploughing their fields,
sowing the seed, trafficking, huckstering, buying and selling:
and at the end winning nothing but bitterness,
For this He was moved to pity.

*From the Upāsaka Sīla Sūtra. Takakusu
XXIV, 1036; translated in 428 A.D.*

TEXTS ORIGINATING IN CHINA AND JAPAN

208. *A Hinayana Sect in Early China*

When Chinese Buddhist pilgrims went to Central Asia and India, they found Buddhism sharply divided into two opposing creeds—the Hinayana and the Mahayana. This was a quite unfamiliar experience; for in China there were never, so far as we know, separate Hinayana monasteries, nor was there (with the exception of the small sect that I am going to discuss) any body of monks which rejected Mahayana doctrines and scriptures. Indian Mahayanists, probably in a minority in India as a whole and subject to constant attacks by their opponents, were astonished to hear that in a remote 'border country' like China only the Mahayana was practised. When at the beginning of the 5th century the Chinese monk Chih-meng[1] visited Pataliputra, he was asked by an Indian friend whether the Mahayana teachings existed in China. Chih-meng replied, "We all follow the Mahayana teachings." The Indian was astonished and suggested that some Bodhisattva[2] must at some time have gone to China and converted the people. To discuss how it came about that the Mahayana was supreme in China would carry us too far afield. But it is certain that some of the beliefs and practices of Mahayanists appeared, superficially at any rate, to have been borrowed from Hinduism, and the accusation of being crypto-Hindus was made against Mahayanists, not only in India, but also in Central Asia. A Chinese named Chu Shih-hsing went in 261 A.D. to Khotan to get a fuller version of the Prajnaparamita.[3] He was successful in finding one; but the Hinayana monks of Khotan complained to the King of Khotan that "a sramana from the

[1] Takakusu LV, 60.
[2] The legend of the Bodhisattva Manjusri's visit to China is probably later.
[3] Takakusu LV, 42.

land of Han" was purposing to corrupt Chinese Buddhism by importing "a Brahmin book". "You are the master of this land," they said to the king. "If you do not make a ruling about this, you will make yourself responsible for the extinction of our great religion and bring deafness and blindness to the land of Han." The king refused to allow the book to be taken to China.

Obviously the suspicion that the Mahayana was only Hinduism in disguise was much less likely to arise in China, where the learned only knew of Hinduism through fragmentary and distorted accounts and the mass of the population thought of Hindus almost exclusively as merchants or as magicians. The chief Chinese opponent of Mahayana was, as we shall see, of Indian origin, and he may well have known a good deal more about Hinduism than the average Chinese. There is, however, no actual evidence that it was this knowledge that prejudiced him against the Mahayana.

Almost all that we know about the 5th-century Hinayanist Fa-tu is contained in a short account given in the *ch'u san-tsang chi chi*,[1] the earliest surviving catalogue of Chinese Buddhist works, finished in about 520 A.D. The account is headed, "Record of how the Indian Fa-tu, an adherent of Hinayana superstition, invented strange rites". After giving the orthodox Mahayana account of the successive stages by which Buddha revealed truths adapted to higher and higher intelligences, the author goes on to say: "But there are some people in foreign countries who accept only the Hinayana. For example, at the very end, in the *nirvana sutra*, Buddha completely revealed his Nature, but these people only accept his earlier teaching. Truly a case of 'playing one's zither with the tuning-pegs glued'."

"In the period Yüan-chia (424–454 A.D.) a foreign merchant, an Indian called Po-le (corresponding perhaps to Sanskrit Bhadrika), stayed for a long time at Kuang-chou (Canton), travelling about from time to time in search of profit. In Nan-k'ang commandery (on the north-west shores of Lake Po-yang, south of the Yangtze) he had a son, whom he named Nan-k'ang, after the place of his birth. When the boy grew up his name was changed to Chin-ch'ieh (probably short for

Sanskrit Kimkara). Later on he was accepted as a Buddhist monk, and became a disciple of Dharmayasas (arrived at Canton from Kashmir in 397–402 A.D.). He then took the name Fa-tu. Though in appearance he was un-Chinese, he knew nothing about Indian institutions, having in fact been born in China. But his nature retained a certain perversity and strangeness, and he had a desire. . . .[1] So he upheld and taught the Hinayana, saying that the Buddhas of the Ten Quarters did not exist. He only worshipped Sakyamuni and did not allow his disciples to read or recite the Mahayana scriptures. He wore his clothes with the skirts thrown back over his shoulders[2] and regarded this as a matter of religion. He used a copper bowl[3] and no other domestic vessel. He got the nuns to make tippets, which resembled sitting-mats; but they were sewn up like bags, and were always carried on the shoulder, never used for sitting on. These things he did as outward signs of the separateness of his community. When they went out into the road, they walked hand in hand.[4] When they confessed their sins at the ceremony of the Uposhadha they only stood facing him with their eyes on the ground; they did not kneel. Fa-tu spoke Chinese perfectly well; but until he took his vows, he always spoke in his foreign language and never let the Chinese know that he understood theirs.

Now there are clear texts in the Monastic Rules which lay down how monks should live, and provide the necessary explanations. If what the Rules say is not accepted, the religious life cannot be carried on. But the Indian Fa-tu, in his blindness and ignorance, pursued false methods of his own. Enlightened members of the Community were all shocked and forsook him. But the nun Fa-hung of the Hsüan-yeh convent, a daughter of the late prefect of Tan-yang, Yen Chün, and the nun P'u-ming[5] of the Hung-kuang convent, a daughter of the governor of Chiao-chou, along with some others, believed in and accepted his doctrines, thinking they were perfect truth."[6]

[1] 'To set things right'? Text uncertain.
[2] This was only forbidden when a monk visited the house of a layman.
[3] The use of copper bowls for cooking in was forbidden.
[4] Forbidden by the Monastic Rules.
[5] A disciple of Dharmayasas.
[6] The teachings of Fa-tu were still followed by certain nuns at Nanking in the 6th century. See Takakusu L, 329.

209. *The Truly So*

You must know that All the Dharmas cannot be defined in words or attained to in thought, and for that reason are called the Truly So (Tathata). It may be asked, "In that case, how can all living creatures accord themselves to the Truly So and achieve entry into it?" The answer is, if you understand that all the Dharmas however much you try to explain them have nothing that you can explain, and however much you may think about them have nothing that can be thought about, this understanding is in itself accordance with the Truly So and is in itself entry into the Truly So.

Next it must be explained that the Truly So, if one tries to express it in words, has two aspects. The first is the Truly So as Emptiness, which makes apparent the final and absolute truth. The second is the Truly So as Not-Emptiness, with reference to its having an essence of its own, a nature free from passion, and being replete with every kind of efficacy.

The Emptiness here referred to means being free since the very beginning from the influence of all defilements; that is, keeping away from the idea of separate forms and having no idle and false notions. For you must know that the Truly So in its own nature is neither form nor formless, nor not-form nor not formless, nor form and formless at the same time. It is not all of one form nor is it of different forms, nor is it the opposite of all of one form nor the opposite of being of different forms. Nor is it of one form and different forms at the same time.

To sum up: all living creatures, owing to their mistaken ideas, make false distinctions at every thought and consequently cannot get into concord with the Truly So. For this reason they call it empty, but if they could get away from their mistaken thoughts, they would realize that it is not really empty. As regards the not-empty aspect of the Truly So, since in essence the dharmas are empty they manifest what is free from error. This is the True Mind, eternal and unchanging, replete with passionless dharmas and called the Not-empty.

From the Ch'i Hsin Lun, Awakening of Faith.
Takakusu XXXII, 576. Probably com-
posed in China in the 6th century.

210. *From the Lives of the Nuns*

The first Chinese Nun

The nun Ching-chien was the daughter of Chung Tan, Governor of Wu-wei (in western Kansu). When young she was fond of study. She lost her parents early and being very badly off she supported herself at one time by giving lessons in zithern-playing and calligraphy to the daughters of fashionable people (at the Capital). She felt strongly drawn towards Buddhism, but had no one to whom she could turn for instruction. But after a while she met a monk called Fa-shih who had a good understanding of the scriptures. In the period Chien-hsing (313–317) he founded a monastery near the western gates of the Palace Precincts (at Nanking). Ching-chien went to see him there; he expounded the Law to her, and she at once had a great Enlightenment. . . . One day she said to Fa-shih, "In the scriptures there is talk of nuns as well as of monks. I should like to be ordained as a nun." "It is true," said Fa-shih, "that in the Western Regions they have the Two Communities, male and female. But here in this respect we remain incomplete." "As a distinction of name is made, does that imply that there is a difference in their way of life," asked Ching-chien. "I am told by people from abroad," said Fa-shih, "that nuns have five hundred rules" (as opposed to the two hundred and fifty rules which monks have to obey); "so there is evidently a considerable difference. I'll ask an instructor (Śīla-upādhyāya)." The instructor said, "On the whole the rules for nuns are similar to those for monks, but there are some small differences. Without knowing those differences it is certainly impossible to receive a nun into the Order. The main Ten Rules she can receive from any senior monk, but without an instructor a nun would be quite at a loss." Ching-chien then had her head shaved and the ten main rules were administered to her by the instructor. Then she and twenty-four of her followers founded the Bamboo Forest Convent at the western gates of the Palace Precincts. There was as yet no nun with the rank of Teacher, and they all came to Ching-chien for advice, which she was able to supply better than many a fully authorized Master.

The instructor who had ordained her was a certain Chih-shan (Prajñāgiri), a monk from the Western Regions, who lived in the country of Kashmir.[1] He was an easy-going, peaceable man with wise ideas, well versed in Meditation and the recitation of the scriptures. At the end of the Yung-chia period (*c.* 313) he came to China, where he supported himself by mendicancy and did much to propagate the religion. But belief was in those days at a very low ebb[2] and hardly anyone went to him for instruction. He returned to Kashmir in the first year of Chien-wu (317 A.D.). . . .

In the period Hsien-k'ang (335–343) the monk Seng-chien obtained copies of the ritual for the ordination of nuns and of the rules for nuns in the country of the Yüeh-chih (Indo-Scythians in Gandhara), and in the first year of Sheng-p'ing (357) on the eighth day of the second month the foreign monk Dharmakarta was asked to set up a platform for the ordination of nuns at Lo-yang. But the monk Tao-ch'ang objected on the ground of a passage in the *Sutra about the Origin of the Rules*,[3] and the ceremony was not carried out. Dharmakarta took ship down the Ss'u River (i.e. went off to Kiangsu?) and Ching-chien with three other women all took their full vows from a senior monk on the same platform. Thus Ching-chien was the first Chinese nun.

Nuns from Ceylon

The nun Seng-kuo . . . when a child at breast would never take more than half the milk. Her parents were proud of this strange singularity. When she grew up her thoughts were concentrated on spiritual progress, but outside circumstances impeded her devotion. Not till she was twenty-six was she able to take orders. Her teacher was the nun Hui-ts'ung. Seng-kuo observed her vows most scrupulously and her Dhyana-vision was untroubled and bright. She would go into Samadhi for whole nights on end, her spirit remaining continuously in Buddha-lands. At such times her body was like a withered

---

[1] Chi-pin.   [2] Taoism was then in fashion.

[3] I think the sūtra referred to is the *Mahāprajāpatī Sūtra* (Tak. XXIV, 952). But in any case it is clear from the Pali Vinaya that a nun receiving full ordination must have a senior nun as instructor. See J. B. Horner, *Women under Primitive Buddhism*, p. 141.

tree, and people of shallow comprehension sometimes suspected (that she was dead?).

In the sixth year of Yüan-chia (429 A.D.) the foreign ship-owner Nandi arrived from the Lion Country (Ceylon) bringing with him some nuns. They went to the Sung capital (Nanking) and lived in the Ching-fu Convent. After a time they asked Seng-kuo whether any other foreign nuns had ever come to China. She told them that they were the first who had ever come. "Then how did previous nuns manage to have nuns as well as monks to conduct their Ordination?" asked the nuns from Ceylon. "We were ordained by a senior monk," said Seng-kuo. "Any woman whose nature prompted her to take vows was accepted. The earnest desire of the candidates gave rise to this expedient, which is in some measure justified by the case of (Buddha's aunt) Prajapati, who was admitted to the Order on the strength of her Eight Declarations of Reverence,[1] and afterwards she in turn acted as Silaupadhyaya (instructress in the Rules) to five hundred ladies of the Sakyan clan."

Such was Seng-kuo's reply. But in her heart of hearts she was not very happy about the situation and consulted the Master of the Three Canons (Gunavarman),[2] who supported her contention. She also asked him if it was possible for nuns who had been ordained already (by a monk only) to be re-ordained (with the assistance of a nun). "Morality, Meditation and Wisdom," he said, "are all progressive states. If an ordination is repeated, so much the better."

In the tenth year (433 A.D.) the ship-owner Nandi came again to China bringing the Ceylonese nun Tessara and ten other Ceylonese nuns. The nuns who had arrived previously could now speak Chinese. They asked the Indian monk Sangha-varman to re-ordain with their assistance three hundred Chinese nuns . . . at the Southern Forest Monastery (at Nanking), receiving them in batches.

3. The Nun Feng

The nun Feng was a woman of Kao-ch'ang (Turfan, in Turkestan). Feng was her surname and as a sign of respect they

---

[1] Of complete submission to male members of the Order.
[2] Arrived from Kashmir in 431.

called her by her surname.[1] She became a nun at the age of twenty-nine, living at the (Chinese) Monastery founded by Mr. Secretary Tu. She lived exclusively on vegetables, ate only once a day and was very scrupulous in observing all the Monastic Rules. She burnt off six of her fingers as far as the palm of her hand and made an offering of them (to Buddha). She used to recite the *Sutra of the Great Decease* in three sessions, each lasting a day. There was at this time a certain Master of the Law called Fa-hui, a man very far advanced in spiritual progress, who was chaplain to all the nuns at Kao-ch'ang. Feng suddenly said to him one day, "Teacher, all is not yet well with you. I am your good friend, and I strongly advise you to go to the Golden Flower Monastery at Kucha (south-west of Turfan). There you will find a monk called Chih-yüeh, and he will teach you the supreme Dharma." Fa-hui took her advice. Chih-yüeh received him with great cordiality and put into his hands a pint-pot of grape-wine, which he begged him to drink. Fa-hui was very much surprised. "I came to you to receive instruction in the supreme Dharma," he said, "but instead of instructing me you offer me wine. I cannot bring myself to drink this unholy stuff." Chih-yüeh caught hold of him, turned him round and pushed him out of his cell. Fa-hui, still carrying the pint-pot, then returned to the quarters allotted to him and thought to himself, "After all, I have come a long way to get this advice. Perhaps there is some meaning in what he did, of a kind I do not understand. I daresay I ought to do as he told me," and he drank the wine at one gulp. He became very drunk, sick, confused and distressed, and finally lost consciousness. . . . When he came to and realized that he had broken his Vows he was overcome with shame, struck himself violently with his staff in deep remorse at what he had done, and indeed came near to taking his own life. As a result of these agonized thoughts he got the Third Fruit (Anāgāmi-phala, involving complete and final severance from the World of Desire). "Have you got it?" asked Chih-yüeh, when he came to see him. "I have," said Fa-hui. He sent no news to the nun Feng, but when, on his return journey, he was still more than two

[1] Just as the great Dhyana-master Tao-i (died, 788) was commonly known by his surname, Ma.

hundred leagues away she called together the other nuns and told them to get ready to go out and meet him. She often had foreknowledge of this kind. The nuns of Kao-ch'ang all revered her as their teacher. She died at the age of ninety-five in the third year of T'ien-chien (504 A.D.).

Takakusu L, 934, 939, 946.

211. *On Trust in the Heart*

'The Heart' means our own fundamental Buddha-nature. The work is a versified statement of doctrine rather than a poem. It is given here because of its immense popularity and influence in China and Japan. I have, I hope, managed to make a version which will be a little clearer to the European reader than previous translations. The work is attributed to Seng-ts'an, the third Patriarch of the Dhyana Sect. It is, however, a statement of average Mahayana doctrine, and not an exposition of beliefs or practices peculiar to the Dhyana Sect.

The Perfect Way is only difficult for those who pick and choose;
Do not like, do not dislike; all will then be clear.
Make a hairbreadth difference, and Heaven and Earth are set apart;
If you want the truth to stand clear before you, never be for or against.
The struggle between 'for' and 'against' is the mind's worst disease;
While the deep meaning is misunderstood, it is useless to meditate on Rest.
It[1] is blank and featureless as space; it has no 'too little' or 'too much';
Only because we take and reject does it seem to us not to be so.
Do not chase after Entanglements as though they were real things,
Do not try to drive pain away by pretending that it is not real;
Pain, if you seek serenity in Oneness, will vanish of its own accord.

[1] The Buddha-nature.

Stop all movement in order to get rest, and rest will itself be
   restless;
Linger over either extreme, and Oneness is for ever lost.
Those who cannot attain to Oneness in either case will fail:
To banish Reality is to sink deeper into the Real;
Allegiance to the Void implies denial of its voidness.
The more you talk about It, the more you think about It, the
   further from It you go;
Stop talking, stop thinking, and there is nothing you will not
   understand.
Return to the Root and you will find the Meaning;
Pursue the Light, and you will lose its source,
Look inward, and in a flash you will conquer the Apparent and
   the Void.
For the whirligigs of Apparent and Void all come from
   mistaken views;
There is no need to seek Truth; only stop having views.
Do not accept either position,[1] examine it or pursue it;
At the least thought of 'Is' and 'Isn't' there is chaos and the
   Mind is lost.
Though the two exist because of the One, do not cling to the
   One;
Only when no thought arises are the Dharmas without blame.
No blame, no Dharmas; no arising, no thought.
The doer vanishes along with the deed,
The deed disappears when the doer is annihilated.
The deed has no function apart from the doer;
The doer has no function apart from the deed.
The ultimate Truth about both Extremes is that they are One
   Void.
In that One Void the two are not distinguished;
Each contains complete within itself the Ten Thousand
   Forms.
Only if we boggle over fine and coarse are we tempted to take
   sides.
In its essence the Great Way is all-embracing;
It is as wrong to call it easy as to call it hard.
Partial views are irresolute and insecure,
Now at a gallop, now lagging in the rear.

                    [1] Assertion and Negation.

Clinging to this or to that beyond measure
The heart trusts to bypaths that lead it astray.
Let things take their own course; know that the Essence
Will neither go nor stay;
Let your nature blend with the Way and wander in it free from
care.
Thoughts that are fettered turn from Truth,
Sink into the unwise habit of 'not liking'.
'Not liking' brings weariness of spirit; estrangements serve
no purpose.
If you want to follow the doctrine of the One, do not rage
against the World of the Senses.
Only by accepting the World of the Senses can you share in
the True Perception.
Those who know most, do least; folly ties its own bonds.
In the Dharma there are no separate dharmas, only the foolish
cleave
To their own preferences and attachments.
To use Thought to devise thoughts, what more misguided than
this?
Ignorance creates Rest and Unrest; Wisdom neither loves nor
hates.
All that belongs to the Two Extremes is inference falsely
drawn—
A dream-phantom, a flower in the air.[1] Why strive to grasp it
in the hand?
'Is' and 'Isn't', gain and loss banish once for all:
If the eyes do not close in sleep there can be no evil dreams;
If the mind makes no distinctions all Dharmas become one.
Let the One with its mystery blot out all memory of compli-
cations.
Let the thought of the Dharmas as All-One bring you to the
So-in-itself.
Thus their origin is forgotten and nothing is left to make us
pit one against the other.
Regard motion as though it were stationary, and what be-
comes of motion?
Treat the stationary as though it moved, and that disposes of
the stationary.

[1] See above, p. 281.

Both these having thus been disposed of, what becomes of the
    One?
At the ultimate point, beyond which you can go no further,
You get to where there are no rules, no standards,
To where thought can accept Impartiality,
To where effect of action ceases,
Doubt is washed away, belief has no obstacle.
Nothing is left over, nothing remembered;
Space is bright, but self-illumined; no power of mind is
    exerted.
Nor indeed could mere thought bring us to such a place.
Nor could sense or feeling comprehend it.
It is the Truly-so, the Transcendent Sphere, where there is
    neither He nor I.
For swift converse with this sphere use the concept 'Not Two';
In the 'Not Two' are no separate things, yet all things are
    included.
The wise throughout the Ten Quarters have had access to this
    Primal Truth;
For it is not a thing with extension in Time or Space;
A moment and an aeon for it are one.
Whether we see it or fail to see it, it is manifest always and
    everywhere.
The very small is as the very large when boundaries are for-
    gotten;
The very large is as the very small when its outlines are not
    seen.
Being is an aspect of Non-being; Non-being is an aspect of
    Being.
In climes of thought where it is not so the mind does ill to
    dwell.
The One is none other than the All, the All none other than
    the One.
Take your stand on this, and the rest will follow of its own
    accord;
To trust in the Heart is the Not Two, the Not Two is to trust
    in the Heart.
I have spoken, but in vain; for what can words tell
Of things that have no yesterday, tomorrow or today?

Takakusu XLVIII, 376.

212. *From the Conversations of Shen-hui*
(8th century A.D.)

1.

The Master Shen-tsu asked Shen-hui: "You say that our Original Nature has the characteristics of the Absolute. In that case it has no colour, blue, yellow or the like, that the eye can see. How then can one perceive one's Original Nature?" Shen-hui answered, "Our Original Nature is void and still. If we have not experienced Enlightenment, erroneous ideas arise. But if we awaken to the erroneous nature of these ideas, both the Awakening and the wrong idea simultaneously vanish. That is what I mean by 'perceiving one's Original Nature'." Shen-tsu again asked: "Despite the light that comes from the Awakening, one is still on the plane of Birth and Destruction. Tell me by what method one can get clear of Birth and Destruction?" Shen-hui answered, "It is only because you put into play the ideas of Birth and Destruction that Birth and Destruction arise. Rid yourself of these ideas, and there will be no substance to which you can even distantly apply these names. When the light that comes from the Awakening is quenched, we pass automatically into Non-being, and there is no question of Birth or Destruction."

2.

"The passions (kleśa)," said the disciple Wu-hsing, "are boundless and innumerable. Buddhas and Bodhisattvas pass through aeons of austerity before achieving success. How was it that the dragon's daughter was instantaneously converted and forthwith achieved Complete Enlightenment?" "Conversion," said Shen-hui, "can be either sudden or gradual; both delusion and the Awakening can come to pass slowly or swiftly. That delusion can go on for aeon after aeon and the Awakening can come in a single moment is an idea that is difficult to understand. I want first of all to illustrate the point by a comparison; I think it will help you to understand what I mean. A single bundle of thread is made up of innumerable separate strands; but if you join them together into a rope and

[1] See Saddharma Pundarika, Ch. IV. (Tak. IX, 35).

put it on a plank, you can easily cut through all these threads with one stroke of a sharp knife. Many though the threads may be, they cannot resist that one blade. With those who are converted to the way of the Bodhisattvas, it is just the same. If they meet with a true Good Friend who by skilful means brings them to immediate perception of the Absolute, with Diamond Wisdom they cut through the passions that belong to all the stages of Bodhisattvahood. They suddenly understand and are awakened, and see for themselves that the True Nature of the dharmas is empty and still. Their intelligence is so sharpened and brightened that it can penetrate unimpeded. When this happens to them, all the myriad entanglements of Causation are cut away, and erroneous thoughts many as the sands of the Ganges in one moment suddenly cease. Limitless virtues are theirs, ready and complete. The Diamond Wisdom is at work, and failure now impossible."

3.

"What is the Void?" asked the Master of the Law Ch'ung-yüan. "If you tell me that it exists, then you are surely implying that it is solid and resistant. If on the other hand you say it is something that does not exist, in that case why go to it for help?" "One talks of the Void," replied Shen-hui, "for the benefit of those who have not seen their own Buddha-natures. For those who have seen their Buddha-natures the Void does not exist. It is this view about the Void that I call 'going to it for help'."

4.

"You must not take it amiss," said Shen-hui to the Master of the Law Ch'ung-yüan and some others, "if I tell you the following story. Nowadays such a lot of people are giving instruction in Dhyana that students are becoming completely bewildered. I am afraid that among these instructors there may well be some that are bent upon leading students of religion astray and destroying the True Law—such teachers being in fact Heretics in disguise, or even the Evil One Mara himself. That is the reason why I tell you this story. Well, it was in the period Chiu-shih (700 A.D.). The Empress Wu Hou summoned the monk Shen-hsiu [1] to serve in the Palace and when he was about to leave his monastery . . . his followers, both laymen and monks, asked him how they were to carry on their spiritual exercises in his absence, and where they were to turn for guidance. 'You will have to go to Shao-chou,' said Shen-hsiu. 'You will find there a great Good Friend. [2] It was to him that the great Master Hung-jen handed on the succession. That is the place to go to for Buddha's Law. They have it all there. If there is anything that you cannot decide about for yourselves, go there and you will be astonished! That Master really does understand the true principles of Buddhism.' Accordingly in . . . the third year of Ching-lung (709) Shen-hsiu's disciple Kuang-chi (affecting to carry out this advice) went to Hui-neng's monastery at Shao-chou and after spending about ten days there he went at midnight to the Master's cell and stole the Mantle of Succession. Hui-neng screamed and his disciples Hui-yüan and Hsüan-wu hearing him scream went to see what was wrong. Just outside Hui-neng's cell they met Kuang-chi, who grasped Hsüan-wu's hand and warned him not to make any noise (as the Master was asleep). However, the two disciples thought they had better go and see if Hui-neng was all right. 'Some one has been in my cell,' said Hui-neng when they came to him. 'He grabbed at the Mantle and carried it off.' Presently a number of monks and some laymen too, both southerners resident at the monastery and visitors from the north, came to Hui-neng's cell and questioned him about the intruder. 'Was he a monk or a layman?' they asked. 'I could not see,' said Hui-neng. 'Someone certainly came in, but whether he was a monk or a layman I can't say.' They also asked whether the man was a northerner or a southerner. As a matter of fact Hui-neng knew who the man was; but he was afraid that, if he mentioned his name, his own disciples might do Kuang-chi some injury. That was why he answered as he did. 'This is not the first time,' Hui-neng went on. 'It was stolen three times from my master Hung-jen, and Hung-jen told me that it was also stolen once from his master Tao-hsin. . . . This mantle is destined to bring to a head the quarrel between the monks and laymen of the South and those

[1] Leader of the Northern School of Dhyana.
[2] Hui-neng, leader of the Southern School.

of the North. They will never meet save with sword or cudgel in hand.' "

For text and translation into French see Jacques Gernet, Entretiens du Maître de Dhyāna Chen-houei, Hanoi, 1949, pp. 37, 40, 43, 95.

213. *A Nice Mountain*

The Dhyana Master Wei-k'uan (755–817 A.D.) settled at the Shao-lin Monastery on Mt. Sung in the thirteenth year of Cheng-yüan (797 A.D.). A monk asked him, "What is the Way?" "This is a nice mountain, isn't it?" he replied. "But I was asking you about the Way, not about the mountain," said the monk. "The mountain is something you understand about," said Wei-k'uan. "The Way is not."

He was asked by a monk whether a dog has the Buddha-nature. "It has," he said. "And have you also got it?" asked the monk. "I!" said Wei-k'uan. "No, indeed." "But All Living Creatures are supposed to have it," said the monk. "I daresay," said Wei-k'uan. "But I am not All Living Creatures." "What are you then?" asked the monk. "A Buddha?" "No, not a Buddha," said Wei-k'uan. "Well really, what sort of thing are you?" asked the monk. "No sort of thing," said Wei-k'uan.

Wei-k'uan belongs to the period when Dhyana teaching, though paradoxical and wayward, still had a rational content. The text will be found in Takakusu LI, 255.

214. *Rain-making*

The Japanese pilgrim Jojin, passing through the Chinese capital, K'ai-feng, on his way to the Wu-t'ai Shan in 1073, was ordered by the Chinese Emperor to pray for rain. Being a member of the Tendai Sect he did not use Tantric spells, but instead set up a Lotus Scripture Altar.

Third month, second day . . . At nightfall I began the ritual according to the Lotus Scripture. A great number of monks and laymen stood round watching. I went on until the hour of the Rat (11 p.m. till 1 a.m.), when, having finished the first part of the ritual, I turned to my own devotions and performed the Observances of the Seven Hours and read the fifth chapter of the Lotus, which I finished at the Fifth Watch (at dawn).

Third day . . . Many of the courtiers came to look, and high ministers too. They were all much impressed by the Lotus Altar. Suddenly at the hour of the Sheep (1–3 p.m.) monks and laymen all went out to the gates. After a time they came back saying that the Empress and other great people had come to the Hall to see the Altar. As well as the Empress there were the Emperor's mother and grandmother, along with about three hundred ladies-in-waiting. The Emperor too, it was said, had come in his coach. This made me more than ever determined to show the magic efficacy of my method. First, because if now, five hundred years after the first propagation of the One Vehicle (Tendai), I could show the superior value of the Lotus, I should win adherents to the One Vehicle. Secondly, I felt bound to repay the Emperor's kindness to me by displaying the efficacy of my method. Thirdly, no previous Master from Japan has ever been entrusted with such a task, and a failure on my part would be a great humiliation for my country. For all these reasons I have carried out the ritual with the utmost single-mindedness, in order to produce a big downpour within the three prescribed days. The Emperor constantly sent encouraging messages, but it grew finer and finer, without the slightest indication of rain. At the hour of the Monkey (3–5 p.m.) the Emperor sent . . . a message saying he would like a report on any dreams I had been having lately. I replied that in the early hours of the morning, while making the offerings, I seemed to dream that someone spoke to me, saying, "The Four Vajrapanis (Thunder-bolt Spirits) are hiding the light of the sun and moon. Within three days it certainly may rain." Afterwards I had an impression that the sun was shining less brightly and that there was a cool feeling coming up from the ground. But I do not know whether the prophecy was false or true. . . . From noon onwards there were races between a number of gorgeously decorated dragon-prowed boats and other lively sports. The Emperor and Empress were watching from boats of their own. Three big boats were moored side by side and spread with brocades.

Outside the gates there was a white swan. It bent down its head, as though inviting our interpreter Ch'en Yung to stroke its neck. When he did so it indicated with its claw a place on its neck that was itching and said "Ku-ku". A most extra-ordinary thing. But I cannot give a full account of everything that happened today, as I could not attend to anything except the rain-making. . . .

Fourth day. A clear sky. In the hour before dawn I thought to myself, "This is the third day. The sky is clear and there is no sign of rain. May the Chief Honoured One and all the Honoured Ones help me!" At the hour of the Dragon (7–9 a.m.) while invoking various subsidiary Powers I fell asleep and in my dream I saw a man in the costume of the Ryo-o dancer and with him another in the costume of the Nasori[1] dancer soaring up to the sky. Thinking about my dream when I woke up I saw that they must be the Red Rain-making Dragon (of the South) and the Green Rain-making Dragon (of the East) going up into the sky, and this gave me great confidence. During the middle part of the day I prayed very earnestly, and suddenly at the hour of the Sheep (1–3 p.m.) the sky became covered and heavy rain began. There was flash after flash of lightning and peal after peal of thunder, and the rain began to come down more and more heavily. Till the hour of the Monkey (3–5 p.m.) it rained very hard; but then the sky cleared. We now heard a rumour that the Emperor was coming to share in our rejoicing. There was a tremendous bustle of preparations and we were expecting him every minute when the Grand Guardian[2] arrived as a messenger from the Emperor. He took a piece of paper out of the folds of his dress and handed it to me. On it was written, "Although you do seem to have exercised a considerable influence on the weather, it has not really rained very much. You had better go on praying your hardest." I wrote in reply, "There is not the slightest doubt that the Dragon Kings have gone up into the sky. However, in accordance with your Majesty's instructions I will continue to pray as hard as I can." The messenger put my

[1] Ryŏ-ŏ and Nasori were Japanese dances performed particularly in connection with horse-races and wrestling.

[2] Presumably a Palace eunuch.

note in the folds of his dress and took it back to the Palace. . . .
So I prayed hard for rain and presently the sky clouded over.
A little rain fell, but the wind kept on blowing it away, and
towards the hour of the Cock (5–7 p.m.), the Grand Guardian
came back saying, "It did look like rain; but the wind at once
blew the rain away. You had better pray for the wind to stop.
If there is anything we can do for you in this respect, please
let us know." I replied that the Wind-deva (Vāyu) had his
place among the twelve devas on our altar, and that I could
ask him to stop the wind. There was nothing else they could
do for me. I then recited the spell[1] of the Wind-deva ten
thousand times, and soon after the hour of the Cock the wind
went down and heavy rain began. It rained hard all night. . . .

Seventh day. The Grand Guardian Chang came and talked
to me. He asked whether in Japan there was anyone who was
so successful in rain-making as I. I replied that there had been
a great many. "For example," I said, "the founder of the
Shingon Sect, Kobo Daishi (774–835). He came to China and
learnt the ritual for obtaining rain according to the *Asking for
Rain Sutra*,[2] his master being Hui-kuo (746–805) of the Green
Dragon Monastery at Ch'ang-an. On his return to Japan he
was asked by the Emperor to obtain rain . . . by the ritual
of the *Asking for Rain Sutra*. The monk Shu-en (died about
834) was jealous of him and by his magic drove all the rain-
dragons into his water-pot. But the staw dragons on Kobo's
rain-making altar soared up straight throught the roof of the
hall, and reaching the sky sent down a great rain. . . . Ever
since then Masters of the Shingon Sect have used this secret
method and never failed to produce heavy rain. . . ." "How
is it," Chang asked, "that you do not use the *Asking for Rain
Sutra*, but use the *Lotus* instead?" "I do not belong to the
Shingon Sect," I replied. "I am not a follower of Kobo's
school, and have therefore never learnt the method of producing rain according to the *Asking for Rain Sutra*. Even in
the Shingon Sect there are at present only two or three Masters

[1] Nama Samanta-Prānam-vāyave-svāhā, 'Praise to the universally
powerful wind'.
[2] Partially translated by Samuel Beal, in *A Catena of Buddhist
Scriptures*, 1871.

to whom this method has been transmitted. They keep it very secret among themselves and it has never been written down; still less would they dream of revealing it to a member of another sect, and I am a member of the Tendai Sect, a follower of Chisho Daishi (814–891). . . . "How many others in Japan," asked Chang, "are as successful as you in bringing rain?" "There are twenty or thirty," I replied, "who are better at it than I, and about the same number who are my equals. As for me, I am just an ignorant sinner, a Japanese monk of the 'dumb sheep' description, who has come here because of a great desire to make the pilgrimages to the T'ien-t'ai and Wu-t'ai Shan." "I find what you say very hard to believe," said Chang, "in view of some recent cases here in China. It took Jih-ch'eng (Sūryakīrti?)[1] fifty-two days to produce rain. The two Central Indian monks Hui-yüan and Hui-chi who arrived in China last year took seven days to produce rain. I do not know of a single case of heavy rain being produced in three days. I also hear that in doctrinal discussions with the great Masters here you have always got the upper hand. I do not believe that you can have many equals in your own country; still less that there are any who excel you." "Since my Ordination," I replied, "I have never once told a lie." He put the papers on which this conversation was written into the folds of his dress and went back to the Palace.

From the *San Tendai Godaisan Ki*.

[1] Born in India in 1016. Arrived in China in 1048.

BIBLIOGRAPHY

I.

(1 = Pali text, 2 = Pali commentary)

VINAYA-PIṬAKA

1. Vinaya-piṭakaṁ, ed. H. Oldenberg, 5 vols., London, 1879–83.
2. Samantapāsādikā, edd. J. Takakusu, M. Nagai, 7 vols., PTS., 1924–47.

SUTTA-PIṬAKA

1. Dīgha-Nikāya, edd. T. W. Rhys Davids, J. Estlin Carpenter, 3 vols., PTS., 1908–11.
2. Sumangalavilāsinī, edd. T. W. Rhys Davids, J. Estlin Carpenter, W. Stede, 3 vols., PTS., 1886–1932.

1. Majjhima-Nikāya, edd. V. Trenckner, Lord Chalmers, 3 vols., PTS., 1888–99.
2. Papañcasūdanī, edd. J. H. Woods, D. Kosambi, I. B. Horner, 5 vols., PTS., 1922–38.

1. Saṁyutta-Nikāya, ed. L. Feer, 5 vols., PTS., 1884–98.
2. Sāratthappakāsinī, ed. F. L. Woodward, 3 vols., PTS., 1929–37.

1. Anguttara-Nikāya, edd. R. Morris, E. Hardy, 5 vols., PTS., 1885–1900.
2. Manorathapūraṇī, edd. M. Walleser, H. Kopp, 4 vols. (concl. vol. in prep.), PTS., 1924–40.

1, 2. Khuddaka-pāṭha, ed. with its Comy. by Helmer Smith, PTS., 1915.

1. Dhammapada, ed. Suriyagoda Sumaṅgala Thera, PTS., 1914.
2. Dhammapada Comy., ed. H. C. Norman, 4 vols., PTS., 1906–14.
2. Buddhist Legends, by E. W. Burlingame, 3 vols., (HOS., 28–30), Harvard U. P., 1921.

1. Udāna, ed. P. Steinthal, PTS., 1885.
2. Udāna Comy., ed. F. L. Woodward, PTS., 1926.

1. Itivuttaka, ed. E. Windisch, PTS., 1889.
2. Itivuttaka Comy., ed. M. M. Bose, 2 vols., PTS., 1934, 1936.

1. Suttanipāta, new edn. by Dines Andersen & Helmer Smith, PTS., 1913.
2. Suttanipāta Comy., ed. Helmer Smith, 2 vols., PTS., 1916–17.

1. Theragāthā, edd. H. Oldenberg, R. Pischel, PTS., 1883.
2. Theragāthā Comy., ed. F. L. Woodward, 2 vols. (concl. vol. in prep.), PTS., 1940, 1952.

1. Therīgatha, ed. R. Pischel, PTS., 1883.
2. Therīgāthā Comy, ed. E. Müller, PTS., 1893.

1, 2. Jātaka together with its Comy., ed. V. Fausbøll, 6 vols., London, 1877–96.

1. Mahā-niddesa, edd. L. de la Vallée-Poussin, E. J. Thomas, PTS., 1916.
1. Culla-niddesa, ed. W. Stede, PTS., 1918.
2. Paṭisambhidāmagga Comy., ed. C. V. Joshi, 3 vols., PTS., 1933–47

ABHIDHAMMA-PIṬAKA

1. Dhammasaṅgaṇi, ed. E. Müller, PTS., 1885.
2. Atthasālinī, ed. E. Müller, PTS., 1897.
2. The Expositor, by Pe Maung Tin, 2 vols., PTS., 1920–21.

1. Vibhaṅga, ed. Mrs. Rhys Davids, PTS., 1904.
2. Vibhaṅga Comy., ed. A. P. Buddhadatta Thera, PTS., 1923.
2. Puggalapaññatti Comy., edd. G. Lansberg, Mrs. Rhys Davids, JPTS., 1914.

POST-CANONICAL WORKS

1. Anāgatavamsa, ed. J. Minayeff, JPTS., 1886.

1. Milindapañha, ed. V. Trenckner, RAS., London, 1928.

1. Visuddhimagga, by Buddhaghosa, ed. Mrs. Rhys Davids, 2 vols., PTS., 1920–21.
1. Visuddhimagga of Buddhaghosa, edd. H. C. Warren, D. Kosambi, HOS. 41, Harvard U. P., 1950.

II.

MAHĀSANGHIKA

Lalitavistara, ed. S. Lefmann, 1902–08.

MAHĀYĀNA SUTRAS

Śāntideva, Śikshāsamuccaya, ed. C. Bendall, 1897–1902.
Saddharmapuṇḍarīka, edd. U. Wogihara, C. Tsuchida, Tokyo, 1933–35.
Ashṭasāhasrikā prajñāpāramitā, ed. R. Mitra, Calcutta, 1888.
Pañcavimśatisāhasrikā prajñāpāramitā: first part ed. N. Dutt, 1934; for later parts the Cambridge Mss. were used.

Śatasāhasrikā prajñāramitā: the first 13 chs., ed. P. Ghosha, 1902–13;
for later parts the Cambridge Sanskrit Mss. were used.
Ashṭādaśasāhasrikā, trsl. Hsüan-tsang, Taishō Issaikyō, no. 220, 479–
537.
Saptaśatikā: first part ed. J. Masuda, Journ. Taisho Univ., vols. 6–7,
1930, part 2, pp. 185–241; remainder after G. Tucci, Mem. R.
Acad. dei Lincei, Cl. di Sc. Mor., Ser. 5a, vol. 17, Roma, 1923.
Vajracchedikā, ed. M. Mueller, 1881.
Prajñāpāramitāhṛdaya, ed. E. Conze, JRAS., 1948, pp. 34–37.
Sukhāvatīvyūha, edd. F. M. Mueller, B. Nanjio, 18
Lankavatāra sūtra, ed. B. Nanjio, Kyoto, 1923.
Ārya-Tārā-nāma-ashṭottara-śataka-stotra, ed. G. de Blonay, Matéri-
aux pour servir à l'histoire de la déesse bouddhique Tārā, 1895,
pp. 48–53.

Mahāyāna Shastras

Rāhulabhadra, Prajñāpāramitāstotra, ed. in Mitra, and Jhosha.
Mātṛceṭa, Śatapañcāśatkastotra, ed. trsl. D. R. Shackleton-Bailey,
Cambridge, 1951.
Asanga, Triśatikāyāḥ prajñāpāramitāyāḥ kārikā-saptati (manuscript).
Vasubandhu, Trimśikā-vijñapti-kārikā, ed. S. Levi, Paris, 1925.
Vasubandhu, Comy. to Asanga's Mahāyānasaṃgraha, trsl. E. Lamotte,
1938.
Sthiramati, Madhyāntavibhāgaṭīkā, ed. S. Yamagucchi, Nagoya, 1934.
Sāramati, Ratnagotravibhāga, edd. E. H. Johnston, T. Chowdhury,
Journ. Bihar Research Soc., xxxvi, 1, 1950.
Candrakīrti, Prasannapadā, ed. de la Vallée-Poussin, 1903–14.

III.

Āryadeva, Cittaviśuddhiprakaraṇa, ed. P. Patel, Visvabharati, 1949
(vv. 24–29, 37–38).
Guhyasamājatantra, ed. B. Bhattacharya, GOS. 53, Baroda, 1931
(ch. 7).
Saraha, Dohākosha:
Apabhraṃśa, ed. M. Shahidullah, Les chants mystiques de Kāṇha
et de Saraha, Paris, 1928; ed. P. C. Bagchi, Dohākosha,
Calcutta Sanskrit Series no. 25c, 1938.
Tibetan in Narthang Tanjur, rGyud 46, fol. 73b–8ob, 193b–222b
(India Office copy).
*Numbering of the verses after Bagchi's text and the Tibetan trsl. of
fol. 193b sq. But see p. 239, note 1.*
Anangavajra, Prajñopāyaviniścayasiddhi, ch. 1–3 (omitting ch. 2, vv.
11–23).
Sanskrit, ed. B. Bhattacharya, Two Vajrayana works, GOS., 44,
Baroda, 1929.
Tibetan: Narthang Tanjur, rGyud 46, folio 31a sq.

Advāyavajrasaṃgraha, ed. H. Śāstri, GOS. 40, 1927, pp. 40–43.
Tibetan: Tanjur rGyud 46, fol. 143–5.
Sādhanamālā, ed. B. Bhattacharya, GOS. 26, 41, Baroda, 1925, 1928 (no. 156).
Hevajratantra, from ch. 1 (manuscript), Comy: Kāṇha, Yogaratnamālā (manuscript).
Stories of the 84 Perfect Ones, Tanjur, rGyud 86, fol. 15a–16b.
The whole series has been translated into German as :
Die Geschichte der 84 Zauberer, trsl. (into German) Gruenwedel, Baessler Archiv V, 1916.
Milarepa, mGur-ḥBum, The Book of One Hundred Thousand Songs.
The cycle here translated for the first time is the seventh of the collection, and begins on folio 29a of a block print in the possession of the India Office Library.

IV.

Taisho Issaikyo: The Tripitaka in Chinese, edd. J. Takakusu and K. Watanaba, 85 vols., Tokyo, 1924–32.

SOURCES

Figures refer to numbers of extracts

GLOSSARY

of

Technical Terms with their Sanskrit Equivalents

*Figures refer to numbers of extracts; B. refers to E. Conze,
Buddhism, 2nd ed. 1953.*

Adamantine, *vajra*. (B., p. 178). See Vajra.
Aeon, *kalpa*. B., p. 49.
All-knowledge, *sarva-jñatā*. Also: Omniscience. 72, 123 (vv. 71-2, 75),
    124, 137, 141, 179.
Aloof, *vivikta*. 33. Also: Isolated.
Ambrosia, *amṛta*. Also: Deathless. 188 (v. 56).
Analytical knowledge, *pratisamvid*. Four: analysis of meanings, of
    dharmas, of definitions, which things are then presented to the
    intellect. Also: Analytical Insight, p. 47.
Applications of Mindfulness, *smṛtyupasthāna*. Four, descr. 32. Also:
    Topics of Meditation, 196.
Apprehension, *upalabdhi*.
Apsara. A celestial nymph. 10, 172.
Arahant. Pali form of Arhan.
Arhat, *arhan*. Descr. 14-19, 69, 96-7, 165. Also: Arahant.
Arising, *samudaya*. Also: Origination, Uprising.
Ariyan, *ārya*. Also: Holy, Saint. May also mean 'noble'.
Assembly, *samgha*. Also: Community (p. 289), Order, Samgha.
Asura. Titanic beings, forever at war with the Gods. See: States of Woe.
Attainment, *prāpti*. Also for *adhigama* p. 47.
Avadhūtī, the central vein in the body, and the Goddess who sym-
    bolizes it.
Avalokiteśvara. The Bodhisattva of compassion. 175-6.

Baseless, *anupalambha*.
Basis: (1) *upadhi*. A remaining substrate of clinging to rebirth. p. 18,
    no. 70, 94, 100.
    (2) *upalambha*. The objective counterpart of Apprehension. 161,
    181.
Becoming, *bhava*. 38, 41, 43, 69, 84.
Being, *sattva*. 66, 149 (v. 110), 157, 164-5.
Birth-and-death, *samsāra*. Also: Circling On, Samsara.
Blessed, *Bhagavatī*. Also: Lady.
Blessed One, *Bhagavan*. Also: Lord.
Bodhisatta. Pali form of Bodhisattva.

Bodhisattva, *bodhi-sattva*. Literally: Enlightenment-being. (B., p. 125 sq.). 121–2, 124–8, 144.

Brahmā. A very high deity, reputed creator of the world. (B., p. 39). 13, 172, 180 (v. 122), 188 (v. 50), 201.

Brahma-faring, *brahma-caryā* (B., p. 58). pp. 28, 33–7, 42, 56. no. 71, 89.

Buddha. 100–120, 173–4, 201.—Five Buddhas: 187, 190.—Seven Buddhas: 196.

Buddha-dharmas, *buddha-dharmā*. Descr. 140. Also: Qualities of a Buddha, Attributes of a Buddha.

Buddha-field, *buddha-kṣetra*. (B., p. 154). 120.

Buddha-nature 213.

Circling On, *saṃsara*. Also: Birth-and-death, Samsara.

Cognition, *jñāna*. Also: Gnosis, Knowledge.—Five kinds: 187, 190.

Compassion, *karuṇā*. 8, 124–5, 127, 188 (vv. 107–8), 189 I.

Complete Nirvana, *pari-nirvāṇa*. Also: Final Nirvana.

Complexes, *saṃskāra*. Also: Conditioned Things, Impulses, Karma-formations. 149.

Compounded, *saṃskṛta*. Also: Conditioned.

Comprehension, *pari-jñā*.

Conceits, *samkalpa*.

Concentration, *samādhi*. (B., pp. 99–105). 23–4, 33–5, 170.

Conditioned, *saṃskṛta*. Also: Compounded. 149–50.

Conditioned co-production, *pratītya-samutpāda*. Also: Conditioned Genesis. (B., p. 48). 39–71. 155.

Conditioned Things, *saṃskāra*. Also: Complexes, Impulses, Karma-formations.

Confusion, *moha*. Also: Delusion; Folly, p. 277.

Conqueror, *jina*. Also: Jina.

Consciousness, *vi-jñāna*. Also for *citta*, no. 6.—15, 34, 43, 48, 49, 52, 110, 149 (vv. 105–7), 181–2, 184.

Consecration, *abhi-ṣekha*. 189 III.

Contact, *sparśa*. Also: Impression. 43. 52.

Covering, *āvaraṇa*. One might also translate 'obstruction'. 146. 173. 179.

Covering of the cognizable, *jñeya-āvaraṇa*. The realistic error.

Craving, *tṛṣṇā*. 43, 51–2, 64, 85, 109.

Deadly Sins, *ānantaryāṇi*. Five: killing mother, father, or Arhat, causing dissension in the Order, deliberately causing the Tathagata's blood to flow. 154; cf. 5.

Deathless, *amṛta*. Also: Ambrosia.

Dedicate, *pari-ṇāmayati*. To transfer one's own merit to the cause of universal enlightenment. 128, 131, 171.

Defilement, *kleśa*. Also: Passions. 201, 209, 212. 2.—27, 179.

Delusion, *moha*. Also: Confusion; Folly. 201.

Deva, God. Literally: 'Shining One'. In no sense a creator, neither omniscient, nor omnipotent; simply a denizen of another world. See also: God. 10, 105, 214.

Dhamma. Pali form of Dharma.

Dharma. (1) The one ultimate reality; (2) an ultimately real event; (3) as reflected in life: righteousness, virtue; (4) as interpreted in the Buddha's teaching: Doctrine, Scripture, Truth; (5) object of the sixth sense-organ, i.e. of mind; (6) a property, as in 140, 171. Translated as 'mental states' in 32, 117; as 'thing', 34, 98; as 'quality', 170; as 'Law', p. 301.

7–9, 21, 24, 27, 39, 42, 69, 77, 92, 96, 101, 103, 118, 122, 134, 158, 188 (vv. 3, 38).

Dharma-body, *dharma-kāya*. The absolute body of Buddhahood free of all definite qualities. The first of the three bodies of a Buddha. (B., p. 172). 118–9, 123 (v. 82), 136–8, 169 (v. 145), 181 (v. 30), 189 I, 190.

Dharmahood, *dharma-tā*. Also: The True Nature of Dharmas. 138, 149 (v. 102).

Dhyāna. Also: Jhana, Meditation, Trance. 196, 202–3.

Dīpankara. A Buddha, the predecessor of the Buddha Gautama who predicted to him that one day he would win Buddhahood. 72, 135.

Disciple, *śrāvaka*. In Mahayana texts a technical term for the followers of the Hinayana.

Discipline, *vi-naya*.

Discrimination, *vi-kalpa*.

Discursive Ideas, *pra-pañca*. Also: Impediment.

Dispensation, *śāsana*. Also: Instruction, Religion.

Efforts, four right, *samyak-prahāna*: descr. 29.

Element, *dhātu*. (1) The four or six material elements, p. 57–8; no. 43, 95, 180, 197. (2) The 18 elements, i.e. the six sense-objects, six sense-organs, six kinds of sense-consciousness. 111. (3) The Element of Dharma. 156. (4) The Element of the Tathagata. 185.

Emptiness, *śūnyatā*. Also: Void. (B., p. 130 sq.). 19, 79–83, 116, 123 (vv. 76, 81), 141, 149–169, 188 (vv. 12, 70, 75, 108–9), 189 III, 191, 209–10, 212 (3).

Enlightenment, *bodhi*.

Essential Original Nature, *prakṛti*.

Ether, *ākāśa*. See: Space.

Evenmindedness, *upekṣā*. 32–3

Extinction, *kṣaya*. The act of extinguishing all worldly elements, as well as the result of that activity.

Eye, *cakṣu*. Five eyes: (1) fleshly eye, (2) heavenly eye, (3) wisdom eye, (4) Dharma-eye, (5) Buddha-eye.

Faculty, *indriya*. Five. 23–4, 36, 116, 170.

Fairy, *yakṣa*. 165.

Faith, *śraddhā*. 23–8, 118, 170.

Family, *kula*. 188 (vv. 26, 50), 190.

Feeling, *vedanā*. 32, 43, 50, 52.
Final Nirvana, *pari-nirvāṇa*. Also: Complete Nirvana.
Fine-materiality, *rūpa*. 69, 70. See: Form, etc.
Foolish common people, *bāla-pṛthag-jana*.
Form, *rūpa*. Also: Material Shape, Sight-object, Fine-Materiality.
Formless Attainment, *ārūpya-samāpatti*. Four, descr. 34–5.
Friendliness, *maitrī*. 34, 124, 154, 168.
Fruit, *phala*. Effect resulting from good or bad actions (see Karma).

Gandharva. (1) A being about to enter a womb. 59–62. (2) A Deva
   belonging to the class of heavenly musicians. 105, 176 (v. 4).
Garuda, *garuḍa*. A mythical bird.
Germ of the Tathagata, *tathāgata-garbha*. The Buddha as he exists in
   embryonic form in all that lives. 169, 185.
Gnosis, *jñāna*. Also: Cognition, Knowledge.
Gods, *deva*. Also: Deva.
Good Dharma, *sad-dharma*.
Grasping, *upādāna*. 43, 53–8, 181, 183 (v. 153).
Ground of Self-confidence, *vaiśāradya*. Four, of a Tathagata. Descr.
   117.—114–5, 170
Group, *skandha*.
Guru. Teacher, or preceptor.

Habit-energy, *vāsanā*. The effects of the latent energy of the bad
   (intellectual) habit, acquired in the past, which makes us view
   things as real. It is broken by meditation on emptiness. 182–3.
   Also: Residue.
Hair Net, *keśoṇḍuka*. Technical term for an optical illusion due to an
   eye-disease. 183.
'Happy Land', *sukhāvatī*. The Buddha-field of Amitābha. 176 (v. 25),
   177.
Heap of Merit, *puṇya-skandha*.
Heavenly Eye, *divya-cakṣu*.
Heretic, *tīrthika*. Non-Buddhist, outsider (literally: a 'ford-maker').
   155, 180.
Hindrances, *nīvaraṇa*. Five, enumerated p. 58. They hinder the attain-
   ment of concentration.
Holy, *ārya*. Also: Ariyan, Saint.

Ignorance, *a-vidyā*. Also: Stupidity, p. 227. no. 43, 46–7, 149 (v. 103).
Ill, *duḥkha*. Also: Suffering.
Illusion, *māyā*. Also: Magical Illusion, Mock Show.
Impediment, *pra-pañca*. Also: Discursive Ideas.
Impression, *sparśa*. Also: Contact.
Impulses, *saṃskāra*. Also: Conditioned Things, Complexes, Karma-
   formations.
Innate, *saha-ja*. Equals absolute truth which is considered as innate in
   all things. 188. 192.
Instruction, *śāsana*. Also: Dispensation, Religion.

Intermediate Existence, *antarā-bhara*. 205.
Isolated, *vivikta*. Also: Aloof.

Jambudvīpa. India.
Jewel, *ratna*. Three, i.e. Buddha, Dharma, Samgha.
Jhana. Pali form of *dhyāna*. Mystic states of serene contemplation attained by meditation. Four, 33. Also: Dhyāna, Meditation, Trance.
Jina, *jina*. Also: Conqueror. Literally: Victor.
Jubilation, *anumodanā*.

Karma. As volitional action, which is either wholesome or unwholesome, it is that which passes in unbroken continuity from one momentary congeries of the skandhas to another, either during the life of a person or after his death, until the result (*vipāka*) of every volitional activity of body, speech or thought, that has been done, is arrived at.
Karma-formations, *saṃskāra*. Also: Complexes, Conditioned Things, Impulses.
Khandha. Pali form of *skandha*.
Kinnara. A mythical bird with a man's head.
Knowledge, *jñāna*. See: Cognition.
Knowledge of All Modes, *sarva-ākāra-jñatā*.
Kos, *krośa*. A distance of about 2¼ miles.
Koti, *koṭi*. A huge number.

Lady, *bhagavatī*. Also: Blessed.
Lakshmī. Goddess of wealth, famed for her beauty. 189 III.
Limbs of Enlightenment, *bodhy-aṅga*. Seven: p. 59.
Lord, *bhagavan*. Also: Blessed One. (In 142, v. 12=nātha.)

Magical Illusion, *māyā*. See: Mock Show, etc.
Mahoraga, *mahā-uraga*. A great snake, conceived as a deity.
Mandala, *maṇḍala*. A mystic circle. pp. 246–8, no. 188 (vv. 11, 24, 98), 198, III.
Mañjuśrī. The Bodhisattva of Wisdom. 153, 200.
Mantra. See: Spell.
Mara. Death, the slayer and foe of what is skilled and wholesome. The Buddhist 'Tempter', the personification of all evils and passions, whose baits and snares are the sensory pleasures. Sometimes identified with the five Skandhas, and with what is impermanent, suffering and not-self. 11, 35, 43, 78, 111, 174 (v. 138).
Mark, *lakṣaṇa*. (1) A characteristic of entities. In this sense one distinguishes special and general marks. Special marks are the features characteristic of different things, 'general' marks those found in all conditioned things, i.e. impermanence, suffering and the absence of a self. (2) The 32 marks of a superman. Physical particularities found in a Buddha's body, as well as in that of a Universal Monarch.

Material Shape, *rūpa*. Also: Form, Sight-object.
Māyā. See: Mock Show.
Means, *upāya*. 188 (v. 95), 189 I.
Means of Conversion, *samgraha-vastu*. Four, 123 (v. 78).
Meditation, *dhyāna*. Also: Dhyana, Jhana, Trance.
Mental States, *dharmā*. 32, 117.
Meritorious Action, *kuśala-mūla*. 171. Also: Roots of Good, Store of Merit.
Mind, *manas*. (For 'thought' p. 58)
Minding, *manyanā*. 112, 159.
Mind-and-body, *nāma-rūpa*. 18, 41, 43.
Mindfulness, *smṛti*. 23–4, 32, 170.
Mind-only, *citta-mātra*. 178–81.
Mock Show, *māyā*. Also: Illusion, Magical Illusion, Maya. 142 (v. 16), 149 (vv. 98, 107), 150–1, 165, 176 (v. 34), 179, 183–4, 188 (v. 53).
Monk, *bhikṣu*. pp. 25, 30; no. 188 (v. 10).
Moral habits, *śīla*. Five, p. 41. Also known as five precepts, or moral rules (B., p. 86).
Morality, *śīla*.
Mudra, *mudrā*. Ritual gesture. 189 I.

Naga, *nāga*. A serpent or dragon, cobra, bull-elephant, great man. 172.
Nibbana. The Pali form of Nirvana.
Nirmana-body, *nirmāṇa-kāya*. The 'body of transformation', by which a Buddha manifests himself to ordinary men and animals. no. 189 I, 190. (B., p. 172.)
Nirvana, *nir-vāṇa*. 72, 76, 78, 84–9, 111, 121–2 (v. 12), 123, 154, 165, 178–9, 186, 188 (vv. 13, 27, 40, 41, 102, 103, 110), 189 I, 201.
Niyuta, or Nayuta. A large number.
Non-attachment, *a-saṅga*.
Non-duality, *a-dvaya*. 160–1, 180–1, 188 (v. 107), 210.
Non-production, *an-ut-pāda*.
Non-substantiality, *niḥ-sva-bhāvatā*. That which has no own-being or self-nature. 189 I.
Notion, *sam-jñā*. Also: Perception.
Not-self, *an-ātman*. 179, 182.
Nun, *bhikṣuṇī*. 3.
Nymph, *apsara*.

Omniscience, *sarva-jñatā*. See: All-knowledge.
Order, *samgha*. Also: Assembly, Community, Samgha. 27
Origination, *sam-ud-aya*. Also: Arising, Uprising.
Outflows, *āsrava*. Four: sense-desire, desire for becoming, wrong views, ignorance. The extinction of the outflows constitutes Arhatship.
Own-being, *sva-bhāva*. Also: Self-nature.

Parinirvana. Also: Final Nirvana, Complete Nirvana.
Passion, *rāga*. Also: Lust, p. 277. no. 186, 188 (vv. 26, 85), 201.
Path, *mārga*. Also: Way. 93, 141, 213.—8–fold: descr. 42.

Perception, *sam-jñā*. Also: Notion.
Perfection, *pāram-itā*. Six, descr. 129–133. See also 29.
Perfection of Wisdom, *prajñāpāramitā*. 129–30, 137, 141–69, 187, 189 I, 191.
Pity, *kṛpā*.
Powers, *bala*. Ten, of a Tathagata. Descr. 116.
Pratyckabuddha. Also: Single Buddha. Oneself-enlightened, but unable or unwilling to teach. (B., 123). 129, 199.

Rakshasa, *rākṣasa*. A kind of demon.
Reality-limit, *bhūta-koṭi*.
Realm of Dharma, *dharma-dhātu*. Also: Element of Dharma, Dharma-element. Expl. 156.
Rebirth 59–66, 205.
Religion, *śāsana*. Also: Instruction (p. 22); Dispensation (p. 43, 49).
Representation-only, *vijñapti-mātra*. 181.
Residue, *vāsanā*. Also: Habit-Energy.
Rest, *nirvṛti*.
Revulsion, *parāvṛtti*. 178–9, 181.
Rishi, *ṛṣi*. 132. Also: Seer.
Root of Good, *kuśala-mūla*. Also: Meritorious Action, Store of Merit.

Sacrament, *samaya*. 187. 189 III.
Sage, *muni*.
Sahā world system. A name for the universe in which we live, and in which there is much to endure (*sahati*).
Saint, *ārya*. Also: Ariyan, Holy.
Sakka, Pali form of Śakra.
Śakra. Name for Indra, the 'Chief of Gods'. 172.
Sambhoga-body; Body of Bliss, in which the Buddhas manifest themselves when they teach the Mahayana Sutras to a select audience of Bodhisattvas, etc. 189 I, 190. (B., p. 172.)
Samgha. The Order of monks and nuns. Also: Assembly, Community, Order.
Saṅkhāra. Pali form of *saṃskāra*. See Complexes, etc.
Samsāra. Also: Birth-and-death, Circling On. 67, 186, 188 (vv. 41, 65, 102–3, 110).
Save, *tārayati*. Literally: To help across.
Saviour, *nātha*. 124, 172, 175 (v. 17), 176 (v. 11).
Seer, *ṛṣi*. no. 134, v. 17. Also: Rishi.
Self, *ātman*. 53–7, 80–1, 96, 106, 111, 131–2, 147, 149 (vv. 106, 117), 155, 180, 182, 188.(vv. 27, 29, 96, 105–6, 112), 192, 195, 197.
Self-existent, *svayam-bhū*. 169 (v. 153), 174 (v. 8).
Self-existing, *svābhāvika*. Literally: Belonging to own-being. 190.
Self-nature, *sva-bhāva*. Also: Own-being.
Sense-field, *āyatana*. There are six, corresponding to the six senses. 43, 52.
Settle down in, *abhi-ni-viśate*.

Sight-object, *rūpa*. Also: Form, Material Shape.

Sign, *nimitta*. A particularly difficult technical term. In the Mahayana we are said to make a datum of experience into a 'sign', when we treat it as pointing to an actually existing entity behind it.

Signless, *a-nimitta*.

Single Buddha, *praty-eka-buddha*. Also: Pratyekabuddha.

Skandha. The five constituents of the personality: form, feeling, perception, impulses, consciousness. Also: group. 14, 32, 54, 148, 187, 188 (v. 92).

Skill in Means, *upāya-kauśalya*. 137.

Skilled, *kuśala*. Also: Wholesome.

Space, *ākāśa*. Also: Ether. 34, 98, 188 (v. 77), 201, 110.

Spell, *mantra*. 121, 146, 187, 188 (v. 14), 189 III.

Śramana. An ascetic. 208.

Stage, *bhūmi*. One reckons ten stages of a Bodhisattva's career, from the time that he decides to win enlightenment to the attainment of Buddhahood. 179, 188 (v. 89), 106.

States of Woe, *apāya*. Conditions in which rebirth is particularly painful, i.e. rebirth in hell, as an animal, as a ghost, as an Asura.

Stations of Brahmā, *brahma-vihāra*. Four: friendliness, compassion, sympathetic joy, evenmindedness.

Stopping, *ni-rodha*.

Store of Merit, *kuśala-mūla*. This translation has often been adopted for stylistic reasons, although it does some violence to the letter. Merit is generally used for *puṇya* (see Heap of Merit), and in no. 128 'meritorious action' renders *puṇya-kriyā-vastu*. Also: Roots of Good, Meritorious Action.

Store-consciousness, *ālaya-vijñāna*. no. 150, 178, 181-2. (B., 168 sq.)

Streamwinner, *srota-āpatti*.

Stupa, *stūpa*. A reliquary, cairn, tope, often bell-shaped, and built in the open to contain relics of the Buddha or his disciples, or to commemorate the scene of their acts. In the course of time it comes to symbolize the Buddha's doctrine. (B., p. 79). 172

Suchness, *tatha-tā*. Also: The Truly So. (B., p. 134). 12, 139, 148, 156, 167, 169 (v. 148), 203, 209-10.

Suffering, *duḥkha*. Also: Ill.

Sugata (su=well, gata=gone). An epithet of the Buddha. Also: Wellfarer.

Superknowledge, *abhi-jñā*. Six: (1) Wonder-working powers, (2) heavenly ear, (3) knowledge of the thoughts of others, (4) ability to recollect one's own previous rebirths, (5) knowledge of other beings' rebirths, (6) knowledge that the outflows are extinct. 33, 123 (vv. 66-71).

Supramundane, *lokottara*. 131, 180.

Sustaining Power, *adhiṣṭhāna*. The mental resolution by which the Buddha upholds, or sustains, the magical creations which do his work of preaching, etc.

Sympathetic Joy, *muditā*.

Tathagata: *tathā-gata*, or *tathā-āgata*. A title of the Buddha. (B., p. 36). 107–8, 113, 118, 134–6, 200–1. Five Tathagatas: 192.

Terrace of Enlightenment, *bodhi-maṇḍa*. The place under the Bodhi-tree where the Buddha won enlightenment. Also: Place of enlightenment 201.

Thought, *citta*. Also: Consciousness. 6; Mind, p. 58 and in 'Mind-only'. 151, 163, 186, 188 (v. 55), 78, 83, 99, 106–7.

Thought of Enlightenment, *bodhi-citta*. A Bodhisattva's decision to win the full enlightenment of a Buddha. In Tantric texts it is symbolized as the fluid of life. 189 III.

Trance, *dhyāna*. Also: Jhana, Dhyana, Meditation.

Triple world, *trai-dhātuka*. Referring to the world of sense-desire, the world of form (or, fine-materiality), the formless world.

True Nature of Dharmas, *dharma-tā*. Also Dharmahood.

The Truly So, *tatha-tā*. no. 203, 209–10. See: Suchness.

Truth, *satya*. Four. Descr. 32, 38. (B., pp. 43–48).

Twin-miracle, *yamaka-prātiharya*. p. 49, (cf. B., p. 104).

Ultimate Reality, *parama-artha*.

Uncompounded, *a-saṃskṛta*. Also: Unconditioned.

Unconditioned, *a-saṃskṛta*. Also: Uncompounded. 98.

Universal Monarch, *cakra-vartin*. Also: Wheel-Turning King. p. 41, no. 172. (B., p. 75).

Unwholesome, *a-kuśala*.

Uprising, *samudaya*. Also: Arising, Origination.

Ushnisha, *uṣṇīṣa*. Top knot of twisted hair, one of the signs of a Buddha. p. 251.

Vaidurya. A precious substance, perhaps lapis lazuli, or beryl.

Vajra: thunderbolt, symbol of the indestructible and irresistible truth, hence applicable as an epithet (see Adamantine) to all things symbolizing this truth. By connotation it is masculine, and as such may be contrasted with the Lotus. 187, 188 (v. 94), 214.

Vetala, a demon. 182.

Vigour, *vīrya*. 23–4, 29–31, 170.

Void, *śūnyatā*. See: Emptiness.

Vow, *pra-ṇi-dhāna*.

Wanderer, *pra-vrajita*. A class of ascetics, male and female, common in India about 500 B.C.

Way, *mārga*. Also Path.

Well-farer, *su-gata*. 12, 13. Also: Sugata.

Wheel-turning King, *cakravartin*. See: Universal Monarch.

Wholesome, *kuśala*.

Wings of Enlightenment, *bodhi-pakṣa*.

Wisdom, *prajñā*. 23–4, 36–8, 170, 189 I.

Wishless, *a-pra-ṇi-hita*. A state in which one makes no plans for the future. The term could also have been rendered as 'aimless'. It is the third of the three 'doors to deliverance', following on emptiness and the signless.

Worship, *pūjā*.

Wrath, *krodha*. 187.

Yakkha. Pali form of Yaksha.

Yaksha, a kind of spirit. 105. Also: Fairy.

Yama, the world of. Yama is the ruler of the Underworld 175 (v. 19).

Yogini, *yoginī*. A woman, human or divine, who co-operates with the Yogin when certain ritual is used for the purpose of gaining enlightenment. 188, (vv. 84–87), 189 III, 190.

ABBREVIATIONS

A. = Anguttara-nikāya
AA. = Comy. on A. (Manora-thapūraṇī)
Asl. = Atthasālinī (Comy. on Dhs.)
B. = E. Conze, *Buddhism*, 2nd. ed., Oxford, 1953.
BD. = *Book of the Discipline*
Comp. = *Compendium of Philosophy.*
Comy. = Commentary
D. = Dīgha-nikāya
DA. = Comy. on D. (Sumanga-lavilāsinī)
DhA. = Comy. on Dhp.
Dhp. = Dhammapada
Dhs. = Dhammasaṅgaṇi
Divy. = Divyâvadāna
GOS. = Gaekwad's Oriental Series
GS. = Gradual Sayings
HJAS. = Harvard Journal of Asiatic Studies
HOS. = Harvard Oriental Studies
It. = Itivuttaka
ItA. = Comy. on It.
Jā. = Jātaka
JPTS. = Journal of the PTS.

JRAS. = Journal of the Royal Asiatic Society
Khp. = Khuddakapāṭha
M. = Majjhima-nikāya
MA. = Comy. on M. (Papañ-casūdanī)
Miln. = Milindapañha
Nd. = Niddesa
PTS. = Pali Text Society
Pts. = Paṭisambhidāmagga
PugA. = Comy. on Puggala-paññatti
RAS. = Royal Asiatic Society
S. = Samyutta-nikāya
SA. = Comy. on S. (Sāratthap-pakāsinī)
SBB. = Sacred Books of the Buddhists
Sn. = Suttanipāta
Thag. = Theragāthā
Thīg. = Therīgāthā
Ud. = Udāna
UdA. = Comy. on Ud.
Vbh. = Vibhanga
VbhA. = Comy. on Vbh. (Sam-mohavinodanī)
Vin. = Vinaya-piṭaka
VinA. = Comy. on Vin. (Saman-tapāsādikā)
Vism. = Visuddhimagga